BEPPE GRILLO'S FIVE STAR MOVEMENT

Beppe Grillo's Five Star Movement

Organisation, Communication and Ideology

Edited by

FILIPPO TRONCONI

University of Bologna, Italy

ASHGATE

Published by
Ashgate Publishing Limited
Wey Court East
Union Road
Farnham
Surrey, GU9 7PT
England

Ashgate Publishing Company
110 Cherry Street
Suite 3–1
Burlington, VT 05401–3818
USA

www.ashgate.com

British Library Cataloguing in Publication Data
A catalogue record for this book is available from the British Library

The Library of Congress has cataloged the printed edition as follows:
Beppe Grillo's Five Star Movement : organisation, communication and ideology / edited by Filippo Tronconi.
pages cm
Includes bibliographical references and index.
ISBN 978–1–4724–3663–4 (hardback) – ISBN 978–1–4724-3664-1 (ebook) – ISBN 978–1–4724–3665–8 (epub)
1. Movimento 5 stelle. 2. Grillo, Beppe, 1948– 3. Italy–Politics and government–21st century.
I. Tronconi, Filippo, editor of compilation.
JN5657.M55B47 2015
324.245'087–dc23

2014030195

ISBN 9781472436634 (hbk)
ISBN 9781472436641 (ebk – PDF)
ISBN 9781472436658 (ebk – ePUB)

MIX
Paper from responsible sources
FSC® C013985
FSC www.fsc.org

Printed in the United Kingdom by Henry Ling Limited, at the Dorset Press, Dorchester, DT1 1HD

Contents

List of Figures

List of Tables

Notes on Contributors

Pasquale Colloca is assistant professor at the University of Bologna, and collaborates with the Istituto Carlo Cattaneo of Bologna. He holds a PhD in sociology from University of Trento. His main research interests include the impact of economic crisis on political attitudes, old and new political cleavages, political values and civic engagement.

Piergiorgio Corbetta is research director at Istituto Cattaneo of Bologna. Now retired, he has been professor of methodology of social research at University of Bologna and also director of the Istituto Cattaneo from 1991 to 2001. In the nineties, he was among the founders of the research group ITANES (Italian National Election Studies). He is author of several articles and books on methodology of social science, statistics applied to social research, political participation and electoral studies.

Maria Elisabetta Lanzone has recently completed a PhD program in political science at the University of Pavia. She is currently a vising scholar at the "Laboratoire Ermes", University of Nice Sophia Antipolis Her main research areas are new parties and political participation. She has published articles and book chapters about new populist expressions in Europe. She is a member of the research team C&LS (Candidate & Leader Selection).

Lorenzo Mosca is assistant professor at the University of Roma Tre. He holds a post-doctorate in political and social sciences from the Max Weber Programme of the European University Institute in Fiesole. He is the author of several articles, book chapters and books on online politics, social movements and political communication.

Gianluca Passarelli is assistant professor in political science at the Department of Political Sciences, Sapienza University, Rome. He is a researcher at the Istituto Carlo Cattaneo and a member of the ITANES (Italian National Election Studies) research group. His main research interests concern: comparative politics, presidents of the Republic, political parties, electoral systems, and electoral behaviour. He is the author of *Monarchi elettivi?* (2008); *Presidenti della Repubblica* (ed.) (2010); *Lega & Padania. Storie e luoghi delle Camicie verdi* (with D. Tuorto, 2012) and several articles in *French Politics*, *Journal of Modern Italian Studies*, *Modern Italy*, *Polis*, *South European Society and Politics*, *Contemporary Italian Politics*, and *Political Geography*. He is currently review editor for the journal *Polis*.

Andrea Pedrazzani is a post-doctoral research fellow at the Department of Social and Political Sciences, University of Bologna. His main research interests include legislative behaviour, executive-legislative relations and intra-coalitional politics. He has published articles in the *European Journal of Political Research*, *Government and Opposition* and the *Italian Political Science Review*.

Luca Pinto is a post-doctoral research fellow at the Department of Social and Political Sciences, University of Bologna. His research interests include party competition and legislative studies. His articles have been accepted for publication in *Party Politics*, *The Journal of Legislative Studies*, *Government and Opposition*, and *International Political Science Review*.

Filippo Tronconi is associate professor of political science at the University of Bologna, Department of Social and Political Sciences, and a regular collaborator of the Istituto Carlo Cattaneo. His research interests cover European political parties, with a specific focus on the ethnoregionalist party family, political elites and legislative behaviour. Recent publications include *From Protest to Power. Autonomist Parties and the Challenges of Representation* (edited with A. Elias, 2011).

Dario Tuorto is associate professor at the University of Bologna, where he teaches sociology of social inclusion and exclusion. His main research topics in the field of political sociology are turnout, populism and party activism. His recent publications include *Lega & Padania. Storie e luoghi delle Camicie Verdi* (with G. Passarelli, 2012) and *Il lavoro difficile. Discriminazione e gruppi discriminate in Italia* (2013).

Cristian Vaccari is lecturer in political science at Royal Holloway University of London and associate professor in political science at the University of Bologna. He studies political communication in a comparative perspective, with a particular focus on digital media. His latest book is titled *Digital Politics in Western Democracies: A Comparative Study* (2013). He is the principal investigator of a comparative research project on social media and political inclusion (www.webpoleu.org).

Augusto Valeriani received his PhD in media studies from the University of Siena. He is currently assistant professor in media sociology at the University of Bologna, Department of Social and Political Sciences, where he lectures in media and international politics. His main scientific interests focus on digital media and politics, journalism, internet and society. On these topics he has authored and co-authored articles in international journals, chapters in edited books and three monographs. His latest book is *Twitter Factor* (2011).

Rinaldo Vignati taught political science at the University of Modena, and Reggio Emilia and public opinion at the University of Milano Bicocca. He currently works at the Istituto Carlo Cattaneo of Bologna. He has written articles about political parties, electoral behaviour and political culture. His last works have been published in *Quaderni di Sociologia, The International Spectator*, *Contemporary Italian Politics*, and *South European Society and Politics*.

Acknowledgements

This edited volume is the result of a research project launched by the Istituto Carlo Cattaneo in spring 2012, soon after the initial success of the Movimento 5 Stelle in that year's local elections. Our first acknowledgement goes to the president of the Istituto Cattaneo, Elisabetta Gualmini, the director, Stefania Profeti, and the administrative manager, Elisa Giardina. Without their support, this book would not have been possible. In a seminar held at the Istituto in December 2013 the initial drafts of the book chapters were discussed also with Giorgia Bulli, Aldo Di Virgilio and Salvatore Vassallo, who offered careful and constructive comments. Chapters 2 and 3 are based on 47 interviews with activists and representatives elected in local and regional assemblies, conducted in two waves. Twenty-five interviews were conducted by Elisabetta Gualmini, Gianluca Passarelli, Filippo Tronconi and Dario Tuorto in Veneto, Lombardy, Liguria, Piedmont, Emilia-Romagna and Campania in the summer of 2012. Twenty-two more interviews were then conducted by Maria Elisabetta Lanzone and Rinaldo Vignati in Piedmont, Lombardy, Emilia-Romagna and Sicily between the end of 2013 and the beginning of 2014. We would like to thank all the activists who generously made their time and knowledge available to us.

Introduction

Filippo Tronconi

In its first participation in a nationwide electoral competition, in February 2013, the Movimento 5 Stelle (M5S, Five Star Movement) obtained an impressive electoral result. Almost nine million Italians chose its symbol on the electoral ballot paper, making it the most voted party in the Chamber of Deputies, if one does not consider the votes of Italians living abroad, with 25.6 per cent of the votes. No parallels can be found in post-1945 Europe of a new party obtaining a similar success in its first electoral participation. Ironically, in spite of becoming the most voted party, the M5S rejects the label of party and all the organisational structures traditionally associated with it. It claims instead to be a non-association, with headquarters 'located' in the blog run by Beppe Grillo himself. It is not just a new party that shook Italian politics in 2013, but a utopian promise of renovation of politics, without the intermediation of parties, where individual citizens are called upon to decide on all the relevant issues through a continuous online discussion.

Officially born in 2009, the M5S came to the forefront of the Italian political scenario in May 2012, where it achieved a first, unexpected success in local and regional elections (Colloca and Marangoni 2013). The success was doubled a few months later, when Grillo's movement became the first party in the regional elections in Sicily, and even the most sceptical observers began to believe (or to fear) that the M5S would play a leading role in the upcoming general elections. Just one year before that breakthrough, this movement was known only among the most well-informed political observers as a bizarre but substantially irrelevant phenomenon. It was led by Beppe Grillo, a comedian with an anomalous professional path. A popular presence on the public TV channels in the 1980s, he was banned from mainstream television after telling a joke on the ruling Socialist Party during a prime time show. After that, he continued his activity in theatres, cultivating a smaller but loyal audience with shows that increasingly focused on current political events, and especially on environmental issues and a harsh criticism of the degeneration of the contemporary capitalist economy. Later on, the same topics will be extensively covered in the blog that Grillo started in 2005.

It is not difficult to discern the basic elements of a populist movement in the catchphrases launched on a daily basis in Grillo's blog. In first place the juxtaposition between the establishment, conceived as corrupt, quarrelsome, self-interested and ultimately unable to offer solutions for the problems of the country, and the people, who on the contrary are considered as fundamentally hard-working, honest and virtuous. The establishment is above all identified with politicians, but often includes those who control economic power (big business leaders, bankers, managers of multinational companies), those who control information, trade unionists, high-ranking bureaucrats. All those representatives of the establishment have been in Grillo's line of fire, first in his theatre shows, then on the blog, and finally during his electoral campaign tours. Politicians are quite obviously the favourite target of his diatribes, but the media system is also frequently criticised for betraying its original mission to be the watchdog of rulers. Big companies are another recurrent theme of Grillo's speeches, most notably in 2003, when the multinational dairy and food corporation Parmalat faced bankruptcy. This came as a bolt from the blue for most in the media, while Grillo had been denouncing its imminent financial collapse for months in his shows, to the point that he was heard as a witness by the judges investigating the scandal. More recently, European and national bureaucrats – especially during the Monti government – have been under attack for hollowing out democratic procedures, taking decisions affecting the lives of millions of citizens without being legitimised by a popular mandate.

The second element frequently recalled as a defining feature of populism is the identification between the leader and his (or, occasionally, her) people. The typical leader of a populist movement is someone who personifies the common sense of 'the man in the street', as opposed to the unnecessary complications and artificial divisions that characterise political elites. The leader is thus able to offer simple and immediate solutions to the problems that affect the community, to which professional politicians are unable to give answers. The direct link between the leader and his or her people is also connected to the rejection of intermediate bodies of representation, and particularly political parties. The anti-party appeal is in fact another crucial defining feature of all populist movements gaining visibility across Europe in the last few decades. In the experience of the M5S the role of Beppe Grillo is indisputable and few – even among its own militants – would argue that the M5S would ever have been born or exist today without its founding leader.

The anti-party appeal is another self-evident feature of Grillo's party, which has interesting consequences also for its internal organisation. Paul Taggart (1995), among others, underlines the contradiction of anti-party organisations that perform typical party functions, such as elaborating policy platforms, selecting candidates and competing in elections for popular votes. The contradiction, Taggart explains, is tackled by proposing solutions that challenge the conventional ideas of parties as organisations, either in the direction of a charismatic leadership or in the direction of a 'devolved, decentralised and depersonalised leadership' (ibid., p. 41). The M5S, quite remarkably, presents both these faces in its organisational model, as we will argue in the following chapters.

The style of communication of the leader is another frequently mentioned feature of populism. Daniele Albertazzi and Duncan McDonnell (2008, p. 7), argue that this is due to the necessity of acting on the political and institutional stage, but at the same time keeping a distance from it and always underlining the leader's closeness to the people. As a consequence, populist leaders tend to adopt a style that breaks the accepted codes of political communication, with the use of direct, at times offensive, language. Beppe Grillo shows these elements in an almost paradigmatic way. The first massive public event he organised was the V-Day, where 'V' stands for 'vaffanculo' (bugger off), generally addressed towards the Italian political elite. He is furthermore known for constantly mangling the names of his opponents and inventing insulting nicknames (Berlusconi is the 'psycho-dwarf', Renzi is the 'little idiot from Florence', Monti is 'rigor montis'). He takes pride in using rude language, against the hypocrisy of the 'politichese' (political jargon). His speeches during campaign rallies are actually one-man shows where the consummate skills of the actor emerge:

> He scorns the stage, roaming among the audience. Apparently consumed with rage, he shouts into the microphone that the country is choking with the rottenness of its ruling class, whether political, religious or corporate – then grabs the head of someone in the audience and clasps it to his chest, stroking the hair, as if providing the spectator a moment's refuge from a cruel world. His short, chubby figure is crowned with a tumbling white mop of hair, his energy belies his 63 years, his commentary shifts from the bitter to the witty and back again in seconds. (Lloyd 2012)

If the characteristics mentioned above allow us to safely place the M5S in the family of populist parties, other elements seem to differentiate it from its European counterparts. The first one of these is ideology. Although the most acute observers of the populist phenomenon warn that we should not automatically identify 'populism' with 'extreme right' (Taguieff 2002; Tarchi 2003; Albertazzi and McDonnell 2008), there is little doubt that the majority of the most successful populist parties display a clear rightist leaning, whether in a neo-liberal or in a nationalist xenophobic variant (Betz 1994). The M5S does not fit into this scheme, nor does Beppe Grillo's biography. Beyond the anti-establishment appeal, the foremost point of reference is to be found in post-materialist and environmentalist values: according to the 2009 'Carta di Firenze' the five stars stand for '[public] water, environment, [public] transport, [sustainable] development and [renewable] energy'. One of the most significant battles fought by Beppe Grillo, in his shows and then on the blog, is against the projected high-speed train connecting Turin to Lyon and other big infrastructure projects that have met with hard opposition from local citizens' associations. More generally, the manifesto of the M5S stresses environmental issues (e.g. waste management, energy, urban quality of life, ethical consumerism) and left libertarian stances related to citizens' empowerment through practices of direct democracy (Passarelli, Tronconi and Tuorto 2013). This brings us to a second element of originality, that is, blind faith in the virtues of the Internet as a tool for breaking the chains of old representative politics, and opening the way to a horizontal exchange of ideas and democratic debate among citizens, and ultimately to the accomplishment of large-scale direct democracy.[1] In this sense, Piergiorgio Corbetta (2013) has coined for the M5S the apt definition of 'web-populism'.

The emergence of populist movements is often traced back to some kind of malaise diffused in a society. Betz (1993, p. 413) maintains that right-wing populism found a fertile soil in Europe in the political climate of the 1980s, 'marked by disenchantment with the major social and political institutions and profound distrust in their working'. These are certainly circumstances that can be observed in the Italian context of 2013 as well. Interestingly, it could be argued that something similar was happening at the beginning of the 1990s, when the Italian political system experienced an unprecedented earthquake that led to the sudden dissolution of the parties that had emerged after the Second World War and to the emergence of two champions of populism like Umberto Bossi and Silvio Berlusconi. Twenty years later, with these two leaders clearly declining, or even marginalised in the political scenario, history seems to be repeating itself. Scandals related to public money mismanagement and corruption are frequent in newspaper headlines, and trust in political institutions is almost without exception at its lowest point. Political parties, in particular, have been depicted as facing a very public 'downgrade' (Bosco and McDonnell 2012), but the technocratic alternative of Monti's government has not proven to be much more effective in dealing with the problems of the country (Di Virgilio and Radaelli 2013). Two more aspects make the current situation look even worse than in 1992. First, the economic crisis has added an increased sense of material insecurity for large quotas of society; second, the European Union, which was once seen as the supranational entity able to rescue Italy from its old vices, is now perceived by a growing share of the population as part of the problem to be solved, and is in turn hit by a deep crisis of legitimacy.

The M5S, however, represents an interesting case study also beyond its specific national context, to the point that it is legitimate to wonder if it can be considered a vanguard of new forms of political organisation likely to spread over the continent (Mosca 2014). The anti-establishment themes it proposes go well beyond the borders of Italy and span throughout Europe. What makes Beppe Grillo's creature unique in the continental scenario is its innovative use of the Internet, both as an organisational and a communication tool, and its ability to position itself beyond the traditional left-right ideological dimension of competition, which allows it to gather votes from a very heterogeneous electoral constituency. This differentiates the M5S from other populist parties across Europe that have recently achieved a remarkable

---

1 'Each one counts as one, but an interconnected and responsible mankind has a value that tends to infinity. The Internet creates communities. Among them, the largest one is the human race, which has never had the opportunity, before now, to be connected, to share, to decide on its own destiny in real time. We are lucky enough to participate to a final change of our History, and we can be both witnesses and actors of it. The Internet redefines the relations between citizen and State, citizens become the State' (Casaleggio and Grillo 2011, p. 188).

electoral success. Most of them, although able to gather voters from previously leftist strongholds stressing issues that are not necessarily related to the ideological cleavage, like Euroscepticism, or immigration, are quite easily recognisable as right-wing populist parties. The UK Independence Party, the Perussuomalaiset (True Finns) and Alternative für Deutschland, to name a few, can be placed in this category. Other recent experiences have more clear similarities with Grillo's movement. The Spanish Podemos, which emerged as the political expression of the Indignados movement, shares with the M5S an extensive use of social media, the idea of participatory democracy and citizens' empowerment, and the emphasis on transparency in its funding. The German Piratenpartei is probably the political experience most often compared to the M5S for its use of the Internet as a tool for internal organisation. Both these parties, however, are clearly distinct from our case, for the fact that they are much closer to the ideal of leaderless organisations, based on an assembly model of decision-making at all levels.[2] On the contrary, Grillo keeps a final word on all key decisions and crucial resources within the M5S, starting from the property of the symbol and the blog beppegrillo.it.

In this book we address these issues looking at the different faces (and contradictions) of the organisation of this party, its use of the Internet, its social base and electoral strategies. The founder Beppe Grillo is introduced in the first chapter, with his unusual path from TV to the stages of theatres, to the virtual stage of his blog, and back to the 'piazzas' as a political leader. The second chapter provides an overview of the organisation of the M5S, its many contradictions and the challenges it poses to traditional political science classifications of parties. In the following three chapters the theme of organisation is tackled from different perspectives: activists, voters and elected officials, respectively. We then move to the Internet (Chapter 6), meant as a tool for organisation, decision-making, communication and identity-building. Chapters 7, 8 and 9 focus on the links between the party and society. While Chapter 7 primarily concerns relations with social movements prior to the participation in the electoral competition, the following two chapters make extensive use of post-electoral surveys to explore the reasons that led some nine million voters to choose the M5S in the February 2013 general elections. Two aspects of this voting behaviour are particularly taken into account: the protest component (Chapter 8) and the ideological component (Chapter 9). In the conclusions we build on the evidence gathered in the previous chapters to address what is probably the most challenging puzzle for the observers that approach the study of this party – and for scholars interested in the emergence and success of new parties more generally. How could a party at its first nationwide electoral competition, founded by an individual entrepreneur only a few years before, without any previous financial and organisational resources,

2 The formal appointment of Pablo Iglesias as Secretary General of Podemos (November 2014) distances this party from the leaderless model. However, the role of Pablo Iglesias is not comparable with that of Beppe Grillo, as the former emerged from a participated democratic process that never took place inside the M5S.

achieve such an outstanding result? What accounts for the most successful electoral breakthrough in a consolidated democracy in the history of the whole of post-war Europe? We argue that the answer is to be found precisely in the original organisational arrangements of the M5S, and in its careful positioning in the political space of contemporary Italy. At the same time, doubts remain on the sustainability of this success, as the very same features that allowed this party to quickly impose itself as one of the main Italian political forces, could represent its potential weak points. If the M5S is not able to adapt to the role of a leading actor in the Italian political scenario, its decline could yet be as fast as its rise.

References

Albertazzi, D. and McDonnell, D. 2008. Introduction: The Sceptre and the Spectre. In: D. Albertazzi and D. McDonnell, eds. *Twenty-First Century Populism. The Spectre of Western European Democracy*. Basingstoke: Palgrave, pp. 1–11.

———, eds. 2008. *Twenty-First Century Populism. The Spectre of Western European Democracy*. Basingstoke: Palgrave.

Betz, H.G. 1993. The New Politics of Resentment. Radical Right-Wing Populist Parties in Western Europe. *Comparative Politics*, 25(4), pp. 413–27.

———. 1994. *Radical Right-Wing Populism in Western Europe*. New York: St Martin's Press.

Bosco, A. and McDonnell, D. 2012. Introduction: The Monti Government and the Downgrade of Italian Parties. In: A. Bosco and D. McDonnell, eds. *Italian Politics: From Berlusconi to Monti*. New York: Berghahn Books, pp. 37–56.

Casaleggio, G. and Grillo, B. 2011. *Siamo in guerra: Per una nuova politica*. Milan: Chiarelettere.

Colloca, P. and Marangoni, F. 2013. Lo shock elettorale. In: P. Corbetta and E. Gualmini, eds. *Il partito di Grillo*. Bologna: Il Mulino, pp. 65–88.

Corbetta, P. 2013. Conclusioni. Un web-populismo dal destino incerto. In: P. Corbetta and E. Gualmini, eds. *Il partito di Grillo*. Bologna: Il Mulino. pp. 197–214.

Di Virgilio, A. and Radaelli, C. 2013. Introduction: The Year of the External Podestà. In: A. Di Virgilio and C. Radaelli, eds. *Italian Politics 2012. Technocrats in Office*. New York: Berghahn, pp. 37–57.

Lloyd, J., 2012. Beppe Grillo: The Anti-Politics Politician. 17 May. *Reuters* [online]. Available at: http://blogs.reuters.com/john-lloyd/2012/05/17/beppe-grillo-the-anti-politics-politician/ [Accessed 4 June 2013].

Mosca, L., 2014. The Five Star Movement: Exception or Vanguard in Europe? *The International Spectator*, 49(1), 36–52.

Passarelli, G., Tronconi, F. and Tuorto, D. 2013. Dentro il Movimento: Organizzazione, attivisti e programmi. In: P. Corbetta and E. Gualmini, eds. *Il partito di Grillo*. Bologna: Il Mulino, pp. 89–122.

Taggart, P. 1995. New Populist Parties in Western Europe. *West European Politics*, 18(1), pp. 34–51.

Taguieff, P.-A. 2002. *L'illusion populiste. De l'archaïque au médiatique*. Paris: Berg.

Tarchi, M. 2003. *L'Italia populista. Dal qualunquismo ai girotondi*. Bologna: Il Mulino.

Chapter 1
Beppe Grillo and the Movimento 5 Stelle: A Brief History of a 'Leaderist' Movement with a Leaderless Ideology

Rinaldo Vignati

The Importance of the Leader and the 'Leaderless' Ideology

One of the many paradoxes of the Movimento 5 Stelle (M5S, 5 Star Movement) lies in the fact that, while it is a political movement with a strong 'leaderist' stamp, its ideology professes an equally strong 'leaderless' nature. On the one hand, according to a survey reported by Roberto Biorcio (2013), 66 per cent of Italians (including M5S voters) believe that 'without Grillo, the M5S would be severely weakened and would break up' and 55 per cent agree with the statement that 'there is little democracy within the M5S because all decisions are taken by Grillo and Casaleggio'. If only those people who state that they intend to vote for the M5S are considered, these percentages fall to 44 per cent and 43 per cent, respectively. These data clearly indicate the importance of the figure of the leader in the Movement's success. Indeed, even among the party's own voters, almost half of those interviewed agreed that without Grillo the M5S would eventually break up.

In stark contrast with this prevalent perception, Grillo and Casaleggio, the two founders of the M5S, have always professed to uphold an ideology which they have defined as 'leaderless'. In a post on his blog on 26 June 2010, Grillo declared his aversion to the very idea of leadership:

> A nation needs citizens, not leaders. 'Leaderism' is the highest form of career that an elected politician who doesn't give a damn for the voters can aspire to. In theory, MPs, Councillors and Euro-deputies are elected in order to implement a program that has been agreed upon: to work in the Regional Assembly, on the City Council, in Parliament. They are paid more than enough for what they do. If your plumber were to spend his time on television enunciating important (and unrequested) 'political' thoughts, writing articles and presenting books, you'd begin to doubt that he was working for you. You'd suspect that he was using his position to gain the visibility in plumbing circles that he would otherwise never have had: to become a local, regional or national leader. It's surreal. And all this happens because you pay him to fix the water pipes in your house. You

> pay a plumber, but if you turn your back for a moment, you find a leader under the kitchen sink.
>
> …
>
> Leaders are usually oversensitive. For them, the approval of the voters is a signal from the heavens; the sign of a glorious destiny that awaits them at the head of the Italian people. Leaders are like shit; they attract bluebottles, usually in the guise of intellectuals, their inspiring muses. Fickle insects always on the lookout for fresher excrement. 'Leaderism' is a social disease. It arises when citizens take no interest in public affairs and give up exercising their duty to point the way and to oversee. If everyone is a leader, no one is a leader. Everyone counts for one. Every citizen is his own leader. If someone you've elected goes around playing the leader, ask him why he is away from his place of work and, with the greatest kindness, because he is a sick person after all, tell him to bugger off. (Grillo 2010)

This aversion to the figure of the leader underlies the slogan 'one counts for one', which is one of the founding myths of the M5S and its idea of direct democracy (for an analysis of the conception of democracy in the M5S, see Floridia and Vignati 2014). This kind of position has often been supported by references to David Graeber, one of the theorists of the 'Occupy Wall Street' movement, who has tried to depict – with the aid of ethnographic examples (see, among others, Graeber 2007) – a direct democracy without leaders or elite. Graeber has been quoted on several occasions by Casaleggio:

> The M5S sees the word 'leader' as belonging to the past; it is a dirty word, perverted. Leader of what? It means that you attribute to others intelligence and decisional capability; it means that you are no longer even a slave; you're an object … Behind the word 'leader' there is nothing. Let's take the case of Occupy Wall Street: a spontaneous demonstration against financial institutions was held in New York. The demonstrators dubbed themselves 'Occupy Wall Street' and invaded the district of the American banks and stock exchange. The phenomenon then spread … but in the various demonstrations, no leader ever emerged: the important thing was the movement. David Graeber, who was among the organisers of the movement, defined it as leaderless, meaning that it gathers together intelligences without having to look to a supreme head. This falls within the very concept of community. (Fo, Grillo and Casaleggio 2013, pp. 10–11)

This ideology is accredited by some observers as a valid description of the M5S. For example, the cyberpunk writer Bruce Sterling interviewed Gianroberto Casaleggio for *Wired* a few months ago. He subsequently wrote that 'the movement is leaderless because leaders get in the way. Instead of leaders, the M5S has Beppe

Grillo, an orator who does not seek public office, and Casaleggio, who until a short time ago rarely said anything to anyone'.

Even some academics (Greblo 2011; Lanfrey 2011; Biorcio 2013) hold a similar view, emphasizing the role of M5S meet-ups and endorsing their independence from leaders. In our opinion, however, despite the fact that the M5S is a complex phenomenon which displays ambivalent features, its 'leaderist' character prevails over the 'leaderless' rhetoric with which it is imbued. A few considerations are enough to demonstrate this. The first concerns the 'commercial ownership' of the party logo, as ratified by its statute, and the ownership of the technological infrastructure that underpins the life of the party. The second concerns the fact that several individual representatives of the Movement, in parliament or in local institutions, have been expelled or disavowed by Grillo. The third regards the fact that the political agenda of the Movement – which issues should be given priority, whether and how a proposal should be put up for voting on the blog, etc. – is always decided by the leader, without any real debate. The fourth – which generalises these last two considerations – regards what we might call the 'metaphysics of the rules', which lies at the basis of the 'founding myth' of the M5S. The speeches of Grillo and other exponents of the M5S frequently contain calls to apply the 'rules' (it is the 'rules' that justify expulsions; it is the somewhat vague 'rules' that dictate the Movement's strategic choices). By appealing to the 'rules' that must be respected, exponents and militants make the functioning of the party depend on a de-personalised claim that is higher than the individual participants and even than the leader. In reality, even a superficial observation of the internal workings of the Movement is enough to reveal that, at decisive moments, the 'rules' are always chosen and imposed without discussion by the leader himself; they are therefore a means by which he maintains command over the party.[1] The last consideration concerns the origin of votes for the Movement. The great success of the M5S in the 2013 general election and the fact that this success was not repeated in the subsequent local elections, in which Grillo did not play a direct role, indicate that the electoral consensus of the M5S depends to a great extent on the words and deeds of its leader rather than on its territorial roots.

Thus, of the two faces that characterise the M5S – 'leaderism' and direct participation – it is the former which has so far prevailed (though the latter should by no means be neglected). The present chapter, which summarises the principal phases of the formation of the M5S, therefore focuses on this singular figure of the comedian who turned himself into a politician.

Analysis of the M5S, and of the relationships between the leader and the organisation, runs up against a methodological, we could almost say epistemological, problem. Indeed, the best literature on political parties is based on a 'realist' postulate (in this regard, the main references are Panebianco (1982) in the specific sphere of the parties, and Crozier and Friedberg (1977) for what

1 To cite just one example, the 'rules' concerning the active and passive electorate in the so-called 'parliamentaries'.

concerns the organisations in general). This approach is founded on the idea that the players involved are interested in extending their own power, both within the party and, prospectively, within the institutions through their control of the party machine. The party is therefore seen as the arena in which struggles are played out among subjects who are motivated by the desire to increase their own power.

In the case of the M5S, however, this postulate does not seem to be applicable. Neither Grillo nor Casaleggio runs in elections. They do not aim to occupy the top posts (or at least they have not so far manifested this aim); rather, they remain to some extent on the sidelines, functioning (according to the rhetoric underlying the Movement's narrative) exclusively as a 'megaphone' for the initiatives autonomously taken by the active components of the Movement, and as 'guarantors' of the Movement's basic principles.

Thus, the debate over this party tends to oscillate between two opposing visions of the role of Grillo and Casaleggio. On the one hand, we find the 'plot theory', according to which the two leaders are claimed to exploit the Movement for banal commercial ends (advertising and marketing of the blog) or to promote obscure economic interests (whereby the Movement is held to be, in reality, a political façade for a variety of unidentified economic interests). On the other hand, we find the notion of the disinterested leader (a leader who does not run in elections? A 'dictator' who does not aspire to office?). Grillo has depicted his 'entry into the political arena' in terms which are in some ways similar to those used by Berlusconi. This latter utilised the gospel reference to 'drinking from the bitter chalice' to describe his duty to go into politics. Similarly, Grillo has explained his progressive entry into the fray as being dictated by politicians' dereliction of their duty, almost as if he had been forced to take part – 'I just want to be a comedian! I can't be the one you come to hear, the Fount of Truth; I can't manage that, it's not part of who I am, it's not in my nature! … I'm a comedian; I'd die for a gag … Straight after the elections, once we are in Parliament, I'll go back to doing theatre, doing my stuff'. And yet it is still not clear what his true intentions are nor what political design it is that drives his and Casaleggio's actions.

A Comedian Turned Political Leader

Who is Grillo and how did he construct his capital of political trust? Born in Savignone (Genova) in 1949,[2] Beppe Grillo became famous as a comedian. He first worked in cabaret before moving into television. In the first half of the 1980s, he became one of television's most successful celebrities. At that time, his comedy centred chiefly around themes of 'custom', only rarely and blandly touching on politics.

2 Grillo's biographic details are narrated by Scanzi (2008) and Caracci (2013), among others. His collections of texts (for the theatre, television and press) are: Grillo (2006a), Ruggiero (2003). For a concise examination of the steps on Grillo's path from comedian to politician, see Vignati (2013a).

In the cinema, he worked only occasionally and with mediocre results. Among the few films he acted in, however, *Fou de guerre* (1985) by Dino Risi, in which he played alongside Coluche, is worthy of note. His meeting with the French comedian deserves attention, in that Coluche, a few years earlier, had been the protagonist of a political adventure that in many ways was a forerunner of Grillo's own exploits – in some of its content at least, if not in its outcome. Indeed, in 1981 the Frenchman ran for President of the Republic, attacking the entire political and economic establishment with catchy slogans that often hinged on the use of popular and openly vulgar language ('Tous ensemble pour foutre au cul avec Coluche' seems to be almost a direct anticipation of the 'Vaffanculo' ('Bugger off') that Grillo would throw at all politicians of his first V-Day in 2007).[3] Coluche's presidential bid initially gained a high profile; he obtained the open support of some intellectuals (Pierre Bourdieu, Gilles Deleuze and Felix Guattari, among others[4]) and won the approval of a sizeable slice of the electorate (according to some surveys, the intention to vote for Coluche reached 16 per cent). Coluche, however, did not carry his candidature through, but withdrew from the race (various hypotheses have been put forward to explain this: the difficulty of obtaining the signatures of the electors needed to ratify his candidature; threats; a promise by Mitterand to support his charitable initiative 'Restaurants du coeur' in exchange for his withdrawal).

It is above all in Bourdieu's reflection on his support for Coluche's candidature that we can discern some features that are common to Grillo's initiative. At the centre of both Coluche's candidature and Grillo's initiative, lies the desire to heal the fracture between politics and the people: 'On reflecting on his support, Bourdieu expressed his concern at the way the political *field* had changed as it became more and more professional and autonomous. It now looked after its own interests rather than those of the people it claimed to represent. Moreover, he drew a comparison between the world of politics and religion; both strongly guarding entry or access to positions which confer "blessing" … The attraction of Coluche's candidature for Bourdieu was, therefore, the way it showed up this attitude of monopolisation among all the politicians and commentators who denounced both him and the people who supported him as "irresponsible"' (Greenfell 2004, pp. 144–5, original emphasis). Bourdieu said that: 'One of the virtues of those who are irresponsible – of whom I am one – is to show up the tacit presuppositions in the political order … I remember that Coluche was not really a candidate but he said that he was a candidate in order to remind everyone that anyone can be a

3 Like Grillo, Coluche had a great ability to twist words in order to 'deconsecrate' the field of politics (the 'élections présidentielles' became 'érections pestilentielles', cf. Ungar 1996). Coluche's presidential candidature is dealt with in the numerous biographies of the French comedian, such as those of Boggio (2006) and Tenaille (2006).

4 On the reasons for the support of Bourdieu, see Swartz (1997, p. 267) and Greenfell (2004, pp. 144–5). On the reasons for the support of Deleuze and Guattari, see Dosse (2010, pp. 301–2).

candidate. All the political-media field became mobilised to condemn this radical barbarity which consisted in questioning the fundamental presupposition that it is only politicians who can talk about politics' (Bourdieu, 2000, pp. 55–6).

Those who are familiar with the issues that Grillo has dealt with during his activity as a political leader will find surprising affinities with the arguments underlined by Bourdieu (the rhetoric of 'irresponsibility'; the idea that politics is everyone's business and not the exclusive domain of professional politicians, etc.). The ability to transcend the separation between left and right is also common to the two comedians (while the pro-Coluche appeal was signed mainly by left-wing intellectuals, support also came from Gérard Nicoud, the leader of artisans and small business people, who was of the opposite political orientation).

This does not mean that Grillo *took his inspiration* from Coluche. Nevertheless, the meeting of the two comedians has an emblematic value that should be borne in mind (the similarities between Grillo and Coluche have also been underlined by Biorcio and Natale 2013, pp. 16–20). Opposition to the closure of the political field is constantly present in every political system (and the comedian – whose propensity is to turn hierarchies on their head and to throw reality into clownish disarray – is the one most willing to represent this sentiment[5]). Normally, sentiments and reactions of this kind remain on the fringe, or display only sudden and transient consensus (as in the case of Coluche). However, Grillo's success, which has been greater, more pervasive and long-standing than any other similar experience, stems from the crisis of the Italian political system (in this regard, we can use the term 'deinstitutionalisation', Corbetta and Vignati 2013a, 2013b) and from the fact that, as we will see, Grillo's alliance with Gianroberto Casaleggio has endowed the Movement with a technological and organisational infrastructure that has proved particularly effective.

Grillo's entry into politics was not sudden; it came about in stages. A watershed moment in Grillo's career was his 'expulsion' – in November 1986 – from national television as a result of a gag aimed at the Socialist Party, the party of the then prime minister Bettino Craxi. Made at peak viewing time on a state TV channel, the gag – which branded the socialists as thieves – led to the comedian's almost total ostracism from national television (on a few occasions he was allowed to make brief appearances, but his scripts were vetted in advance in case they contained any potentially offensive material). From then on, Grillo found his ideal setting in shows in theatres and sports arenas, where he had direct contact with the audience. The greater freedom offered by these occasions prompted him gradually to redefine his repertoire, which increasingly centred around scathing criticism of the political class and economic powers (big industry, finance), and which, more and more often, targeted specific individuals by name.

5 The role of the comedian as a natural counterpoint to power has been underscored by one of the best-known supporters of Grillo and the M5S, the Nobel Prize winner for literature Dario Fo (Fo and Manin 2013).

A major step on the path that was to lead Grillo to political prominence was taken in the autumn of 1993, when he returned (with great success) for two evenings to state television. In Italian politics, 1993 was an important year. The great change that would be brought about by the elections held the following March was already looming; under the onslaught of judicial enquiries and faced with a slump in the opinion polls, the governing parties had already got wind of the approaching storm.

Seen today, Grillo's 1993 TV show reveals some themes which would become central to his political proposal. It featured a Grillo who meditated on the figure of the comedian who says things that a comedian is not entitled to say (when he seemed to be taking himself too seriously, he would put on a clown's red nose and go back to his proper role, occasionally quipping 'I shouldn't be saying this; I'm a comedian' – a refrain that would often follow his outbursts[6]). To tell the truth, in the show, Grillo's criticism of politics was fairly low key. In the name of feisty consumerism, his main target was the economic and financial world, and politics took a back seat. At a time when the political class was being hammered by judicial enquiries, this choice was somewhat unorthodox, since politicians would have made far easier targets. Instead, most of his arrows were aimed at entrepreneurs and the big names in finance. As the real power was in their hands, it was these figures who should come under public scrutiny. Subsequent years (from the foundation of the blog onwards), however, would see a progressive shift in this stance, with politicians increasingly becoming scapegoats for widespread social unease. Beyond this, however, the show revealed a few points that Grillo would later develop on his blog and in the Movement. First of all, there was his emphasis on some issues (water as a public asset, the environmental repercussions of human behaviour, etc.) that would become central to his 'program'. Secondly, there was his use of two arguments that would later characterise his political discourse. One of these was the active role of the citizen – the power which citizens themselves must be aware of: 'we have done great things; these people now know that we know a bit more ...'. The other was the contrast between the future (innovation, renewal) and a 'dead' governing class, incapable of understanding these changes: 'these people are dead ... We'll bury them with a loud raspberry'. This was a way

6 After Grillo's entry into politics, his dual nature as comedian and politician prompted his critics to accuse him of ambiguity and to downplay the true size of his following (if thousands attend his rallies – it was often claimed – it is only because they want to see a comedy show free of charge). However, this dual nature was subtly exploited by Grillo himself as a kind of 'Catch-22': when the politicians ignored him, he could accuse them of being deaf to society; when they paid attention to him, the fact that they were hanging on the words of a comedian made them look ridiculous. For example, when Prime Minister Prodi talked about him on the TV programme *Porta a Porta*, Grillo commented that 'It's like the BBC broadcasting a speech to the nation by Gordon Brown, who then addresses himself to Mr. Bean'.

of criticising the political and economic elite that would repeatedly feature in his future political speeches.

For purposes of the present analysis, however, the most interesting aspect of Grillo's show is that, for the first time, he triggered collective action from the stage by prompting his audience to target a common objective. After harshly criticizing the state telephone company (SIP) for charging high prices for certain telephone services, which, he claimed, unjustly inflated users' telephone bills, he urged every member of the audience to send a postcard to the company chairman demanding that the charges be abolished. For the first time, Grillo's spectators were not passive; by uniting, they felt the strength that they could exert. This initiative was successful, so much so that the telephone company announced a few days later that customers would soon be able to deactivate the numbers in question. The target of the protest (a monopolistic company) and the strategy of action (sending a protest message) were forerunners of the objectives pursued and the methods adopted by the blog 10 years later, as we will see.

Those spectators who had not followed Grillo between 1986 and 1993 were therefore faced with a very different comedian, one who no longer made fun of the strange habits of the Americans or of the Italians on holiday, but utilised the same comic weapons (frequent appeals to common sense, care not to get hoodwinked, the taste for hyperbole and paradox, etc.) in order to criticise the economy and finance. Grillo increasingly intervened in 'serious' issues (the debt of developing countries, biotechnologies, information, the multinationals) and began writing newspaper articles fairly regularly. Gradually the comedian turned himself into an 'opinion-maker' or, as is often said, a 'guru'.

In those days, the positions adopted by Grillo – albeit endowed with a certain independence – could undoubtedly be located on the left of the political spectrum. He was influenced by the themes of critical consumerism, ecology and a certain anticapitalist stance of a Catholic stamp. Before his entry into politics, his audience was chiefly leftist (the festivals of the main left-wing party – PCI/PDS/DS – frequently offered him the stage; leftist newspapers often praised his civic commitment and contributed to building the public's faith in his work of 'counter-information').

The Birth of the Blog (and the Cyber-Entrepreneur Behind the Scenes)

The decisive turning-point was reached on 26 January 2005, with the foundation of the blog (www.beppegrillo.it), which soon became the blog with the largest following in Italy and was also frequently quoted by foreign media. In 2008, *The Observer* rated it as the ninth most influential blog in the world, while in the same year *Time* magazine included it in its list of the world's 25 best blogs.

The issues dealt with by the blog were a direct follow-on from those which Grillo had tackled as an opinion-maker. His favourite issue, the one with which he was chiefly identified, at least in the early days, was that of temporary employment.

At that time, a fierce debate was raging in Italy over workers' rights to job security. Some argued that these should be reduced in order to favour the creation of new jobs in an economic environment that was becoming more complex and dynamic; others felt that they were the bulwark of workers' dignity and had to be defended. Grillo was of the latter opinion. Assuming the role of spokesman for the hopes and disappointments of numerous young people engaged in temporary and underpaid jobs, he gathered many of their stories through his blog and later assembled them in his book *Schiavi Moderni* (*Modern Slaves*) (2007), which can be downloaded free of charge from the website. This issue, which was certainly the most popular that Grillo dealt with, earned him considerable criticism (many accused him of sullying the memory of Marco Biagi, the expert on employment law who had given his name to a labour market reform law much criticised by the blog, and who had been murdered by terrorists).

The blog opposed the war in Iraq, accusing the Berlusconi government of lying to the Italian people and to the president of the republic and of having initiated a mission that was anti-constitutional. After reading the declarations of the president of the foreign commission, Gustavo Selva, who admitted that the intervention was 'a war disguised as a peace mission', Grillo urged people to send the president of the republic an email asking him 'to bring our "peacemakers" back from Iraq immediately and to replace them with this government that talks bullshit'. According to Grillo (2007, p. 42), 'a million emails were sent in a few months'.

Another recurrent theme was ecology (opposition to incinerators and activism in favour of renewable energy sources), which was often linked to criticism of official science (viewed as being subservient to powerful economic interests). Among the actions promoted in this area, there was the raising of funds to buy the equipment needed for research by a group of specialists in the field of nanoparticles and the pollution caused by them.

Italian finance and the harm caused by 'capitalism without capital' also came under constant criticism. For instance, the blog promoted the purchase of a page in *la Repubblica* demanding the resignation of the then governor of the Bank of Italy, Antonio Fazio, who was involved in a banking scandal, and then a campaign to 'fire' the board of directors of the telephone company Telecom. Powerful economic interests – large multinational groups, monopolistic companies, international finance – were a constant target of Grillo's attacks. In opposition to such interests, he earned the trust of broad sectors of public opinion by becoming the champion of small savers – who had purportedly been swindled by misleading financial instruments – and of those workers who suffered the consequences of the strategies of delocalisation and the management errors of the large companies.

Even before the creation of the blog, faith in Grillo in the economic field had been nurtured by his anticipation of the collapse of Parmalat. Back in 2002, a year before this large food manufacturer went bankrupt, Grillo had warned that the debt status of Parmalat was unsustainable. For this reason, following the bankruptcy, the comedian was summoned by the magistrates to testify, as an informed witness, in the ensuing court case. Thus, in all of these instances, Grillo became the champion and spokesman for the interests of the man in the street (small saver, small shareholder, worker) against powerful interest groups, while at the same time criticizing the negligence of the supervisory institutions and a less-than-free press.

But the theme which progressively came to the fore was Grillo's criticism of the political 'caste', which can be summed up by the slogan 'Clean up Parliament'. On 22 November 2005, he paid for the publication, again with the financial contribution of the followers of the blog, of an appeal ('Clean up Parliament!') in the daily *International Herald Tribune* for the resignations of 23 Italian MPs who had been definitively convicted of various crimes.

As we have seen, the blog became a vehicle for the promotion of political actions of various kinds (purchase of newspaper pages, additions, fundraising, etc.). In a booklet (*Un anno di blog*) accompanying the DVD *Incantesimi* (2006), Grillo defined the blog as 'the tool that we have for creating true democracy – a new form of democracy that has been called 'direct democracy'. People can now keep themselves informed, at all times and from different sources, about the issues that concern them: energy, water, health care and the government; and they can express their opinions without going through the filters of the party mandarins and newspaper editors. We are moving away from giving the politician *carte blanche* and towards the participation of the citizen' (Grillo 2006b). Doubts have been expressed as to the true ability of Grillo's blog to fulfil these promises of participation (cf. Chapter 6). Several critics claim that the blog does not exploit the potential of this instrument, but rather makes a one-way use of it: 'centralised, with a founding nucleus, the post, which is handed down every day from on high, is a series of comments that cancel one another out through their overabundance and their lack of feedback. Each post gets hundreds, sometimes thousands, of comments. It is impossible to read them all. The system is not geared for dialogue. Grillo never replies. It is a solo performance, a soliloquy, a monologue which imposes a dominant thought and leaves the commentators with the ephemeral glory of an uninfluential, invisible space' (Trocino 2011, pp. 117–18). Instead of opening the door to a new form of participation and communication on an equal footing, the blog is seen as serving to free the leader from the 'nuisance' of journalistic mediation and from the obligation imposed by the traditional media to take part in debate with others (journalists or television interviewers). Such criticism seems to be confirmed by Grillo's intolerance, ever since the foundation of the blog, of interviews – which he has increasingly rarely granted – and of cross-questioning in general (De Maria, Fleischner and Targia 2008).

The birth of the blog stemmed from Grillo's decisive meeting with Casaleggio Associati, the company of web marketing and strategies presided over by Gianroberto Casaleggio. Casaleggio himself is a singular figure, who likes to depict apocalyptic scenarios (as in the video *Gaia*, available on YouTube and the butt of numerous parodies) and who has built up a successful business enterprise (see Oggiano 2013, among others) in the field of the Internet, of which he is also a utopian theorist (and, in many ways, a little naïve, Casaleggio 2004). His vision of politics and society (as far as can be judged from his writings and his rare public statements) attributes to technology (specifically to information technology) the role of a dynamo of social change.[7]

Grillo, a leader able to seduce crowds with the skill of a born performer, found in Casaleggio a managerial organisation, albeit very much *sui generis*. The partnership between Grillo, who stood in the spotlight, and Casaleggio, who remained behind the scenes, constituted one of the most controversial aspects of the political experience of what was to become the 5 Star Movement (De Maria, Fleischner and Targia 2008, p. 177; Orsatti 2010). Indeed, the role of Casaleggio has been criticised by the exponents of the movement who, over the years, have been expelled. According to them, Casaleggio's role is not one of mere technical support, as was initially depicted; rather, he is claimed to contribute to defining the political contents. In the opinion of some observers, it is Casaleggio who has been responsible for some of Grillo's swings to the right.

Some of the stances adopted by Grillo's blog have aroused arguments because they appear to be in contradiction with his history and with his original political collocation. This is particularly true of the issue of immigration. In 2000, Grillo criticised the 'natural racism' of Italians (Scanzi 2008, p. 118), while since the foundation of the blog, he has increasingly frequently spoken out against immigration and against Italy's excessively soft approach to this phenomenon (see, for example, the posts of 5 October 2007 or 10 May 2013).

The political collocation of Grillo, and later of the M5S, is a matter of debate (Corbetta and Vignati 2013b; Vignati 2013c). On this question, two main interpretations have so far emerged. One of these holds that Grillo is above all a son of 'Berlusconism', of the 'non-pedagogic and non-orthopedic' conception of politics that characterises the founder of Forza Italia (Orsina 2013), or else of the 'populist toxins' that Berlusconi injected into the Italian political system (according to the interpretation spread by *la Repubblica*, an influential newspaper in public debate in Italy). The other interpretation (which we advocated in Vignati 2013a, pp. 34–6, 2013b, pp. 80–81) is that the success of the M5S – at least in the early stages – found nourishment chiefly in the arguments and social environments that had, in the previous decade, supported the galaxy of the 'anti-Berlusconi'

7 In an interview, Casaleggio (2013) provided a list of authors who had inspired him: Steven Johnson (*Emergence. The connected lives of Ants, Brains, Cities, and Software*, 2001), Duncan Watts (*Six Degrees. The Science of a Connected Age*, 2004), Howard Rheingold (*Smart Mobs: The Next Social Revolution*, 2002), Malcolm Gladwell, (*The Tipping Point: How Little Things Can Make a Big Difference*, 2000), Lawrence Lessig (*Free Culture*, 2004), Albert-Laszlo Parabasi (*Linked. The New Science of Network*, 2002); while the scientific and intellectual quality of these texts is somewhat mixed, their unifying feature may perhaps be seen in a vision of social change that is *induced and guided* by the new communication technologies – change constructed through horizontal networks that are able to bypass hierarchies and mediation and through 'emerging' systemic phenomena arising from molecular changes in individual behaviours.

movements; analysis of the issues championed by the blog (on which, among politicians, Berlusconi was the most frequent target of criticism and invective) and surveys on the profile of the supporters of the early initiatives reveal this proximity. The ability of Grillo (and Casaleggio) lies precisely in the fact that onto these issues they managed to graft openly 'antipolitical' language and issues of diverse provenance (such as opposition to immigration or hostility towards the tax authorities) and succeeded in constructing around these an organisation that was efficient (at least in the phase of electoral consensus-building).

For what concerns closeness to the political parties, Grillo manifested a preference for the centre-left coalition up until the 2006 general election. In 2006, he advocated support of the centre-left coalition led by Prodi, albeit with scant enthusiasm (as the choice of the 'lesser evil'). During the course of Prodi's brief legislature, however, his faith in the centre-left gradually waned (the law on prison pardons, which in 2006 led to the early release of some thousands of prison inmates, was mainly responsible for the change). Grillo's arguments with some members of the government became increasingly heated (the minister of justice, Mastella, being the favourite target) until, on the occasion of the 2008 general election, he urged voters to abstain, claiming that there was no difference between Veltroni and Berlusconi, the leaders of the two main coalitions: 'The answer to this regime is not to vote. It's the only democratic weapon we've got left' (Grillo 2008).

More generally, we can say that, during the 15th legislature (2006–2008), Grillo's relationship with institutional politics and representative democracy changed. Initially, the blog constituted a sort of goad to be used on politicians: citizens were to inform themselves, to become active, and to make their proposals heard, but it was the politicians – defined as our 'employees' – who were to translate these proposals into laws within the political institutions. Although politics was seen as largely discredited, it remained the repository of the right/duty to govern and therefore its least discredited components (mainly identified as centre-left parties) had to be goaded into action. In January 2006, the initiative dubbed 'citizens' primaries' (consultation of followers of the blog on the principal political issues, the results of which were delivered to Prime Minister Prodi) provided an example of this mechanism (the blog as a point of collection for citizens' petitions, so that the politicians would know which objectives to pursue). Symbolically, delivering the results of the 'citizens' primaries' to Prodi and, some time later, the arrival in the senate of the three laws that had been proposed by popular initiative and promoted through V-day (see below) were the culmination of the phase in which Grillo acted as the voice of the people demanding to be heard in government circles. The scant attention that was paid towards these two initiatives (the proposed laws were not scheduled for debate, while, according to Grillo's reconstruction, Prodi slept during the meeting in which the results of the citizen's primaries were presented to him) marked a schism; from then on, it was no longer possible to hope for anything from *this* political class. Citizens had to become directly engaged and no longer delegate.

A fundamental step in the constitution of the political base of the future 5 Star Movement was taken through the creation of local discussion groups by means of the platform of Meetup.com (on this point, see Chapter 3). This initiative – which was intended 'to give all those who follow my blog the chance to meet together, to discuss and take initiatives' – was announced in a post on 16 July 2005. Within a short time, numerous groups formed, which gave rise to a few national meetings (the first held in Turin on 17 December 2005). During that meeting, Grillo called himself the 'amplifier' of the activities of the groups. The Meet-ups would become the basis for the constitution of the 5 Star civic lists, whose foundation can be traced back to a post of 25 January 2007, and which took concrete form after the success of a watershed initiative in the story that we are tracing – the so-called V-day.

V-Day and the Civic Lists

In 2007 two events took place which significantly marked Beppe Grillo's political collocation. One was the so-called V-Day. The other is less well known, but is important because it clearly sanctioned Grillo's break with the left. The event was his last participation in the 'festa dell'Unità' (the celebration of the main party on the left – PCI, PDS, DS, in its various incarnations).

The idea of V-Day was launched by the blog on 14 June 2007. The letter 'V' has a threefold meaning: it recalls Winston Churchill's victory sign; it stands for 'vendetta', as in the comics by Alan Moore and David Lloyd; and, more prosaically, it is the first letter of 'vaffanculo' (bugger off), an imperative resoundingly addressed to Italian politicians. Held on 8 September in over 200 venues, V-Day obtained enormous (and, to many observers, unexpected) success. Grillo himself turned up at the Bologna gathering, where he reeled off a long list of 'vaffanculo'. During the event, signatures were collected for three laws proposed by popular initiative (one to bar the election to parliament of persons definitively convicted of crimes; one to limit MPs to a maximum of two terms in Parliament, and one to modify electoral law so that votes could be cast for individual candidates rather than for fixed lists). This initiative was a great success; instead of the 50,000 signatures required by the constitution (art. 71) for laws proposed by popular initiative, some 336,144 were collected.

A week after V-day, on 15 September 2007, Grillo attended his last 'festa dell'Unità'. Until then, he had been regarded by the left as a travelling companion – albeit not easy to control – whose positions were close to those of the leftist party (he had regularly participated in the 'feste dell'Unità'). On this occasion, however, he harshly criticised the leadership of the DS and the centre-left government, as indeed he had already done on V-day. This marked a definitive split and, therefore, the conquest of an autonomous political position, separate from the traditional parties.

The success of V-day prompted Grillo to call for another demonstration of the same type a short time later (27 October). This time, the 'caste' of journalists was targeted. Like the first event, this demonstration was held at several venues throughout the country (Grillo was in Turin), and again signatures were collected. Three abrogative referendums were called for: one to abolish the professional register of journalists, one to abolish the public financing of newspapers, and one to abolish the Gasparri law on the system of radio and television (the initiative did not have a successful outcome: the Supreme Court judged that the procedures followed had been improper). In his speech, Grillo did not only deal with the issue of the day (the press); confirming his political ambitions and the fact that the theme of the demonstration was, more than anything else, a pretext to affirm his own strength through his ability to draw crowds, he directly attacked the president of the republic: 'He ought to be the president of the Italian people, not of the parties'.

The antipathy between Grillo and Giorgio Napolitano has always been strong – and reciprocal. Indeed, Grillo has often spoken out against the role assumed by Napolitano (culminating in his demand for the president's impeachment on 30 January 2014). Equally numerous, however, have been the president's statements against forms of populism and 'antipolitics', in which the allusion to the leader of the M5S is evident. That these two figures should perceive each other as enemies was inevitable. On the one hand, Grillo – to quote Bourdieu's observation on Coluche – questions 'the fundamental presupposition, that it is only politicians who can talk about politics'. On the other hand, in the deep crisis in which the Italian party system has found itself in recent years, Napolitano has ended up playing a far more active role than his predecessors. Indeed, his interpretation of his role as guarantor of Italian political institutions has led him to be identified by some as a bulwark in defence of the political class's monopoly on politics, and therefore as an obstacle to citizens' requests to participate in political activity.[8]

As mentioned earlier, 25 January 2007 was the founding moment of the civic lists: on the blog, Grillo started from the premise that 'the parties are anachronistic, finished, self-recommending'. He went on to identify the municipalities as the setting in which politics should be renovated, through the creation of civic lists and finally of 5-star municipalities (the stars indicating the cornerstones of the political proposal: energy, connectivity, publicly owned water supplies, refuse collection, social services).

Through this move, Grillo intercepted a phenomenon – that of the civic lists – which had been growing for several years; an expression of detachment from the parties and of the search for alternative settings in which to carry out political activity (Norris 2002), the civic lists significantly modified the political choices offered in administrative elections. The relationship between Grillo and the civic lists is the principal node around which the various interpretations of the M5S

8 The book which Marco Travaglio (2014), a journalist close to the M5S, has devoted to Napolitano summarises the same type of criticism that has characterised the positions of Grillo and the M5S towards the president of the republic.

turn. Those observers who highlight the role of the Movement's founder and his ability to attract the support of voters (hence considering the civic lists as mere local appendices of the leader) define the M5S as a populist and 'leaderist' party. By contrast, those who underline the formation 'from below' and the autonomy of the civic lists (hence accepting Grillo's claim to be a 'megaphone' for their autonomous petitions) consider the M5S to be a party capable of profound democratic and participatory renewal. In reality, both of these aspects are to be found in the original political project, even though – as we claimed in the first section – the 'leaderist' aspect has so far prevailed.

It was especially after the success of V-Day that the idea of creating the civic lists took shape. On 10 October 2007, Grillo provided the first indications of how to create these lists, which he called 'viruses of participatory democracy'. His prescription was to fulfil four requirements (candidates must not be members of any other party or political movement; they must have no criminal convictions, even if not definitive, nor any criminal proceedings pending; they must not have served more than one electoral term, at any level; they must reside within the ward of the municipality or region in which they are candidates) and to ensure three commitments (candidates must give up their electoral mandate 'if they no longer possess, or are shown never to have possessed, one or more of the above-described minimum requirements; the list must publish candidates' curricula online and open a blog to allow citizens free exchange of opinions and criticisms with members of the lists'; the list 'must not ally itself with other parties or lists, unless certified by the blog, in order to govern the municipality or region'). The lists, bearing various names and symbols – the most common being 'Amici di Beppe Grillo' (Friends of Beppe Grillo) – ran for the first time in the elections of April 2008 in 17 municipalities and the Sicilian Regional Council; their percentages were low but encouraging. The blog (17 April 2008) expressed satisfaction over the results, which had been achieved 'without advertising, without public funds, and without support from television channels or newspapers'. This reference to the absence of public financing and television or press support would later become one of the leitmotifs marking the difference between the lists linked to Grillo and the traditional political parties.

On 8 March 2009, the first national meeting of the 5 Star Civic Lists was held in Florence, where Grillo presented the main points of the programme 'Carta di Firenze' (Florence Charter). The objectives to pursue chiefly concerned ecology or issues connected with it, such as energy, transport and mobility, and connectivity. Between 2009 and 2011 the civic lists certified by the blog participated in an ever greater number of municipal and regional elections, achieving increasing success, especially in the regions of the centre-north (Piedmont and Emilia-Romagna being the regions where support was greatest).

The history, or the chronicle, of Grillo's entry into politics follows two parallel pathways: on the one hand, the increasingly numerous local meet-ups carrying out their day-to-day, low-profile work of organisation and propagation; on the other, Grillo's sporadic search for the media event, for the provocation that draws a reaction from other political players – a reaction that is often clumsy, graceless and generally ineffective (swinging between warnings of danger to democracy and aping the comedian's sarcastic language). One of the provocations that obtained the greatest media coverage was Grillo's attempt to run as a candidate in the October 2009 open elections (improperly called 'primaries') for the post of secretary of the Partito Democratico (Democratic Party, PD). The rejection of his candidature on the part of the PD leadership enabled Grillo to portray himself as a representative of a civil society whose desire to participate was rejected by the political parties which 'monopolised' the political sphere.

Shortly after the rejection of Grillo's candidature in the PD primaries, the Movement was born. This was hailed as 'the voice of millions of people who have no say on television or in newsreels, but which will be the voice of the Italy of tomorrow. The Italy of people who are honest, transparent, clean, who don't want nuclear power stations, incinerators, refuse tips filled with toxic waste'. 'This movement will not delegate to others; I can guarantee that. It is a first-person movement; the first person plural: we, the citizens'. The actual baptism of the movement took place on 4 October 2009 in Milan, where it was announced that the M5S would run in the 2010 regional elections, and a 122-point programme was presented. In his speech, Grillo summarised these as: the abolition of some of the most controversial laws passed by Berlusconi's governments in the spheres of justice or employment; the limitation to two terms for all elective offices, the non-eligibility of those convicted of crimes, and the obligatory discussion of law proposals made by popular initiative; the provision of incentives for renewable energy sources, and opposition to incinerators and nuclear power stations; scrapping of the 'great infrastructure projects', such as the Tav (high-speed rail link) and the bridge over the Strait of Messina.

The political importance of the Movement began to emerge clearly in the 2010 regional elections. The M5S presented lists in five regions (out of 13, Piedmont, Lombardy, Veneto, Emilia-Romagna and Campania), achieving notable results especially in Emilia-Romagna (6 per cent for the list; 7 per cent for the presidential candidate) and in Piedmont (where the incumbent president, Mercedes Bresso of the PD, narrowly lost, partly on account of the votes cast for the M5S candidate, a fact which would cause considerable argument).

It was, however, in the municipal elections of May 2012 that the Movement became a prominent political force. On that occasion, the number of municipalities in which the M5S managed to present its own list rose markedly. Moreover, for the first time, the movement succeeded in winning some municipalities, among which one regional capital (Parma), and frequently reached double-figure percentages (Vignati 2013b). This undeniable success, however, brought with it some difficulties: governing a city proved to be a complicated business (the M5S mayor of Parma was forced to accept the start-up of the incinerator he had opposed during his election campaign, and appointing the municipal government (*giunta comunale*) proved long and arduous – a symptom of the Movement's limited 'relationship capital'). Moreover, in the months that followed, a few cases of dissidence – and consequent expulsions decided upon authoritatively by Grillo – emerged within the Movement, episodes which brought to light the problems of internal democracy.

Success in the General Election and the Limits of Grillo's Leadership

In spite of these difficulties, however, support for the M5S grew rapidly after the municipal elections, as indicated by the opinion polls, reaching a level of around 20 per cent. Confirmation of the Movement's political stature came in the regional elections in Sicily in October of the same year, when the M5S (with Grillo personally taking part in the election campaign through spectacular media stunts, such as swimming across the Strait of Messina) became the most voted party (Colloca and Vignati 2013).

A few months later, the general election confirmed the importance of the party, which garnered 25.1 per cent of the votes cast(Chamber of Deputies), obtaining 109 deputies and 54 senators. However, the months following the opening of the new parliament saw further difficulties (the disagreement of a few deputies with the policies of the M5S leadership led to their expulsion, while the party appeared isolated and unable to impact on parliamentary manoeuvres). Since then, voter support has manifested contrasting signals. While the opinion polls of people's intention to vote have continued to attribute a share of around 20 per cent to the M5S, the party has displayed a substantial incapacity to transform this support into a stable identity. Indeed, the various regional and administrative elections held since the general election have often yielded disappointing results. Examples can be seen in the regional elections (April 2013) in Friuli-Venezia Giulia (in which the M5S stopped at 13.7 per cent and its candidate at 19.1 per cent), in the May 2013 administrative elections (in which the M5S, though winning another provincial capital, Ragusa, obtained far fewer votes across the board than in the general election) (Corbetta and Vignati 2013a), in the provincial elections (October 2013) in Trentino-Alto Adige (in which Grillo's party won only 5.8 per cent in Trento and 2.5 per cent in Bolzano), and in the regional elections (February 2014) in Sardinia (in which the M5S did not manage to present a list). The contrast between support at the national level (which boomed in the general election and has been confirmed by subsequent surveys) and the difficulty (or at least the slowness) of the party in putting down firm roots at the territorial level, as manifested by the local elections, reveal the lasting dependence of the M5S on its leader Beppe Grillo.

Dependence on the leader is a factor of intrinsic fragility for any organisation, and this contributes to the uncertainty of the long-term prospects of the M5S. In addition, the characteristics of this same leadership have displayed peculiar shortcomings. If a leader is a political entrepreneur who activates lines of conflict latent in society, who is politically able to interpret social unease or even simply a widespread mood, and to give voice to this mood (Grillo has often used the metaphor of the 'megaphone'), then Grillo certainly has the charisma of the leader. If, however, the word 'leader' also means – as the etymology of the term suggests – one who guides, then Grillo is not a leader in the full sense. He has a great ability to gather support, but is unable to guide it from an organisational standpoint and towards concrete objectives.

In their treatise entitled *The Psychology of the Leader*, the English social psychologists Haslam, Reicher and Platow write that: 'no charismatic promise and no promissory notes last forever. In the end, leaders must deliver … Ultimately, leadership can only thrive if the group is made to matter … This is where it becomes important to collaboratively initiate structures that can channel the efforts of group members' (Haslam, Reicher and Platow 2011, pp. 212–13). They go on to add that: 'leaders must know not only how to mobilise people but also how to direct that so as to best achieve results' (ibid., p. 188).

The same conviction has been expressed by Ernesto Galli della Loggia, historian and editorialist of *Corriere della Sera*: 'It is one thing to stir up a crowd at a political rally, but leading a group of parliamentary deputies in accordance with a given strategy is quite another. Grillo has proved that he has charisma, but he is proving unable to transform it into leadership' (*Corriere della Sera*, 5 June 2013). Bruce Sterling, who, in the above-mentioned article for *Wired*, revealed himself to be very sympathetic towards the ideas and practices of the Movement, has compared Grillo to 'Garibaldi leading the charge' and Casaleggio to 'Mazzini publishing clandestine republican tracts'; what the M5S still lacks in order to 'give life to a new Italy' is 'a Cavour in Parliament'. Beyond this picturesque (and, in the case of Casaleggio-Mazzini, somewhat doubtful) comparison, it is certainly true that, alongside a personality able to grab media attention and whip up support, the M5S has so far lacked a leader capable of transforming this consensus into truly incisive political action.

References

Biorcio, R. and Natale, P. 2013. *Politica a cinque stelle*. Milano: Feltrinelli.

Boggio, P. 2006. *Coluche. L'histoire d'un mec*. Paris: Flammarion.

———. 2013. Le tre ragioni del successo del Movimento 5 stelle. *Comunicazione politica*, 13(1), pp. 43–62.

Bourdieu, P. 2000. *Propos sur le champ politique*. Lyon: Presses Universitaires de Lyon.

Caracci, R. 2013. *Il ruggito del Grillo*. Bergamo: Moretti & Vitali.

Casaleggio, G. 2004. *Web ergo sum*. Milan: Sperling & Kupfer.

Casaleggio, G. 2013. Casaleggio: La democrazia va rifondata. Interviewed by S. Danna. *Il Club della Lettura – Il Corriere della Sera*, 23 June. [online] Available at: http://lettura.corriere.it/la-democrazia-va-rifondata/ [Accessed 30 April 2014].

Colloca, P. and Vignati, R. 2013. Tra continuità e cambiamenti. Le elezioni regionali siciliane del 2012. *Istituzioni del federalismo*, 34(1), 1, pp. 265–302.

Corbetta, P. and Vignati, R. 2013a. Beppe Grillo's First Defeat? The May 2013 Municipal Elections in Italy. *South European Society and Politics*, 18(4), pp. 499–521.

———. 2013b. Left or Right? The Complex Nature and Uncertain Future of the 5 Star Movement. *Italian politics & society*, 72–3, Spring-Fall, pp. 53–62.

Crozier, M. and Fridberg, E. 1977. *L'acteur et le système. Les contraintes de l'action collective*. Paris: Éditions du Seuil.

De Maria, F., Fleischner, E. and Targia, E. 2008. *Chi ha paura di Beppe Grillo?* Milano: Selene.

Dosse, F. 2010. *Gilles Deleuze & Felix Guattari: Intersecting lives*. New York: Columbia University Press.

Floridia, A. and Vignati, R. 2014. Deliberativa, diretta o partecipativa? Le sfide del Movimento 5 stelle alla democrazia rappresentativa. *Quaderni di sociologia*, 58(2), pp. 51–74.

Fo, D., Grillo, B. and Casaleggio, G. 2013. *Il Grillo canta sempre al tramonto*. Milan: Chiarelettere.

Fo, D. and Manin, G. 2013. *Un clown vi seppellirà*. Parma: Guanda.

Galli Della Loggia, E. 2013. Se il carisma non basta, *Corriere della sera*, 10 June.

Graeber, D. 2007. *There Never Was a West, or: Democracy Emerges the Spaces in Between*. Oakland: Ak Press.

Greblo, E. 2011. *Filosofia di Beppe Grillo*. Sesto San Giovanni: Mimesis.

Greenfell, M. 2004. *Pierre Bourdieu: Agent Provocateur*. London and New York: Continuum.

Grillo, B. 2006a. *Un anno di blog*. Booklet accompanying the DVD *Incantesimi*. Milan: Casaleggio Associati.

———. 2006b. *Tutto il Grillo che conta*. Milan: Feltrinelli.

———. 2007. *Tutte le battaglie di Beppe Grillo*. Milan: Casaleggio Associati.

———. 2008. Comunicato politico numero 4. *Beppegrillo.it*, [blog] 6 March. Available at: http://www.beppegrillo.it/2008/03/comunicato_poli_2.html [Accessed 4 June 2014].

———. 2010. Il leader. *Beppegrillo.it*, [blog] 26 June. Available at: http://www.beppegrillo.it/2010/06/il_leader.html [Accessed 4 June 2014].

Haslam, S.A., Reicher, D.S. and Platow, M.J. 2011. *The New Psychology of Leadership: Identity, Influence, and Power*. Hove and New York: Psychology Press.

Lanfrey, D. 2011. Il Movimento dei grillini tra meetup, meta-organizzazione e democrazia del monitoraggio. In: L. Mosca and C. Vaccari, eds. *Nuovi media, nuova politica? Partecipazione e mobilitazione online da MoveOn al MoVimento 5 Stelle*. Milano: Franco Angeli, pp. 143–66.

Norris, P. 2002. *Democratic Phoenix: Reinventing Political Activism*. Cambridge: Cambridge University Press.

Oggiano, F. 2013. *Beppe Grillo parlante*. Milano: Cairo.

Orsatti, P. 2010. Grillo e il suo spin doctor: la Casaleggio Associati. *Micromega*, 5, pp. 197–204.

Orsina, G. 2013. *Il berlusconismo nella storia d'Italia*. Venezia: Marsilio.

Panebianco, A. 1982. *Modelli di partito*. Bologna: Il Mulino.

Ruggiero, L., ed. 2003. *Grillo da ridere (per non piangere)*. Milano: Kaos.

Scanzi, A. 2008. *Ve lo do io Beppe Grillo*. Milano: Mondadori.

Swartz, D. 1997. *Culture and Power: The Sociology of Pierre Bourdieu*. Chicago: University of Chicago Press.

Tenaille, F. 2006. *Coluche, même pas mort*. Paris: Calmann-Lévy.

Travaglio, M. 2014. *Viva il re!* Milano: Chiarelettere.

Trocino, F. 2011. *Popstar della cultura*. Fazi: Roma.

Ungar, S. 1996. The Coluche Effect. In: S. Ungar and T. Conley, eds. *Identity Papers: Contested Nationhood in Twentieth Century France*. Minneapolis: University of Minnesota Press, pp. 259–71.

Vignati, R. 2013a. Beppe Grillo: dalla Tv ai palasport, dal blog al Movimento. In: P. Corbetta and E. Gualmini, eds. *Il partito di Grillo*. Bologna: Il Mulino, pp. 29–63.

———. 2013b. The Challenge of the 5 Star Movement. In: A. Di Virgilio and C. Radaelli, eds. *Italian politics 2012*. New York: Berghahn, pp. 78–94.

———. 2013c. La provenienza degli elettori del Movimento 5 stelle: indagini campionarie e Modello di Goodman a confronto. In: I. Diamanti and L. Ceccarini, eds. *Sondaggi ed elezioni. Le regole del gioco e della comunicazione*. Firenze: Sise, pp. 424–44.

Chapter 2
The Organization of the Movimento 5 Stelle: A Contradictory Party Model

Rinaldo Vignati

Introduction

It is not easy to describe the organization of the 5 Star Movement (M5S), both because the characteristics of the party are practically unique, and because its structure is continuously and rapidly evolving. It is therefore difficult to link the party to previous organizational models, and even more difficult to capture it in a snapshot that can freeze its structure in a given moment and which is able to grasp the different facets and the different geographic expressions of this structure.

The organizational theory on which the M5S is based is radically innovative. In the writings and declarations of Grillo and Casaleggio, the party is one of those mediating structures which – thanks to the power of the Web – are destined to disappear. The Movement's two leaders enunciate this in various passages of their books:

> Parties live on money, on lobbies, on territorial structures: headquarters, press offices, employees, newspapers. On the Internet, all this is worthless; it's not needed. (Casaleggio and Grillo 2011, p. 8)

> Parties belong to history. (Grillo in Fo, Grillo and Casaleggio 2013, p. 161)

> If we introduce direct democracy, we no longer need parties: on an egalitarian basis, you can decide anything, whether at the local or national level. (Casaleggio in Fo Grillo and Casaleggio, 2013, p. 191)

> A leader has to do with a party, and we want parties to disappear completely; we want new community rules, and we want these community rules to be applicable by everyone; and at the end of this process we want the Movement to be no longer necessary, because there are the citizens, there is a community. I know a lot of people might ask: but if there are no parties, who will sit in parliament? How can a parliament exist without parties? There will be the movements, the committees, all of which will be an expression of the demands that come from civil society. (Grillo in Fo, Grillo and Casaleggio 2013, pp. 79–80)

This utopian conception finds expression in a statute which, in order to distinguish itself from those of the traditional parties, prefers to call itself a *non*-statute. This is a totally original document which has nothing in common with the statutes of the parties that we have known so far. Even forms of parties *sui generis* and of a highly personalized character, such as the Lega Nord and Forza Italia, have adopted statutes that more or less conform to the 'traditional' party models; this means having restricted bodies charged with party management and periodic general assemblies to choose the leadership, in a blend, which varies from party to party, of the *top-down* principle of appointment and the *bottom-up* principle of election.

The statute of the M5S, by contrast, is a slim document of only seven articles (Movimento 5 Stelle 2009). The first of these defines the Movement as a 'non-association' (article 4 subsequently specifies that 'it is not a political party, nor is it intended that it should become one in the future'): it is a 'platform and vehicle for debate and consultation which originates from and finds its epicentre in the blog beppegrillo.it. The "headquarters" of the "MoVimento 5 Stelle" coincides with the Internet address beppegrillo.it'. The third article establishes that the name and symbol of the Movement are 'registered in the name of Beppe Grillo, the only title-holder of the rights to their use'. This is the most controversial article, in that it depicts the party as a sort of commercial enterprise headed by a 'boss', who is its owner; as such, it leads to the extreme manifestation of those forms of 'personal party' (Calise 2000)[1] that have been seen in recent decades. The use of the Movement's name and symbol have been at the centre of some of the arguments that have led to the expulsion of some exponents of the M5S.

Article 5 of the statute states that:

> Enrolment in the Movement does not require any greater formalities than does registration with a normal Internet site. The Movement is open to all Italian citizens who have reached the age of majority who, on application for enrolment,

1 Another feature that attributes this character to the M5S is the ownership of the so-called operating system, the instrument which – by linking the party's base with its elected representatives – should be the means of implementing that direct democracy which underpins the political project of this Movement. This system is characterized by a rigidly proprietary structure, which has been contested by some exponents on the ground. See, for example, the circumstantiated criticisms of the operating system advanced by Davide Barillari, a member of the Lazio Regional Council and the promoter of an alternative initiative for electronic democracy (the Lazio Movement's 'Electronic Parliament'). Barillari highlighted certain limits of the platform and advocated greater participation by the party's base in defining the platform itself, starting from the contribution of the Lazio Movement's experience (Lazio's Electronic Parliament *'is at the complete disposal of the national staff and of all the activists; we can unite our efforts')*. On 19 September 2013, Grillo indirectly cut short these discussions by peremptorily concluding one of his posts on the blog: 'P.S: it must be remembered that no certified applications exist outside those of the blog' (Grillo 2013a).

> are not members of political parties or of associations whose objectives contrast with those described above. Application for membership of the Movement is to be forwarded by Internet; on application, aspiring members are to certify that they are in possession of the requisites specified in the previous paragraph.

In order to join, 'no membership fee is required' (article 6); however, on the 'blog www.beppegrillo.it voluntary subscriptions may be made for the collection of funds dedicated to financing individual initiatives or demonstrations'.

Article 4 indicates the purpose of the M5S as the wish:

> To bear witness to the possibility of realizing an efficient an efficacious exchange of opinions and democratic debate outside the bonds of associations and parties and without the mediation of directive or representative organisms, thereby conferring on all Internet users the role of government and direction that is normally attributed to the few.

This rejection of 'mediation' means that, unlike the statutes of the traditional parties, the regulations of the M5S do not envisage any organ charged with ensuring internal democracy; rather, they limit themselves to indicating a few generic rules for the choice of candidatures. Thus, article 7 states that:

> On occasions of, and in preparation for, electoral consultations …, the M5S will constitute the center of collection of candidatures and the vehicle for the selection of those subjects who will be authorized, on each occasion and in writing, to use the name and symbol 'MoVimento 5 Stelle' in the setting of their participation in each electoral consultation. These candidates will be chosen from among Italian citizens whose minimum age corresponds to that established by the law for candidature for the elective offices in question who have not been convicted of any criminal offence and who are not the subjects of any penal proceedings, regardless of the nature of the offence involved. The identity of candidates for each elective office will be publicized on a dedicated website created within the framework of the blog; discussions regarding such candidatures will likewise be public, transparent and unmediated. The rules concerning the procedure of candidature and designation for national or local electoral consultations may be more precisely determined in accordance with the type of consultation and in the light of the experience that will be gained over time.

Clearly, a document like this – which does not define organs or modalities for the making of decisions – has no value in regulating the internal life of the Movement; rather, it serves only as the efficacious provocation of a politician who has not forgotten that he is a clown and who uses this dual identity to wrong-foot his opponents. Anyone, among the politicians of the traditional parties, who might dare to criticize the 'non-statute' as being undemocratic would lay himself open to criticism that the practice of the parties deviates – often in a highly visible manner – from the democratic principles sanctioned by their own statutes, and that these organizations are increasingly propped up by a 'leaderistic' principle that turns the participation of their base into a mass that their leaders can manoeuvre.

This awareness – of the shortcomings of the 'normal' political parties, of their failure to keep their promises to allow participation in debate – is the source of the reasoning which leads the exponents of the M5S to accept the peculiarities of the Movement, such as the 'non-statute' and the uncontested role of Beppe Grillo.[2] Referring to a television debate in which an exponent of the Democratic Party (PD) had claimed that the online consultations of the M5S were skewed because they were conditioned by Grillo and Casaleggio's indications as to how to vote, one of the interviewees said:[3]

> If it's true that providing indications on how to vote influences and conditions everyone, then why, dear Democratic party, in your primaries, do you let *the party* indicate which candidate should win? So the primaries are false, then … Let's try to agree on this, folks … Do these indications create a bias, or not? If they do, then you, Democratic party, shouldn't give any indication as to who has to win (City Councilor, Parma, February 2014).

> They [i.e. the parties; the reference is to a television debate in which an exponent of the PD claimed that it was easy to manipulate the votes cast by the M5S base – 'just get 50 people to vote … '] pass it off as normal, as democratic: a practice that is completely antidemocratic. (City Councillor, Parma, February 2014)

In answer to the assertion that the M5S does not have 'places' in which to discuss its policies, one activist replied:

> That's not true; it's a lie, so don't spread it around. In a traditional party, the opinion of a boy in a local branch counts for bugger all! Here, it counts for more! Ask Renzi. Ask one of the PD. That lot said they were going to do one thing, and two minutes later they did the exact opposite [the reference is to the handover of the government from Letta to Renzi in February 2014]. Did the militants have any say in it? No! They hold the primaries, which have to be done in a certain way. Who decides how? Someone in a secret secretariat, because there

---

2 This is one of the most recurrent arguments in the sympathetic press. In this regard, a good example is provided by Scanzi (2014).

3 47 interviews with activists and representatives elected in local and regional assemblies were conducted in two waves. Twenty-five interviews were conducted by Elisabetta Gualmini, Gianluca Passarelli, Filippo Tronconi and Dario Tuorto in Veneto, Lombardy, Liguria, Piedmont, Emilia-Romagna, and Campania in the summer of 2012. Twenty-two more interviews were then conducted by Maria Elisabetta Lanzone and Rinaldo Vignati in Piedmont, Lombardy, Emilia-Romagna, and Sicily between the end of 2013 and the beginning of 2014.

was already an agreement between the majority and the opposition … And no one goes and asks the PD voters what they think. Come and ask us in the M5S about democracy. (Activist and candidate, Milan, February 2014)

I think the PD's statute is well written, but look what it's become. (City Councillor, Ravenna, February 2014)

Personal Party? Charismatic Party?

The essential point in this statute lies in the definition of the ownership of the party brand, which is recognized as belonging to Beppe Grillo. This makes the party the property of its leader in the strict sense, and he can grant or revoke its use as he pleases. This takes to the extreme a tendency that has characterized Italian political parties since the end of the so-called First Republic and the disappearance, or radical transformation, of those parties which had characterized its political panorama. As Calise (2000) points out, in the wake of transformations in the system of the media and changes in electoral legislation, a party that can be defined as 'personal' has gradually come to the fore. 'The personal party has asserted itself outside of parties endowed with rules, procedures and careers. The appearance of organization with which the leader endows himself as he acts is only an extension of the body of the chief' (Prospero 2012, p. 115). In different ways, examples of the personal party have been Forza Italia (later the Popolo della Libertà), l'Italia dei valori and the many celebrity-led micro-parties that have been formed at the periphery to contest municipal and regional elections, or at the centre in the continuous change that has characterized the composition of parliamentary groups in recent legislatures. Moreover, growing elements of personalization have also increasingly characterized those parties which are the more direct heirs of the formations of the First Republic, such as Alleanza Nazionale and then the Partito Democratico (Bordignon 2014).

In press debates, the M5S has frequently been traced back to this model, which is often evoked through the even stronger term of 'partito padronale' (party of the boss). Is this an adequate description, or it is an exaggeration dictated by the dynamics of political-journalistic polemics?

To answer this question, we have to try to define the different components of the M5S more precisely. At the top, around the two leaders, there is what everyone calls 'the staff', which is not clearly defined:

There are seven or eight youngsters: IT people and those who receive the thousands of documents that need to be checked. There's Beppe [Grillo], the lawyers who advise Beppe, and Gianroberto [Casaleggio]. (City Councillor, Ravenna, February 2014)

> We're talking about four or five people. But then, they haven't got that much work to do, except in the run-up to elections, when they have to certify the lists, check that the complete lists come in with the penal certificates attached and grant the use of the symbol. Otherwise, the rest of the time is devoted to taking care of Grillo's blog. (Regional Councillor, Bologna, February 2014)

Officially, the task of the staff is limited to ratifying the lists that are presented in elections, i.e. checking that the candidates who make up the lists fulfil the requirements (the staff therefore acts as a 'guarantor' to ensure that the basic principles of the Movement are respected). Relationships with those who are elected in local elections and with their respective groups – as is confirmed by all the interviewees – are sporadic or even totally absent:

> I hear from Grillo about three times a year; from Casaleggio even less, about twice a year … I don't really have any reason to hear from them. I'd have more reason to hear from my colleagues in Sicily or Lombardy, to find out what they are doing, for example about the refuse program. I can't even think of one reason why I should need to talk to the staff. (Regional Councilor, Bologna, February 2014)

At one time – until the upsurge of votes for the M5S in 2012 – the staff also played a training role, organizing (in Milan) periodic meetings with candidates and elected representatives on the most important issues of the program (public water supply, environment, etc.) and on communication. These meetings were subsequently discontinued when the number of local lists and elected representatives became too great to manage.

The 'party in central office', in addition to the two leaders and their small staff of assistants, also comprises the so-called Gruppo comunicazione (Communication group), which was created to support the activities of the parliamentary groups. The existence and modus operandi of this group have caused not a few problems, raised principally by some MPs who have since been expelled from the Movement.

> 37–38% of the budget of the parliamentary group is spent on the Communication group; we've taken on people to assist us with communication. Seeing these people, with this public money that we give them, writing posts in which they offend the very people they are supposed to be helping to communicate, it's just not on. Since then, I reckon things have changed a bit. He [Claudio Messora, head of the Communication group] was put there, we know, by, by … [he hesitates] … We know that in our code of behavior[4] we have given Beppe Grillo the freedom to choose the members of the Communication group. To tell the

4 Candidates for election to Parliament are required to sign a 'code of behaviour' which prescribes the constitution of 'communication groups' for M5S deputies and senators (cf. Mello 2013, pp. 277–8).

> truth, I reckon he picked the wrong people altogether. (Luis Alberto Orellana, Senator, during the assembly of the meet-ups and the activists of the Province of Pavia, 7 February 2014)

> Ever since I came out with a few criticisms, the Communication group has acted like I no longer exist. [Orellana cites the example of a hearing in commission, the communiqué of which, drafted by the Communication group, makes no mention of him] That's the situation I find myself in … I think that if you make a dialectical internal speech and the reaction of some people is to ostracize you, not to let you make yourself heard … that's really sad; I'm pretty upset by this situation. (ibid.)

Moreover, on several occasions the party's central office has sanctioned not only MPs but also local exponents of the party, revoking their mandate and forbidding them to use the Movement's symbol. Such cases have often been highlighted by the press. The most emblematic is that of Valentino Tavolazzi in Ferrara, an exponent of the Movement from the outset and recognized nationally, and other exponents who had organized a meeting in Rimini to discuss the Movement's internal democracy. Other notable cases have involved Giovanni Favia, Federica Salsi, Raffaella Pirini, some militants from Cento, and Fabrizio Biolé.[5] While some of these cases might be explained in terms of personal incompatibility, others have greater significance from the political and organizational standpoint. In this regard, the case of Tavolazzi appears to be particularly emblematic. Together with other exponents, Tavolazzi was expelled from the M5S for having requested a discussion of the Movement's internal democracy and for attempting to constitute forms of coordination 'from below' through regular, extended assemblies aimed at drawing up a common policy on the main aspects of the work of local administrations. Tavolazzi himself interpreted the reaction of the party leadership (particularly Casaleggio) as being prompted by the fear that, in Emilia-Romagna, there might emerge a Movement that would no longer be dependent on Grillo, but which would be able to organize itself autonomously and to establish equally autonomous forms of discussion and definition of policy:

> From the second half of 2010 onwards, the fear arose that, through these assemblies and this organized way of proceeding, the Movement might take on a rigid, party-like character. … Casaleggio thought that the Movement in Emilia-Romagna could become a center of political power as a result of the fact that its organizational capability was patently superior to that of the average of the Movement. In the rest of Italy these things were not done. … Such a united, strong, cooperative Movement which had so many members throughout

5 An overview of all these cases is provided by a few volumes of a journalistic nature which were published after the great electoral success of the M5S: Pucciarelli (2012), Carbonaro (2013), Mello (2013) and Oggiano (2013).

> the territory, which organized political initiatives in the municipalities and put up stands every week: these were signs of a Movement that could stand on its own two feet. We didn't need to read Grillo's posts on the blog in order to know what to do. (V. Tavolazzi, City Councilor, Ferrara, former exponent of a certified list, July 2013)

Likewise, the Piedmontese Regional Councilor Fabrizio Biolé, who was also expelled from the Movement, interprets the case of his own region – albeit less 'dramatic' than that of Emilia-Romagna – in much the same way. In his view, the dissolution – demanded, or at least advocated, by Grillo – of the association that the Piedmontese meet-ups had created in 2010 to prepare for the regional elections constituted a watershed moment in the affairs of the M5S in Piedmont and revealed Grillo's true intention: to prevent the constitution of organizational forms or intermediate structures between the apex and the base of the Movement:

> The association [created for the regional elections] was dissolved around about June 2010 on Grillo's insistence … because this association was a formal reality with a name, linked to a council group, it meant that it paralleled a party-like form. That was what they were afraid of. It was understandable from their point of view. … If we look at the principles of the non-statute, this association clashed with them. (F. Biolé, Regional Councillor, Piedmont, former M5S exponent, July 2013)

These episodes – the arbitration of the leader in decisions regarding expulsion and the political will to prevent the formation of an organization that was in some way independent of the leader himself – seem to justify the definition of the M5S as a personal party.

Nevertheless, the M5S distinguishes itself from the personal party in that, in this latter model, relationships are, for the most part, built on economic foundations. This, for example, is the case of a party like Forza Italia, which Maraffi (1995, p. 248) describes in terms of the Weberian category of 'patrimonialism' (in the early days of Forza Italia, much of the personnel was drawn from the companies of its leader). Support for the personal party is generally based to a large extent on 'clientelism' and the relationships between the center and the periphery involve exchanges that lead to the formation of a class of grandees, bigwigs and 'capibastone' ('enforcers'), who are charged with controlling portions of the territory and who, over time, may gain such independence as to hold the centre to ransom. In the M5S, by contrast, though elements of an economic and 'proprietary' nature do exist – as we have seen – allegiance to the leader is not based on economic considerations, and voter support is largely independent of the intermediation of local notables and 'capibastone'.[6] In some respects, the

6 The low percentage of preferential votes (Colloca and Vignati, 2013; Vignati, 2013) obtained by the M5S in the local elections is a clear indication of this.

Movement's centralization seems to be more closely linked to the features of the 'charismatic party' (Panebianco 1982) and stems from the leader's ability to arouse enthusiasm. It is this characteristic which gives rise to the rejection not only of the bureaucratic apparatus typical of a traditional party, but also of a personal apparatus founded on the role of local notables. The relationship is exclusively between Grillo (and his close entourage) and the party's base, without any intermediation that might distort the leader's message.

Nevertheless, the exponents of the Movement firmly reject the notion that the party is dependent on Grillo.

A Meta-Organization? A Franchise System?

One of the organizational principles on which the M5S is hinged is that of the complete autonomy of its local branches. This principle, at least, is essential to the image which the party's exponents have of the Movement:

> I've been involved for a few years and I've never felt these political impositions. We've never, *never* had any interference; they don't even know what we're talking about. We're 100% free. (City Councillor, Ravenna, February 2014)

> Grillo has never poked his nose into either the regional or the municipal program. (City Councillor, Parma, February 2014)

> Grillo has never had anything to do with me at the local level. (City Councillor, Crema, March 2014)

A few anecdotes (the videos shot during the election campaigns for the administrative elections show that, on arriving in some towns, Grillo sometimes does not know who is the candidate for Mayor that he has come to support) would seem to confirm this principle of non-interference by the centre and therefore of the complete autonomy of the local branches. The independence of the local groups and the absence of a higher level (e.g. a provincial or regional secretary) is claimed as a basic principle of cohabitation within the Movement:

> Solving local problems is left to the local branch. If you can't get on together, work it out for yourselves! (City Councilor, Voghera)

> They've got to work things out for themselves! For example, if there are two people in the same territory and each one claims to be the true representative of the Movement, I reckon the citizens of that territory (who know the people and what they've done in the territory) have to work it out for themselves. They call a meeting to decide who should apply for certification. Otherwise, if there are

two applications for certification, the blog won't say a word about it and won't certify either of the two; and I reckon that's right.

[Question: But you are a City Councillor in the provincial capital. Wouldn't you be seen as the person who could settle the argument or arbitrate in such situations?]

No. I wouldn't have the authority to do so, nor would I even be prepared to do so. It would be authoritarian to intervene …

[Question: But doesn't this create chaos?]

Well, it does cause bit of difficulty, of course. But that's the way we've been from the start and we've built up our local groups in this way, handling personal friction on our own. Asking a third party – me or a regional councilor, or even Grillo – to intervene is inconceivable (City Councilor, Brescia, March 2014).

The principle of 'work it out for yourselves 'seems to have been confirmed in a few cases in which different groups have wrangled over the question of who is the rightful representative of the Movement. In these cases, the leadership has preferred not to grant any of the contenders certification of their list, thereby passing up the chance to participate in important electoral contests (a case in point being that of the regional elections in Sardinia in 2014).

This conviction among activists and the elected representatives of the Movement finds correspondence in some descriptions of the M5S that have appeared in the sociological and political science literature. For instance, Lanfrey (2011, p. 145) describes the M5S as a 'meta-organization', or as a 'network of micro-organizations that are largely heterogeneous in their manifestations and partially coordinated at the central level'. Originally formulated by Ahrne and Brunnson (2008), the concept of meta-organization fits into the framework of a broader emergence of organizations with 'post-bureaucratic' characteristics (Bimber 2003).

While this concept appears to provide an efficacious description of the M5S, it may, in reality, be misleading. First of all, it risks being insufficiently specific; indeed, all parties, even traditional ones, are witnessing a progressive growth in the autonomy of individual local branches (often emanations of local lords, who haggle with national leaderships over their respective ambits of power). In this sense, then, the nature of the 'meta-organization' may perhaps be more accentuated (and more overtly claimed) in the M5S; but the same trend can be seen to some extent in all parties. Here, I am referring to that trend described by Mair (1994, p. 17), who wrote of a 'quite widespread consensus that the relevant relationships are now more *stratarchical* than heierarchical, and that each face of the party is now increasingly autonomous of the others', a diagnosis which, in his view, was a harbinger of great risk ('it may also be the case that mutual autonomy will develop to a degree in which the local party will become essentially unconcerned about any real input into the national party, and vice versa'). Expressed in the terms used by Panebianco (1982), this may be regarded as a trend towards increasing deinstitutionalization, or towards a loss of the systematic nature of the organization itself. In the last 20 years, political parties in Italy have been subjected to this process of deinstitutionalization to a far greater extent than those in other European countries.

Secondly, the concept of 'meta-organization' risks bringing with it improper value judgments (by endowing this model with connotations of freedom and independence of its components, which are deemed to be absent in the traditional bureaucratic party models). These judgments clearly emerge in the second part of Lanfrey's essay in particular, in which he attributes Grillo's coordinating intervention to the 'result of some of the Movement's failed attempts at national coordination' (Lanfrey 2011, p. 164), rather than to the leader's desire to command – a view which seems to clash with some of the events in the Movement's history, as we will see. In short, Lanfrey's description – which is in line with that of Greblo (2011) – ends up by giving credence to the representation that the Movement has always given of itself, to its mythology.

A more realistic, and more neutral, description of the M5S seems to be that of the model of the 'franchise system', which has been applied to the Movement by some authors (Bordignon and Ceccarini 2013, among others). Originally formulated by Carty (2004), this concept – with its clear analogy with an organizational model of entrepreneurial extraction – seems to lend itself well to defining the organization of a party propped up by a statute whose central point concerns the ownership of the brand. Carty's analysis starts from the presupposition that 'most parties are no longer, if they ever really were, definitively hierarchical' and arrives at a fundamental point according to which 'the relationships between a central organization and its local franchises can vary enormously, and indeed need not be the same for each individual franchise within a single organization. Large, rich or important units may well have a level of independence and power not shared by smaller or less vital outlets'. In other words, the franchising '*contract*' that binds local branches to the head office may vary, granting more or less freedom to manoeuvre, imposing more or less stringent bonds and exercising more or less pressing control. In this way, the concept of 'franchise system' appears to be more flexible, and therefore more appropriate, than that of the 'meta-organization', which takes the autonomy of local organizations for granted.

In the face of a party of this kind, the researcher's challenging task is therefore to identify the '*contract*' that binds the various branches to the headquarters. This means identifying the modalities that govern the reciprocal rights and duties and the reciprocal spheres of autonomy. This contract (the *real* one) is not necessarily formalized. Indeed, in politics, not everything has to be said; the reality of political relationships needs to be hidden, to some extent, behind the rhetoric.

In the case of the M5S, the non-statute smacks almost of trickery, given that this document, as has been seen, is a long way from describing the profile, confines and characteristics of a real organization.

The M5S seems to be merely a *party in public office*, a party centred entirely around its elected representatives:

> If you've got elected representatives on the City Council, you obviously have to address yourself to them. (City Councillor, Parma, February 2014)

> I always refer to the elected councilors. (Regional Councilor, Bologna, February 2014)

> The locomotive of the group's activity is the City Councilor. (City Councillor I, Crema, March 2014)

> The Movement exists in the territory if an elected representative exists, or else if there is a certified electoral list. It does not exist in any other form. This is something that is difficult to understand at times, even for insiders. (Former M5S Regional Councillor, Turin, July 2013)

Some regard this aspect – the central position of elected representatives and the absence of an extra-institutional structure – as a limitation:

> Precisely because the base is so fluid, you have problems forming a stable group. We have a very high turnover. People might come in because they're interested in a particular issue and they just follow that one issue; then, when that's finished with, they disappear ... A lot of people in the street come up to our stands and ask: 'Where are you? How can we contact you?' And then, because there is no secretary answering the phone and no fixed office, they necessarily turn to the City Councilor. ... The elected representatives are the only ones who have the time, who are doing it full-time, even though they are often wrapped up in internal business. And this is a paradox for a movement because ... you risk having them stuck inside and a movement that doesn't exist outside the institutions. (Activist and candidate, Milan, February 2014)

> Our group works, but it's no bed of roses ... I mean, there are a lot of people who expect us [i.e. the city councillors] to organize the stand ... The group does manage to attract very able people, but then they drift away. (City Councillor II, Crema, March 2014)

On the other hand, any extra-institutional structure is seen as a danger which would distort the essence of the Movement and is therefore to be avoided:

> The lack of structure is a handicap and it'll be felt in the next regional elections, too, in the organization. It will be difficult. As I see it, the problem is that no structure, apart from a fluid one like this, can exist without immediately evolving

> into a party organization. When you coordinate things, there's always a chief, someone who presides. (Regional Councilor, Bologna, February 2014)
>
> Grillo abhors the figure of the 'capibastone' [enforcer], I mean, what has always happened in parties. For example, when it's election time, who decides on the lists in a party? It's the regional referent who decides which names go on the list, who is the candidate for Mayor, etc. He is the 'capobastone'. ... In the end, this system based on 'capibastone' leads to failure. (City Councilor, Parma, February 2014)
>
> If you create party functionaries, you ruin everything. (Activist and candidate, Formigine, February 2014)
>
> The idea of the party, with provincial or regional coordination, is no good, because then factions form: there's the chief who forms his own faction; you have to have membership cards. (Activist, Voghera, March 2014)

The formalization of a structure is seen as a negation of the trust deemed necessary as a basis for a voluntary association like a party:

> In my opinion, wanting to formalize everything is a sign of lack of mutual trust within the group. So then we have to lay down rules, because that way, if you break the rules, you can be sanctioned. (City Councillor, Brescia, March 2014)
>
> We do have a structure, but it's a structure made up of trust, not of pigeonholes in the pyramid of power. (Activist and candidate, Formigine, February 2014)

This absence of a structure of the extra-institutional Movement therefore places the elected representatives in a central position. Indeed, as emerges from some of the above quotations, it is the elected representatives who constitute the point of reference; it is to them that the citizens turn. Thanks to their visibility, and to the greater competence that they have gained by being inside the institutions, they are the ones who assume the leadership of the Movement's local groups.

Moreover, it is the elected representatives who are the nodes that form the territorial networks. These networks arise in a non-formalized manner, through contacts which stem from personal acquaintanceships and affinities or, in a completely voluntary manner, through instruments such as mailing lists or Google groups (as happened among city councillors in Lombardy; through the online posting of deliberations and motions presented in the various city councils, they became – in the words of a Crema city councillor – 'a real fighting machine'). Thus, above the level of the citizen, the embryos of organization are created, in a manner that is spontaneous and not directed from the centre, thanks to the initiative of individual exponents.

There are therefore marked differences between one locality and another, depending on the number (and level) of elected representatives present, and depending on the style and 'authoritativeness' of the most prominent exponents in the specific territory. If Brescia is, as the city councillor claims, a 'haven of peace', where there is no particular friction or squabbling, this is probably due to the presence of Vito Crimi, one of the Movement's exponents closest to Grillo; having run for the presidency of the Regional Council in 2010, he was elected to the Senate in 2013, and is thus universally recognized as authoritative. Elsewhere, however, were such a figure is lacking, conflicts among the various components are more likely to arise.

This network of relationships above the level of the municipality facilitates the exchange of 'good practices' and the implementation of training activities. The attitude of the leadership tends to be one of *laissez faire*. Nevertheless, the tweet sent out by Grillo in February 2014, a few days before a meeting organized by the mayor of Parma with the future candidates in the administrative elections, stated that this initiative 'has in no way been agreed upon with the staff or with me'; this sounds like a clear warning that such autonomous initiatives are subject to the control, and perhaps also censure, of the leadership.[7]

Between the Base and the Leadership: Controlling Elected Representatives

The elected representatives of the M5S therefore find themselves squeezed between the *party in central office*, which, as has been said, hangs the sword of Damocles over their heads, in the form of the threat of disavowal and withdrawal of the right to use the party symbol, and the *party on the ground*, on which their remaining in office depends. In several cases, this dependence has been endorsed through the organization of periodic assemblies, to which the elected members present their resignation and apply for renewal of their mandate (the first to do so were the regional councillors elected in Emilia-Romagna in 2010; their example was then followed in many other instances, such as in the City Council of Milan).

These assemblies, as the regional councillor for Emilia-Romagna puts it, generally turn out to have a 'foregone and unanimous conclusion' (he jokingly speaks of 'assemblee che si concludono in maniera piuttosto bulgara'). Watching the videos of these assemblies, many of which can easily be seen on YouTube,

7 The newspapers have reported various initiatives on the part of the mayor of Parma which indicate a desire to establish areas that are independent from Grillo's control (maintenance of contacts with some expelled MPs; criticism of some internal affairs, such as how candidates for the European elections are chosen). As the first M5S mayor of a provincial capital, Pizzarotti enjoys greater independence and freedom of movement than others. Grillo has to deal more cautiously with him than he would with other exponents. However, a few posts on the blog in April 2014 suggest the possibility that he might be censured or even expelled.

is quite enlightening, both when they end in the unanimous confirmation and acclamation of the elected representatives, and when – more rarely – they conclude with the accusation of a representative who is deemed wanting.

That meetings of this kind raise problems is apparent not only to anyone who, like us, scrutinizes them critically from the outside through the YouTube videos, and not only to anyone – like the above-mentioned senator – who finds himself under accusation in front of a hostile audience. It is also noted by those who – like the exponent quoted below – agree with how the organization of the party works. Indeed, on the one hand, the importance of being 'continuously' under the scrutiny of the citizens is acknowledged; on the other, there is the fear of having to submit to indications given by those who have not analyzed the issues in depth:

> Let's not forget that we are in a representative democracy, for the moment. This means that, while respecting the program, we take decisions inside the institutions; and we explain why we have taken those decisions, and we assume responsibility for those decisions. It's not feasible to import direct democracy into a structure of representative democracy. Things don't fit together. … You've got representatives of the institutions, who have civil and penal responsibilities, who have to take part in all the commissions, in all the meetings, who have greater knowledge and awareness of the issues than other citizens – who perhaps participate only occasionally. Those who don't have the means, the time or the will to go into the issues can't be allowed to decide everything. Of course, they can make a contribution, but you can't reduce everything to voting by show of hands. It's a more complex business. We take the decisions and we accept responsibility, praise or criticism from those who come after us. … Not all citizens are able to get the information and to analyze all the issues. Even we don't know everything, but because we sit on the commissions and can study the issues, our view is a bit more complete. In short, a lot of these people were obsessed with voting by show of hands. Unfortunately, I must say, some of the people who approach the Movement see things in this way: everything is reduced to a show of hands … If we have to take a decision on the budget, which is the thorniest question, and I go to a meeting where there are 10 people; first of all, why should 10 people in the room be deciding for the 8–9,000 who voted for us? … I risk my reputation every day, on the council, in the newspapers. I'm not prepared to put myself in the hands of someone who hasn't had the means, time or will to analyze an issue in depth, as if I were a puppet who just does what he is told to do. (City Councillor, Ravenna, February 2014)

The scenario in which an elected representative is accused by the party on the ground was the case of the assembly held on 7 February 2014 by the Movement in the Province of Pavia, which placed the senator Luis Orellana under accusation.[8]

8 The video of the assembly is available on Youtube at: http://www.youtube.com/watch?v=0RunZy_dGbU [accessed 23 February 2014].

The assembly turned into a somewhat grotesque mixture of a family discussion in which the wayward behaviour of one of the members is analyzed lovingly but pitilessly, a meeting of a self-help group whose members encourage one another towards a common objective, and an end-of-60s Maoist group's session of self-criticism, dominated by the overwhelming and ferocious unanimity of the speeches. As can be seen from the video concerning Orellana, the outcome of the meeting is not the result of an open confrontation between positions; it is clearly preordained. Indeed, the video reveals the complete lack of any dialogue between the two sides; the same accusation is repeated in various tones in each speech and the accused is obliged to listen, his weak defensive rebuttals making no impact whatsoever on how the debate is continued.

What is even more interesting is that the outcome of the discussion had no immediate, practical, binding effect. It remained confined to the local level, taking on a political effect as 'no confidence from the territory' only after Orellana's position had been openly questioned by the central leadership, that is to say by Beppe Grillo. At that point, the discussion, which was diffused by the blog, came to national prominence and served to endow the decision of the leadership with democratic legitimation (in that it came 'from below').[9] When that happened, the discussion by the provincial assembly in Pavia became known to the public, and the Pavia meet-up published a communiqué – promptly diffused by Grillo's blog – in which Orellana was declared to have been 'disavowed by the territory'.[10]

9 Grillo (2014a) revoked his confidence in Orellana after the latter had distanced himself from Grillo's refusal to enter into a dialogue with Matteo Renzi when the government was being formed. Before this, the leadership had already expressed its reservations towards Orellana (Grillo 2013b).

10 The same formula – 'disavowed by the territory' – cropped up in the blog a few days later with regard to another two MPs, Bocchino and Campanella, guilty of advocating that the M5S should open up to negotiations and alliances with other political forces (Grillo 2014b). The ensuing discussion of this measure on the blog is quite significant, for two reasons. Firstly, because the modality of the debate and the type of arguments used (words such as 'betrayal' frequently recur in the comments to this post) shed light on the culture of the Movement. Secondly, the discussion highlights the fluid nature of its organization. The legitimacy of the no-confidence 'measure' implemented against Bocchino and Campanella by the territory of Palermo was contested by some commentators on the grounds that some of the meet-ups that had endorsed the measure were allegedly bereft of certification and that the decision to implement the measure had been taken by minorities within each of the meet-ups involved. Likewise, with regard to the measure implemented against Orellana, the very existence of a '*provincial assembly*' entitled to pronounce on the question of confidence or no-confidence in an elected representative had been contested, in that it was contrary to the non-statute and the principles of the Movement. On the one hand, this type of contestation highlights the fluid state of the Movement and the impossibility to precisely establish its confines and to identify its various ambits of power; on the other hand, it illustrates how the central leadership utilizes this fluidity in order to strengthen its own power (in the discussion on the blog, the 'procedural' objections are submerged by a flood of comments defining the two senators as traitors and forces vociferously calling for their expulsion).

The problem with 'assemblies' of this kind is the lack of any definition of their composition, modality of convocation or real powers.

The M5S is, at one and the same time, and paradoxically, characterized by an obsessive cult of the *rules* – which are invoked whenever the Movement is called upon to make any sort of choice – and by an informality that is wholly refractory to rules.

The Orellana affair is thus emblematic of how the Movement works: its central leadership utilizing its appeal to the base, to the territory – with its power to legitimize in a democratic sense – in order to isolate and weaken the elected representatives and their autonomy. As soon as an elected representative is criticized by the leadership, certain mechanisms are set in motion at the base. These mechanisms, which are typical of the conformism generated by a closed group (and one which construes this closure as an asset because 'we are at war', 'we are fighting a battle'), lead to the increasing isolation of the elected representative, since the other exponents have an incentive to distance themselves from their colleague who has been criticized.

At each level, the *party in public office* manifests some peculiar weaknesses vis-à-vis the *party in central office*. Firstly, its representatives are, for the most part, outsiders – people endowed with scant personal political resources (this applies above all to the most important office, that of the MP; as the candidates for parliamentary office are often chosen from among those who are not elected in the administrative elections, seats in Parliament have in many cases gone to less prominent individuals with limited local support at the base). These people are therefore entirely dependent on the party. This is a key variable in determining the type of relationship between the single exponents and the party. For example, Panebianco (1982) pointed out that Communist Party MPs, who had fewer personal resources that their Christian Democrat counterparts, also had less power in their dealings with the central structure of their party. The rules governing the choice of M5S parliamentary candidates match exactly with this strategy: i.e. ensuring that candidature depends on substantially random factors, thereby preventing, as far as possible, candidature from being conditioned by the personal resources of the aspiring candidate (personal support, visibility, previous experience). Secondly, the fact that M5S MPs are limited to two terms of office[11] exposes them to an obvious reprimand if they should adopt independent positions that differ from those of the leadership. Indeed, they may be accused of trying to further their own career and of seeking the visibility that might enable them to find hospitality in other political parties where the two-term limitation does not apply. This was, for

11 The commitment of M5S representatives elected to institutions is limited to two electoral terms. This rule is not codified in the 'non-statute' and has sometimes aroused controversy, particularly with regard to how to consider those mandates which terminate before their natural expiry owing to the early dissolution of the assemblies. This point prompted debate particularly when Biolé (Piedmont) and Favia (Emilia-Romagna) were expelled.

instance, the reprimand meted out to Favia; his criticisms of Casaleggio were seen by many as an attempt to get himself noticed, given that he was approaching the end of his second term, and thus the end of his parliamentary career under the flag of the M5S:

> The two-term limit means that no one thinks about their own future as a politician … You can't carve out a career for yourself: you know, first the City Council, then the Provincial Council, then the Regional Council, then a seat in Parliament … No! They all know they'll be going back to doing other things. And we've already seen the likes of Favia get kicked out; they had served their two terms, but they were elbowing their way to the front, saying 'hey, I'm still here, get me elected'. They were told 'no!' (Activist and candidate, Milan, February 2014)

Thirdly, the elected representatives find themselves squeezed between the risk of having their use of the party symbol revoked by the leadership and the plebiscitary appeal of the leadership to the rank and file. Indeed, Grillo's organizational practice seems to be aimed at using his direct appeal to the base in order to weaken the individual exponents and prevent them from taking up autonomous positions (Floridia and Vignati 2014). Censure on the part of the base – skilfully manipulated (as in the case of Orellana) – is always lying in ambush. In this respect, the *party on the ground* is a formless mass without clear confines, and can easily be manoeuvred by the appeal of the leader, who is the repository of trust and an indispensable resource for the gathering of support. Active participation in the assemblies is largely restricted to convinced militants – that is to say, those who most closely identify with the aims of the organization, as defined charismatically by the leader – while the remainder of the base, among whom more moderate positions may be found, do not participate or participate half-heartedly or less actively.

The Movement does offer the possibility of a career, albeit brief (two terms). Moreover, this opportunity is open to anyone, even to those who, on account of their limited competence and experience, would be very unlikely to make a career for themselves in other political parties. This prompts the consideration that, among the incentives acting on the rank and file, the rational aspiration to a career may, paradoxically, be stronger than it might appear at first sight:[12] that

12 Here, the reference is to the classic distinction between believers and careerists (Panebianco 1982). Placing a limit on the number of terms – a policy also adopted in various ways by libertarian left-wing parties, such as the Greens in Germany – is deemed to encourage believers and to discourage career-seekers. In the M5S, however, for the reasons mentioned (the substantial 'randomness' of the 'call', which does not depend on the skills possessed or the work done), may, paradoxically, produce an opposite effect, drawing in a large number of 'career-seekers', who see a way of getting in without the effort of going through any 'cursus honorum'.

the Movement may be rationally exploited for the purpose of self-interest by individual activists. In other words, these individuals might be attracted to the Movement not only by the persuasive skills of its leader and by his ability to manipulate the symbols and liturgies of support, but also as a result of a rational assessment of the potential costs and benefits (this is applicable not only to individual MPs and elected representatives at the various levels, but also to all aspiring candidates – anyone can hope to be 'called', and therefore has the same potential worth as any other elected representative). This has rightly prompted some analysts to speak of an 'instrumental' (Lanfrey 2011, p. 153), 'utilitarian' (Biorcio 2013, p. 50) relationship between the activists, the rank and file and the leader of the Movement, thus inverting the image of dependence on the leader.

Conclusions: A 'Super-Organism'?

Each of the factors indicated above hides an element of weakness for the organization, or at least for its long-term prospects. If its candidates are chosen according to substantially *random* criteria, how can a capable, competent, political class be created? If Favia's dissent was motivated by a desire to be noticed, in the hope of obtaining a new mandate when his second term expired, then how will the Movement be able to survive once most of its current representatives have entered their second term? If compliance and allegiance are propped up by rational, instrumental considerations of self-interest, will the Movement continue to find the resources that feed it (the growth in the polls that generates enthusiasm, the sharing of objectives and the hope of seats in institutions)?

The point at which the M5S still finds itself today is that of its institutionalization, its possibility to become consolidated and to endure over time. Electoral success does not, in itself, ensure institutionalization.[13] The essential test of whether or not a party can be regarded as fully institutionalized is its ability to survive its own leader, the figure who – thanks to his resources (economic or charismatic) – has led the party to success in the polls. In this regard, the difficulties currently faced by Forza Italia and the Lega Nord, in the wake of Berlusconi's judicial problems and Bossi's fall from grace, clearly bear witness to the incomplete institutionalization of these parties.

From this point of view, the prospects of the M5S remain uncertain, since its development is still closely dependent on its leader and remains linked to the conformation of the 'Movement party'. As has been argued by Kitschelt,

13 Although somc authors (such as Pedahzur and Brichta 2002) suggest that the concept of institutionalization should be redefined in such a way as to include electoral success among its features (in reality, this choice seems to be motivated only by the desire to make it easier to operationalize the concept empirically, in order to facilitate comparative research; from the conceptual standpoint, however, it only gives rise to confusion).

'movement parties' 'are not impossible, but comparatively rare phenomena' (Kitschelt 2006, p. 288).

Those exponents of the M5S whom we interviewed revealed an awareness of the structural shortcomings that afflict the Movement. Founded with the aim of carrying out a circumscribed activity of scrutiny and monitoring of the other parties (what Grillo called 'fiato sul collo', 'breathing down their necks'), the M5S then became a federation of local lists and subsequently, in a very short time, found itself faced with the 'obligations' of a fully-fledged political party: starting with the need to draw up a programme that would not be limited only to the traditional battles fought by movements (opposition to career politics and its costs, protection of the environment, etc.) but which would embrace all political issues.

The principal strategic choices are made exclusively by the leadership. The attempt at coordination 'from below' in Emilia-Romagna (of which Tavolazzi was the main protagonist) – coordination which, through periodic assemblies, might have led to the formation of a political force that would have greater independence from the centre – was nipped in the bud. By contrast, the organizational strategy implemented by the leadership has been driven by a deliberate will to 'fragment' the Movement's base.

At the local level, the fluidity of the group and uncertainty regarding its boundaries, as we mentioned earlier, have thrown up certain problems. These were succinctly expressed by a Milanese exponent whom we interviewed (and also emerged in different words in other interviews): the tendency to 'argue over nothing', a 'high turnover of personnel and so the inability to attract skills' and the fact that 'the elected representatives are totally wrapped up in institutional business' and do not have the time or resources to bring a more solid and stable structure to the Movement.

Most exponents of the M5S seem to be aware of these problems – that without roles and codified structures the Movement is unlikely to be able to face national political challenges. Indeed, they all hope that the Movement, being a continuously evolving political entity, can tackle and solve, day by day, the problems that arise:

> The great thing about the Movement is that it is always a work in progress: each time, we add a step of difficulty … We tackle problems as they crop up. (Activist, Formigine, February 2014)

For what concerns the role of Grillo (and of his 'staff'), it can be said that it never really comes under analysis; rather, it is exorcised by means of peremptory statements:

> To be honest, I don't have time to think about the staff! As I am the representative of the list, and as I need certification, I sent off the envelope with all the candidates' judicial certificates. My dealings with the staff ended there. (City Councillor, Monza, February 2014)

Grillo's role is therefore reduced to that of a 'megaphone', an amplifier, a catalyst of consensus, who does not, however, intervene in locally decided political actions.

In this undoubtedly simplistic way of conceiving Grillo's role, we find the problem which still weighs heavily on the future prospects of the M5S, that is, its inability to conceptualize politics, its inability to create rules and instruments that allow its internal pluralism to be expressed. An organization is not a monolithic entity; rather, it is an arena in which players with a plurality of objectives are called upon to act. The organization must therefore find instruments for regulating the interaction among these various objectives; otherwise, it risks exploding in divergent directions or ending up holding itself together by authoritarian means; it must therefore balance efficiency and democracy. The absence of these instruments may work in a movement that has a circumscribed objective (on which unanimity of intentions can be taken for granted), but it cannot work if this 'movement' intends to enter into the institutions and proposes to compete in the electoral arena, as this means addressing the whole spectrum of political questions.

The fact is that the 'utopia' of Grillo and Casaleggio yearns for a community-based future in which politics, and power, are outdated.[14] In the present, however, the relationship with power is schizophrenic. In the confrontation with the outside world, the need for strict discipline is justified (which justifies – because 'we are at war' – authoritarian measures of expulsion). By contrast, in internal relationships (as the Movement is a microcosm in which the community-based future is claimed to have already been realized), power – instead of being acknowledged and regulated – is hidden beneath rituals and liturgies[15] that celebrate the community (in the sociology of organizations, there is ample literature on liturgies – from Meyer and Rowan, 1977 onwards).

We have already mentioned the difficulty of identifying the 'contract' which binds the headquarters of the M5S to its local branches. But we do have what may be the *What is to be done?* of the M5S, the text which indicates the principles that guide the political action of its leaders. It is a text which has received scant attention from the studies on this political entity; or rather, it has been almost completely ignored (we have sometimes seen it erroneously attributed to Gianroberto Casaleggio). Entitled *Tu sei rete*, it is an ebook in which Davide Casaleggio (2012) – Gianroberto's son and a prominent member of the 'staff' – analyzes the importance of the concept of the network and the utility, in both economics and

14 On several occasions Grillo has enunciated the objective of achieving '100% consensus'; at that point, the Movement itself would be dissolved and political parties would no longer exist.

15 Chief among these liturgies are the periodic online votes, a celebration of the 'direct democracy' of which the M5S is the bearer. It should be noted that the rules, modalities and timing of these votes are always decided by the centre in an authoritarian manner. In addition, it should be noted that, for instance in the case of the choice of the electoral system (February 2014), voting was preceded by assessments by an 'expert' (Aldo Giannuli), whose statements strongly influenced perceptions of the issue.

politics, of being able to understand, and manipulate, the language of networks. Both in marketing and in politics, knowing how networks interact and organize themselves confers power ('network theory enables us to identify the informal structures of organizations, to foresee their evolution and also to design them with a view to achieving new objectives'; 'the phenomena of self-organization and emerging properties can be designed or directed towards an objective by providing them with a context and rules for interaction'). Mr Casaleggio Jr makes use of the metaphor of the anthill: 'anthills provide the best example of self-organization. The ants follow a series of rules that are applied to the individual and which give rise to a highly organized, but not centralized, structure'. Particularly interesting in this thesis is the reflection concerning the relationship between the individual and the Internet:

> It is necessary that the components be very numerous, that they meet by chance and that they be unaware of the characteristics of the system as a whole. *An ant must not know how the anthill works, otherwise all the ants would aim to get the best and least tiring jobs, thus creating a problem of coordination.* (Casaleggio, 2012, our italics)

It is truly curious that a text which reveals so much about the organizational affairs of the 5 Stars Movement has so far been almost completely ignored. The metaphor of anthill is revealing. The M5S contains some features of a personal party, of a charismatic party and of a franchise system. But the best way to understand the M5S may be to describe it as an experiment in building a 'super-organism'.[16]

References

Ahrne, G. and Brunnson, N. 2008, *Meta-organizations*. Cheltenham: Edward Elgar.
Bimber, B. 2003. *Information and American Democracy. Technology in the Evolution of Political Power*. Cambridge: Cambridge University Press.
Biorcio, R. 2013. Le tre ragioni del successo del Movimento 5 stelle. *Comunicazione politica*, 13(1), pp. 43–62.
Bordignon, F. 2013. *Il partito del capo*. Milan: Apogeo; Santarcangelo di Romanga: Maggioli.
Bordignon, F. and Ceccarini, L., 2013. Five Stars and a Cricket. Beppe Grillo Shakes Italian Politics. *South European Society and Politics*, 18(4), pp. 427–49.
Calise, M. 2000. *Il partito personale*. Roma: Laterza.
Carbonaro, M. 2013. *Grillo vale uno: il libro nero del Movimento 5 stelle*. Pavona di Albano Laziale: Iacobelli.
Carty, R.K. 2004. Parties as Franchise Systems: The Stratarchical Organizational Imperative. *Party politics*, 10(1), pp. 5–24.

16 On the concept of 'super-organism', see Hölldobler and Wilson (2009).

Casaleggio, D. 2012. *Tu sei rete*. Milan: Casaleggio Associati.
Casaleggio, G. and Grillo, B. 2011. *Siamo in Guerra*. Milan: Chiarelettere.
Colloca, P. and Vignati, R. 2013. Tra continuità e cambiamenti. Le elezioni regionali siciliane del 2012. *Istituzioni del federalismo*, 34(1), 1, pp. 265–302.
Floridia, A. and Vignati, R. 2014. Deliberativa, diretta o partecipativa? Le sfide del Movimento 5 stelle alla democrazia rappresentativa. *Quaderni di sociologia*, 58(2).
Fo, D., Grillo, B. and Casaleggio, G. 2013. *Il Grillo canta sempre al tramonto*. Milan: Chiarelettere.
Greblo, E. 2011. *Filosofia di Beppe Grillo*. Sesto San Giovanni: Mimesis.
Grillo, B. 2013a. Il sistema operativo del M5S. *Beppegrillo.it* [blog] 19 September. Available at: http://www.beppegrillo.it/2013/09/il_sistema_oper.html [Accessed 24 February 2014].
———. 2013b. I nuovi Scilipoti *Beppegrillo.it* [blog] 4 September. Available at: http://www.beppegrillo.it/2013/09/i_nuovi_scilipoti.html [Accessed 24 February 2014].
———. 2014a. Orellana sfiduciato dal territorio. *Beppegrillo.it* [blog] 21 February. Available at: http://www.beppegrillo.it/2014/02/orellana_sfiduciato_dal_territorio.html [Accessed 24 February 2014].
———. 2014b. Bocchino e Campanella sfiduciati dal territorio. *Beppegrillo.it* [blog] 23 February. Available at: http://www.beppegrillo.it/2014/02/bocchino_e_campanella_sfiduciati_dal_territorio.html [Accessed 24 February 2014].
Hölldobler, B. and Wilson, E.O. 2009. *The Superorganism: The Beauty, Elegance, and Strangeness of Insect Societies*. New York: Norton & Company.
Kitschelt, H. 2006. Movement Parties. In: R.S. Katz and W.J. Crotty, eds. *Handbook of Party Politics*. London: Sage, pp. 278–90.
Lanfrey, D, 2011. Il movimento dei grillini tra meetup, meta-organizzazione e democrazia del monitoraggio. In: L. Mosca and C. Vaccari, eds. 2011. *Nuovi media, nuova politica? Partecipazione e mobilitazione online da MoveOn al Movimento 5 stelle*. Milan: Angeli, pp. 143–66.
Mair, P. 1994. Party Organizations: From Civil Society to the State. In: R.S. Katz and P. Mair, eds. *How Parties Organize. Adaptation and Change in Party Organizations in Western Democracies*. London: Sage, pp. 1–22.
Maraffi, M. 1995. Forza Italia. In: Pasquino, G., ed. *La politica italiana. Dizionario critico, 1945–1995*. Roma: Laterza, pp. 247–60.
Meyer, J.W. and Rowan, B. 1977. Institutionalized Organizations: Formal Structure as Myth and Ceremony. *American Journal of Sociology*, 83(2), pp. 340–63.
Movimento 5 Stelle. 2009. *Non statuto*, available at: https://s3-eu-west-1.amazonaws.com/materiali-bg/Regolamento-Movimento-5-Stelle.pdf [Accessed 24 February 2014].
Oggiano, F. 2013. *Beppe Grillo parlante*. Milan: Cairo.
Panebianco, A. 1982. *Modelli di partito*. Bologna: Il Mulino.
Pedahzur, A. and Bricht, A. 2002. The Institutionalization of Extreme Right-wing Charismatic Parties: A Paradox? *Party Politics*, 8(1), pp. 31–49.

Prospero, M. 2012. *Il partito politico. Teoria e modelli*. Roma: Carocci.
Scanzi, A. 2014. Sulla (mancata?) democrazia interna di M5S e Pd. *I blog de IlFattoQuotidiano.it* [blog] 26 February 2014. Available at: http://www.ilfattoquotidiano.it/2014/02/26/sulla-mancata-democrazia-interna-di-m5s-e-pd/894631/ [Accessed 4 June 2014].
Vignati, R. 2013. Le elezioni amministrative di maggio. *Il Mulino*, 62(6), pp. 1,061–8.

Chapter 3
Between Blog, Social Networks and Territory: Activists and Grassroots Organization

Maria Elisabetta Lanzone and Filippo Tronconi[1]

Introduction

For a long time political parties have been considered the basic organizational unit through which citizens were involved in the democratic life of their countries. Mass participation in politics is, in fact, one of the main functions that parties fulfil in contemporary political systems (Neumann 1956). For decades, it seemed that mass parties, first described by Maurice Duverger (1951), were able to guarantee such participation. This was due to the widespread presence of party structures at local level that enabled the recruitment of a greater number of citizens and the coordination of their activities across the whole country. The subsequent decline of the mass-party organizational model, first described by Otto Kirchheimer (1966), concerns this specific side of their activities. Parties kept on working as efficient organizations for electoral purposes, ensuring that campaigns were centralized and professionally managed (Panebianco 1982), and ensured their own survival through an effective use of financial and communicative resources of the state (Katz and Mair 1995). Yet, along with the centralization of resources and a more professional form of communication, came the diffused marginalization of the so-called party on the ground (Katz and Mair 1993) – namely, of militants and party members. Consequently, neither group found enough stimuli in the parties anymore, both in terms of personal identification and of their perception of effective political actions. Many of the above-mentioned authors have highlighted the dangers that could originate from a detachment between controlling the *res publica* (a function that parties still fulfil) and creating a link between citizens and their elected representatives within the institutions (something that present-day parties can no longer guarantee) (Lawson and Merkl 1988). Attempts to restore the main role of membership through more open rules for the selection of candidates

1 This chapter is the result of a joint reflection of the two authors. However, for bureaucratic purposes only, the final draft of sections 2, 6, and 7 is to be attributed to M.E. Lanzone, and the final draft of sections 3, 4, and 5 to F. Tronconi. The first and last sections have been drafted jointly.

and party leadership alike (Scarrow, Webb and Farrell 2000; Hazan and Rahat 2010) – should thus be considered as a reaction to the decrease in legitimacy previously discussed.

Italy is no exception to this general situation. On the contrary, the crisis that originated in the nineties with the scandal of the *Mani Pulite* (Italian for 'clean hands') accentuated the decreasing legitimacy of parties, even though the beginnings of such a phenomenon can be traced back to the Eighties (Morlino 2001; Bardi 2002). According to data produced by van Bienzen, Mair and Poguntke in 2012, more than one third of the members dropped out of Italian political parties between 1980 and 2007. However, not only has the membership of Italian parties dropped dramatically in recent decades, but, according to the polls, even the level of trust in political parties has reached a historic low. According to Piero Ignazi (2004), Italian political parties – in a similar way to their European counterparts – present a contradiction: on the one hand, they have become stronger (in terms of resource control) and more open (while recruiting candidates and party leaders); but on the other hand, they are not as alluring nor legitimate as they once were. Such a lack of legitimacy results in a blatant and growing inability to recruit militants and engage them in party activities.

The Movimento Cinque Stelle (M5S) stands out as a counter-trend within such a dismal context. Its capability to attract citizens and promote their active involvement in politics is surprising, and it is certainly worth careful analysis. As we shall see in later sections of this chapter, a whole cohort of young adults first approached politics precisely because of Beppe Grillo's 'call to arms'. Local-based organizational units were built later by this new group of militants, thanks to their innovative use of social networks – innovative, at least, in the Italian context. This often surprised the militants themselves: during the interviews we conducted with them, it was often stated that the idea of 'doing politics' had never occurred to them before getting involved in the M5S.

This chapter will look at the activists in the Movement, at their origins and their role within the association, whereas for more generic considerations on the organizational aspects of the M5S we refer the reader to Chapter 2. Web based documents, as well as 47 face-to-face interviews with activists and elected members of the Movement, will provide a starting point for our analysis. First, we will take into consideration the birth of the first organizational units on the online platform meetup.com – something that has often been defined as the most important organizational innovation that the M5S came up with. We will then move on to focus on the workings of this peculiar recruiting procedure, and on what motivates those citizens approaching the Movement. Focusing our analysis solely on meetup.com would be a mistake. The Movement, in fact, has quickly succeeded in going beyond 'virtual' interactions, mixing online and offline models of organization. Among them, the assembly of activists plays a major role, and as the electorate grew, attempts were made to build supra-local organizational structures, even though this too implied new impediments and contradictions. The electoral success also forced the Movement to face a traditional problem: that of the militant membership base maintaining a connection with, and an effective form of control over, elected representatives. Finally, the main results of our analysis will be summarized in the concluding section of this chapter.

Meetups: Origins and Diffusion

Officially, the M5S was born in a theatre in Milan on 4 October 2009. However, local branches for the movement existed well before this. In 2005 Beppe Grillo started urging followers of his blog (and also the audiences of his shows) to Meetup and to create groups that would later evolve into civic lists and then specific local M5S groups. His chosen tool was the Meetup[2] platform. In a blog post that dates back to 16 July 2005, Grillo wrote:

> I had to think of a way to give my blog followers the chance to Meetup, discuss issues, step forward, see one another in person – to turn an online debate into a moment of change. I talked about it with my collaborators, and I decided to use Meetup. Meetup is a website that allows to arrange with little effort meetings between people sharing similar interests, everywhere in the world and also in every Italian city … I created a category, I called it 'Beppe Grillo', and a group was activated in Milan named 'Gli amici di Beppe Grillo' ('Beppe Grillo's friends'). I will try to meet the groups throughout Italy while I am on tour, every time I take part in an event. I'm not promising anything, but I will do everything possible. Let's try. (Grillo 2005)

Grillo's initiative of setting up this online platform can be seen as the moment when the M5S was born as an organization. It did not take long to become successful. The first groups were established: Milan, Rome, Naples, and then Vicenza, Salerno, Turin, Florence, Bologna, and La Spezia. The first meet-ups dealt with the same environmental issues that Grillo had been discussing during his shows: support for the public water system, opposition to major building projects and uncontrolled urban development throughout Italy, as well as his commitment to renewable energy sources. This foundation displayed early versions of some of the features that would later become typical of the organizational structure of the Movement: first of all by using the blog beppegrillo.it both as an 'ideological' cornerstone and as the driving organizational force of the movement; secondly, showing support for devolution, and the bottom-up formation of local groups.

2 The Meetup platform (www.meetup.com) was launched in 2001 to give people who share the same interests and passions, and who live on the same territory, the chance to meet one another – that is, to turn the online interactions that happen on websites or forums specializing in specific topics into face-to-face interactions. Howard Dean (USA Democratic Party presidential candidate) was the first one to sense how much political potential the platform had, and he used it in his campaign for the 2003 primary elections.

Eliassen and Svåsand's (1975) and Panebianco's (1982) analytic categories are useful when describing the M5S formation process as a peculiar mixture of *penetration* and *diffusion*. The former implies a 'centre' both actively promoting and coordinating the creation of peripheral branches; the latter, on the other hand, describes the federation process of local experiences, born independently from one another. Such a difference in the original party model had major consequences on the organizational consolidation. Parties that originate by diffusion processes tend to maintain decentralized structures. This remains true even after many years because the local elites preserve high levels of independence from national leaderships. On the other hand, parties that originate by penetration processes usually have a stronger and more cohesive leadership. (Panebianco 1982, p. 107).

As for the M5S, Meetups are born on the territory, independently from one another, and with no central control or coordination – thus resembling a model of a party that originated through diffusion. However, as we have seen, the M5S was born because of specific inputs from the centre, and Beppe Grillo and his blog have always been considered the party's reference points and indispensable guide. These elements could therefore define the origins of the M5S as a case of penetration. These partially conflicting features are useful for understanding some aspects of the vertical structure of power within the party, both at its origin and in later years, as explained in Chapter 2.

In the beginning, meet-ups were only open to Grillo's many blog followers – in March 2008 *The Observer* mentioned Grillo's blog as one of the 50 most influential blogs in the world. Soon enough, however, the public events Beppe Grillo organized – particularly, the 2007 and 2008 V-days – made his political initiatives known to a greater public and the first 'certified' civic lists 'Gli Amici di Beppe Grillo' ('Friends of Beppe Grillo') were also recognized. The number of meet-ups increased exponentially after the regional elections in 2010 and again after the local elections in 2012. Thereafter the Movement entered the competition with its own political symbol and was able to successfully elect a mayor in four cities (Parma being the most important of them) as well as winning dozens of seats in city councils (Pinto e Vignati 2012; Colloca e Marangoni 2013).

At present, there are 1,217 Meetups,[3] as opposed to 35 created during the first year (2005): Figure 3.1 shows their constant increasing trend.

Meetups steadily increased during the first two years, reaching a peak in 2007 (+62 units). From then on there was a continual upward trend until 2011 (with a yearly average of +29 units). A significant increase, however, started in 2012, when the number of groups doubled, from 239 to 560. This was the year of the electoral boom, when the Movement got its first mayors elected (in May), and then

3 The figure, updated to 30 November 2013, was derived from the official Meetup register on Beppe Grillo's blog (http://beppegrillo.meetup.com/all/). The creation date refers to the one officially indicated on each group's page (as at 30 November 2013). Some groups may have occasionally been re-founded or reorganized, and some of the names might have changed.

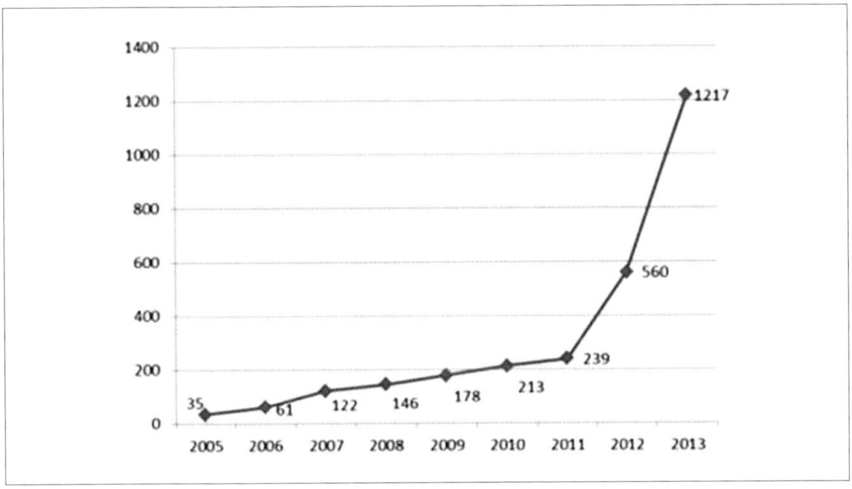

Figure 3.1 Total number of meet-ups at the end of every year
Note: The figure for 2013 is limited as at 30 November.

triumphed in the Sicilian regional elections (in October). Following the success in the parliamentary elections, in 2013 the number of new groups rose significantly (657 new groups in 11 months: 117 per cent increase compared to the previous year).

If we exclude the 25 Meetups located abroad and other 161 supra-local (provincial and regional) or thematic groups, 1,030 groups are active at municipal level.[4] However, they are not equally distributed on the national territory. For the purposes of our analyses we have considered four phases: the first from June 2005 and September 2009 (when the movement was officially founded) and includes the two V-Days; the second phase (October 2009 to May 2012) ends with the local elections in the spring of 2012; the third phase from May 2012 and February 2013 (until the national elections); the last phase starts with the national elections in February 2013.

Figure 3.2 shows the rate of increase divided into territorial areas.[5] It can be noted that new groups are mainly created in the north and in the 'Red Belt' during the first two phases, and that they start growing again at a faster rate in the south after May 2012, particularly in line with the regional elections in Sicily. In the centre, groups increase at a more constant pace.

4 This figure includes the only Meetup in the Aosta Valley.

5 The chart accounts for the number of groups created in Italy at municipal level during each phase; 132 in phase one; 62 in phase two; 346 in phase three and 490 in the last phase. The territorial areas are divided as follows: the north includes Piedmont, Aosta Valley, Lombardy, Liguria, Trentino-Alto Adige, Friuli-Venezia Giulia and Veneto; the 'Red Belt' includes Tuscany, Emilia-Romagnia, Marche and Umbria; the centre includes Lazio, Abruzzo, Molise and Sardinia; the south includes Campania, Calabria, Apulia, Basilicata and Sicily.

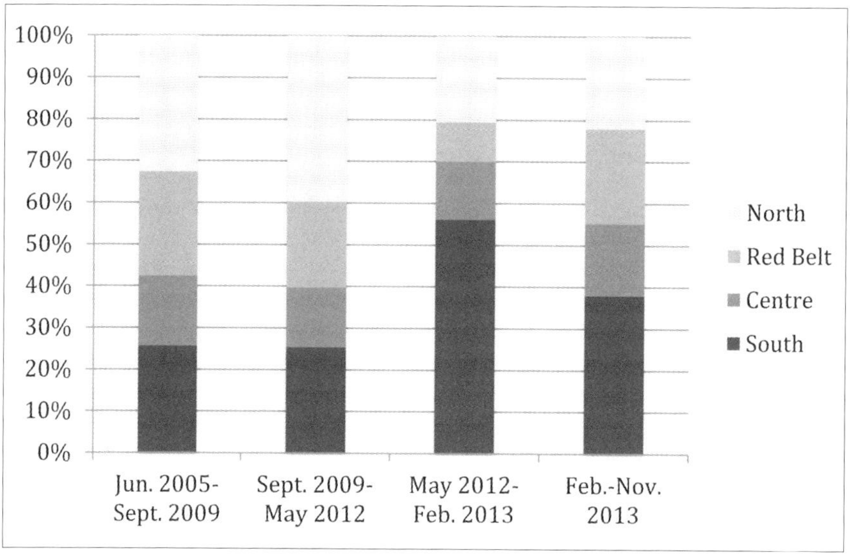

Figure 3.2 Creation of meet-ups in different phases and geographical areas (percentage values)

The Three 'Places' of Recruitment: Beppegrillo.it, the Meet-Up, the Assembly

As we have seen, the main channel through which Beppe Grillo was able to connect and start the first activist groups, even before the Movement was officially founded, was through the Meetup platform. Nevertheless, the Movement's activity does only take place on a virtual platform. The 'piazza' remains crucial, especially during the events where Beppe Grillo himself is present, which receive intense media coverage. These events, the most important of which are the two aforementioned V-days, are fundamental platforms which allow Grillo to make his political activities and the embryonic structure of the Movement known to a wider public. They also work as a trial stage for the local groups, who engage themselves in the organization of the event and in obtaining signatures for different citizens' initiatives:[6]

6 During the first V-Day (8 September 2007), the M5S obtained signatures for an initiative regarding candidacy and eligibility criteria for the Parliament, members of parliament's mandate suspension and the modification of the electoral law with the introduction of the preference vote. During the second V-Day (25 April 2008), signatures were obtained in support of three abrogatory referendums concerning the public financing of the publishing industry and the reorganization of the national public broadcasting company.

> The group in Turin has existed since 2005 and, together with other cities like Milan and Bologna, was one of the first to be created. However, its bulk was created in 2007 in conjunction with the first V-Day, during the summer and until September 8th. At the time many people – around one hundred – got involved, and I was among them. Then, our group was joined also by many activists from the whole urban area and even from the rest of the district, where no official groups existed yet. (Regional Councilman, Turin, October 2013)

> In September 2007, after the first V-Day, together with some friends I decided to start a local group in Caltanissetta. So I decided to send an email to those who had took part in the initiative, who had come to our stalls and left their contact information. In the beginning, we had some trouble scheduling the meetings: we did not know what to discuss, nor how. Then we understood that we had to concentrate exclusively on local issues. At that point we were a local movement, not a political party with national aspirations … (Regional Councilman, Palermo, November 2012)

> The primordial soup from which the Movement would emerge in 2009 was the Meetup; everything concerning the net of Meetups, the friends, the so-called 'friends of Beppe Grillo'. In Monza, a meet-up was created in 2007; it took part in the first V-Day and then in the second V-Day in 2008 … But until the second V-Day all interactions were mainly online or during regular meetings that never led to any real activity on the territory: we had never taken to the streets, we had never taken part in any specific local conflict. (Activist, Monza, June 2012)

Almost inevitably, then, the first local groups start off with the creation of virtual forums on Meetup, which eventually evolve into real-life communities. Local activities, which tend to tackle environmental issues, initially consist of informative meetings and the creation of residents' associations focused on specific goals for the benefit of the local community, such as the opposition to the opening of an incinerator, the management of urban green areas and the request for cycling lanes. Goals tackling national issues were added later, on occasion of the two V-Days, such as obtaining the signatures for the citizens' initiatives and the referendums. It is only since 2009 that these experiences of mobilization have started dealing with political agendas: this change of direction can be read as an important factor, leading the groups to participate in the electoral competition.[7]

7 In particular, in May 2009 the Charter of Florence ('Carta di Firenze') was presented, stating the main programmatic points of the Movement. In October of same year Grillo officially announced the creation of the Movement, presenting the symbol with which it has since then run for election. The previous year, Grillo already consented to municipal lists being presented at local elections. These lists were presented only in a few dozen municipalities, and did not obtain remarkable results. Only in one case (Treviso) it led to one city councilman being elected (Vignati 2013, p. 50).

It is the interaction between online and offline mobilization that represents the main communication and recruitment channel for the M5S in its beginning. This interaction involves three 'places': the blog beepegrillo.it, the meet-ups and the local groups' periodical assemblies (Lanfrey 2011). The first two are, of course, virtual arenas; still they are crucial for the organization of the Movement and for its recruiting system. The blog has never been the comedian's private diary. By contrast it is the main reference point both in terms of contents (it is where the main mobilization campaigns are launched and the Movement's catchphrases are presented), and organizational matters. For instance, as discussed at the beginning of this chapter, the invitation to use the Meetup platform to create the first mobilization groups in different cities was issued from the blog. Moreover, it is through the blog that national political initiatives are launched and that major organizational developments are communicated (the creation of M5S, the electoral manifesto, the decision to run for general elections, etc.). Later on, the blog became the place where lists of candidates could be 'verified', where candidates and elected members presented their activities, and where thematic forums could be joined.[8]

Meet-ups constitute the local sites for aggregation rather than for organization. Since there are no physical premises, they are the virtual places where those who are drawn to the Movement can meet, and the first forums for public discussion about local issues. Other 'electronic showcases' (like the Facebook group) have subsequently been provided, but the meet-ups are the first place where supporters can get together:

> When someone asked you 'Did you know that the M5S is active in Garbagnate' you went on the Internet and googled Meetup. Among the first results you had the Meetups, because maybe the group on Facebook came a bit later on. The only way to be seen today is on the web. (City Councilman, Garbagnate Milanese, July 2012)

From virtual, the interaction soon becomes personal:

> The web created us, and brought us together. People come to us through the web, we use Facebook we use the general Meetup. Then of course we need to look each other in the eye, we need to reach those who have no access to the Internet. The web is a tool, that's the thing, a very simple tool, which anyone can use, that helped us to win during our electoral campaign. (City Councilman, Parma, July 2012)

Meetup graduates from a discussion forum to an instrument to organise mobilization in a more traditional way – the third 'place' we mentioned earlier. Local groups meet on a regular basis to decide upon which themes to scrutinize and which

8 www.beppegrillo.it/movimento [Accessed 30 April 2014].

political initiatives to support, and, before election, to discuss candidacies and the electoral campaign. It is during the electoral campaigns that the Movement, apparently in countertrend to the other parties, rediscovers 'labor-intensive' communication modalities, typical of mass-parties and 'pre-modern' electoral campaigns (Farrell 1996; Farrell and Webb 2000). These are based on the activist's presence and visibility and on the leader's public rallies. On the other hand, the Movement is almost invisible in traditional media (newspapers and television).

The centrality of the Meetup in shaping the organization of local activist groups has some relevant consequences. First, Meetup has almost completely prevented the formation of vertical hierarchies. With the exception of the 'organiser' (the person who subscribes to the platform and owns the passwords), all participants are on the same level and can equally take part in the discussion, no matter how long they have been members of the group. Moreover, the platform works perfectly to guarantee a public and transparent discussion, and can help in organizing real-life meetings between participants.

> Thanks to Grillo's hyped-up public image too, Meetup is the chance we have to raise issues that are developed further. People participate, which is nothing new, this is clear. The only new element is that there is no structure within the Meetup, there is no leader. (Activist, Naples, June 2012)

The horizontal relations between activists and the absence of a strict hierarchical structure is a central aspect to the very identity of the Movement, and a difference from traditional parties that activists are proud of:

> We had to choose our Mayor candidate [for local elections of 2012]. I had joined the Movement only a couple months before, I was eligible and so I put myself forward in the public meeting ... and so that night we decided, we voted, there were questions, introductions ... And despite being a latecomer, I was chosen to be a candidate. ... For me that was a kind of evidence proving the quality of the project, and of the Movement's democratic nature: the latecomer, not the eldest or highest one in rank, becomes the candidate for Mayor, the spokesperson. (City Councilman, Monza, June 2012)

However, there is another aspect which, despite not being mentioned very often, could be even more important. Social networks (Meetup is no exception) favour weak interactions among participants, which is unlikely to happen in traditional parties – or even in voluntary associations – where there is a strong moral bond. It could be argued that Meetup allows people to keep a foot both in and out of the Movement. One can follow a discussion without participating actively and, when one decides to do so, one can act directly, without having to go through a long learning process, in order to learn the formal and informal rules regulating the life of a traditional political organization, which usually appear incomprehensible to newcomers. Through the online forum one can get an impression of actually contributing to the life of the Movement, to the choice of issues and the elaboration of a political movement; expenses are extremely low both in terms of time, learning and emotional involvement. Moreover, the Movement's rhetoric constantly describes politics as being not only for professionals or for those who have sophisticated skills. On the contrary, inexperience and amateurism are seen as antidote to the careerism of professional politicians. Only a small portion of online participants decides to get more involved in the Movement, but Meetup offers the possibility to reach an extremely wide potential audience (enhanced by the popularity of Grillo's blog). Thus the Movement has had an enormous advantage over traditional organizations, one that they have been able to capitalize on so far. At the same time, one should not take the easy access to discussions as a sign of a more intense involvement by the supporters in the decision-making process nor as an index of greater democracy within the organization, as will be discussed later.

Civic Commitment and Opposition to Traditional Participatory Channels: What Motivates the Activists

The common ground many people have with the M5S, and what drives them more than anything else to join it, is their scepticism over the role of parties as channels through which ordinary citizens can communicate their questions to government institutions. New members often lack any prior political experience, but some of them had tried to join other parties and ended up being disappointed by the experience. Beppe Grillo's blog has been a catalyst for their protests, and forming new local groups through Meetup has also been a response to their resentment towards a non-legitimate political class. Activists are not generally individuals who are uninterested in, or indifferent to, political life, since they do respond to the call of a movement that aims specifically at giving back the *res publica* and its management to citizens. Moreover, the profile of the typical M5S voter, as identified in Chapter 4, is not that of a typical marginalized subject – one who does not participate in political life due to a lack of means (either pecuniary or cultural). By contrast, the first M5S activists are mostly employed, well-informed men with a medium to high level of education. For the most part, in spite of having both the necessary resources and the will to engage themselves politically, these activists have come across challenging obstacles whilst trying to enter more traditional participatory channels. They may be referred to as those who were disappointed by politics – or, even better, those who were rejected by politics:

> That is the question: if you want to join a party, you have to become the canvasser for someone who is already being a canvasser for someone else who may or may not have promised them a position somewhere. (City Councilman, Garbagnate Milanese, July 2012)

Disowning traditional parties also indicates an opposition to the idea of political professionalism. M5S activists see themselves as common citizens who make their competences and experiences temporarily available to the community:

> Activists are common people who devote their time to political participation. Doing politics with us means making your competences available to the community – even just for a couple of hours. Belonging to the Movement means accepting a certain kind of life-style. If I can prove to myself that such a thing is possible, then I become an example for others to imitate. (Activist, La Spezia, June 2012)

All activists share the 'negative' common ground of refusing, and distancing oneself from those who traditionally play a role in the field of institutional representation. Yet, their political views diverge from one another. This is not, however, the kind of disagreement that divides people. On the contrary, according to the activists, this kind of disagreement turns out to be another positive factor – the proof that the M5S political experience marks a break with twentieth-century ideological divisions. These divisions are now perceived as an artifice, as masks behind which parties hide their self-referential qualities: violent disagreements while in public, and convenient understandings behind the curtains:

> The left-right divide is part of a big theatrical trick. Righteous ideas are neither right-wing nor left-wing. Labels don't make good things happen. (Activist, Naples, June 2012)

> The Movement as a political subject does not have any cultural matrix. Left and right are two sides of the same coin. The words 'Left' or 'Right' don't mean anything to us. (Activist, Piacenza, July 2012)

This is not a new idea. Katz and Mair (1995, p. 24) pointed out that the weakness relating to the cartel-party model was to be found in the tendency parties had to restrict competitive environments and enlarge collusive ones – especially in terms of access to public resources. This provides a great mobilization opportunity for new parties, which are by definition extraneous to the cartel. These parties can now capitalize on their positions as outsiders to attract anyone who was disappointed by politics, in spite of their ideological positioning. It is therefore not surprising to find some heterogeneousness within the M5S, both in terms of ideology and of the activists' (political) backgrounds. Some of them are former Lega Nord (LN) electors who were originally attracted by the anti-establishment views that the M5S supported, at least at its origins (Cento Bull and Gilbert 2001; Passarelli e Tuorto 2012). Other activists – probably, the majority of them – were drawn to the M5S by Beppe Grillo's environmentalist struggles: his opposition to major public works (first of all, his struggle against the construction of the high-speed railway between Turin and Lyon. See Chapter 7 in this volume), and his concern with renewable energies, waste management, and public water management. These themes are the ones discussed more widely (along with the ever-present concern about setting moral standards in politics) in many local groups – the themes that gave the Movement's political action its first consent and visibility.[9] This is not a new subject matter. Elsewhere in Europe, green and left-libertarian parties have built their electoral successes on the politicization of those issues. On the other hand, environmental struggles in Italy were always perpetrated exclusively by ad hoc and often locally-rooted movements and residents' associations, whereas national parties rarely gave visibility to environmental issues. Beppe Grillo's political programme manages to respond to the environmental-minded group within the electorate, and it succeeds in doing so starting from local communities. The intuition that led to using Meetup – a platform that was created specifically to put people belonging to the same community, and sharing the same interests and passions, in touch with one another – proved to be extremely effective.

The Activist Assembly as the Main Decision-Making Institution

Although Meetup has proven itself to be an extraordinary recruitment tool, its drawbacks, in terms of organizational management, soon became evident. The decision-making moment in all local groups (or, at least, all the groups that we have been able to get in touch with through our interviews) is never a result of an online poll. Meetup does not just serve as a recruitment tool, but also as a discussion forum. It is the 'place' where important issues are raised, where research materials are shared and where different views are compared to one another:[10] Thus the agenda for upcoming meetings is often established online. Nonetheless, the activist assembly always remains the cornerstone for local M5S groups: it is during the assembly – that is, during a face-to-face meeting between the activists – that relevant decisions are made, starting from decisions about candidacy.

9 These are also the main themes in the first political program presented by the M5S. The so-called Carta di Firenze ('Charter of Florence') (2009) opens with the following statement: 'Town Halls subject our daily lives to huge conditioning. They can either poison us with incinerators or start waste sorting. They can open playgrounds for children or ports for financial speculators. They can build parking lots or kindergartens. They can either privatize water or keep it under their own control. It is necessary to begin again doing politics starting from the Five Star Town Halls with civic lists for Water, Environment, Transportation, Development, and Energy'.

10 A Sicilian regional council member explains, 'We have always thought of Meetup as a possibility to keep on having meetings [he refers to the weekly activist assemblies]; to keep on having discussions; as the chance to share our experiences online; maybe also as a chance to share newspaper articles, to store away the marks they leave, to create an archive. Even though the weekly meeting lasted two hours, it felt like the Meetup meeting was on 24/24' (Regional Councilman, Palermo, November 2013).

It is, therefore, of crucial importance to establish who does and who does not belong to the activist assembly. In the specific case of the M5S – a so-called movement party that recently experienced an electoral boom, and that is now beginning its foray into institutional arenas – the dilemma is whether or not to keep the Movement as open as possible to civil society. This would mean having low barriers of entry for new potential members while, on the other hand, setting up enough obstacles to avoid careerists and opportunists from getting involved with the Movement, or simply to prevent the organization from becoming unmanageable because of a sudden membership increase.

Since no guidelines have been given by central authorities in the Movement, each local meet-up is free to give itself its own organizational regulations. Therefore, most local groups give themselves more or less formalized rules that leave their assemblies open to the public, but only recognize as activists – and, thus, only accord the right to vote to – those who were regularly present and active within the Movement in the previous months. Some Meetups even went as far as to draw up official documents that formally regulate access to the Movement and the different roles members may hold in it. Gela (Sicily) is an example of this tendency. The internal regulation the Gela group has given itself stated that:

> The assembly holds sovereignty over decisive issues and/or general guidelines for the Movement. It is the cornerstone for the Movement itself, the most important unit in which every decision is made about the direction the Movement is going to take. Every attendee, whether a supporter or an activist, is free to express their opinion, but only the activists can vote. The assembly approves the Movement's participation in, or support of, campaigns, struggles, and political stances; it elects members and has the power to emanate motions of no confidence against them; it approves the Movement's expenses, its contracts and its important obligations; it singles out appropriate referents for the work groups that are necessary to realize the projects that were approved. (Movimento Gela Cinque Stelle, 2012, pp. 6–7)

This same document explains how to establish which position one holds within the Movement: 'The Movement is made up of Internet Users, Supporters and Active Members'. Internet Users 'are those who have signed up to our Newsletters, those who are registered on our Website (www.gela5stelle.it), on the Meetup (http://www.meetup.com/m5sgela/), on the Facebook group Movimento 5 stelle – Gela (http://www.facebook.com/groups/263101240418694), or on Twitter. They are not recognized in any way within the Movement'. Supporters 'are those who joined the "Meetup", and they can participate both in the general assemblies and in any other initiatives. Those who only participate occasionally in the meetings and campaign stalls are Supporters; those who do not distinguish themselves by any form of Movement-related merit are Supporters. … Supporters do not have the right to vote and cannot participate in the activist assemblies'. And finally, the Activists 'are those who usually take part in the meetings and in the stalls, and those who distinguish themselves by some form of Movement-related merit. Activists are the only ones who can hold a position within the Movement. They have the right to vote during the assemblies. Their presence during the assemblies will be registered in the Attendance Register' (Movimento Gela Cinque Stelle, 2012, p. 2).

Many other local groups among the ones we have been able to get in touch with through our interviews, or whose statement we have been able to read, have given themselves similar regulations. In Monza the distinction only applies to the group of the supporters (those who have enrolled themselves for the Meetup) and that of the activists (only those who have taken part in at least two assemblies, one thematic work group, and two local-based ventures such as collecting signatures and flyering in the last three months are allowed to enter this group). Only the activist assembly is entitled to define the political course of action of the Movement and to elect its spokesperson (Movimento 5 Stelle Monza 2011, p. 5).

The distinction between supporters and activists exists elsewhere too, but it is less formalized. In Palermo, for instance, activists (and, consequently, those who are entitled to vote), are simply those who 'work somehow continuously, either in person or online, within [thematic work] groups' (Movimento 5 Stelle Palermo, 2013).

Supra-Local Coordination

The M5S' electoral successes, along with its widespread diffusion throughout Italy, have forced many local groups to deal with the problem of setting up new, supra-local organizational units. This necessity becomes particularly clear whenever contesting regional elections becomes an option. On such occasions, there is the need to set some shared rules in order to piece together electoral lists and to choose candidates for regional chairmanships. Those decisions are not always made without internal conflicts, although, up until 2010, when the M5S first took part in regional consultations, the groups were still so small they required no more than informal agreements between different local realities. After the elections, it was decided whether to make those supra-local organizational units permanent features – at least in those regions where the M5S achieved representation.[11] Communications between M5S regional councillors and local Meetups in Emilia-Romagna take place in entirely informal situations: meetings between city councilmen and regional councillors, and those focusing on specific issues, are only held occasionally – or, even more informally, elected members of different ranks relate to one another on a personal basis. The situation in Piedmont is not very different from what is described above. Here too, the creation of some form

11 Regional councillors from the M5S were elected in Piedmont and in Emilia-Romagna in the 2010 round of voting: in Sicily (2012), and Lombardy, Lazio, Molise, and Basilicata (2013).

of regional coordination – something that came to be perceived as a necessity – proved to be difficult because of logistics and particularly financial problems.[12]

> We held some [regional meetings] in 2010, when I was elected, but we ascertained that they were not manageable. There are 350 kilometres between the Northernmost and the Southern most areas in Piedmont, and we cannot ask volunteers to spend 50 Euros on gas every time … (Regional Councilman, Turin, October 2013)

The lack of fixed forms of coordination is not solely due to practical problems. In some cases, more deeply-rooted forms of political resistance are also contributing to it. Many are afraid that shifting focus from local realities may result in a hierarchical form of organization that would go against the very nature of the movement. Indeed, the strictly horizontal and fluid nature of the organization – the most prominent features since its beginning – can only be maintained at local level, through the interaction of a few dozen people living in the same area. From the activists' point of view, there is no bigger risk than that of coming to resemble the very same parties they loathe, starting from their bureaucratized, self-referential organizational units. When asked whether the absence of regional reference units was perceived as a setback, a Regional Councilman from Emilia-Romagna answered:

> It most certainly is a drawback …, and it will be a drawback also when regional elections are held: it will surely be complicated. In my opinion, the problem is that no structure exists aside from this fluid one, that does not immediately evolve into a party-like organization. When you coordinate there is always a boss, someone who is the chairperson for a period of time – you can call them Secretary, President, etcetera. Not to mention what happens when you start dealing with money, which is always a nightmare. (Regional Councilman, Emilia-Romagna, January 2014)

Upon being asked whether the autonomy every local group benefits from represents some kind of problem, a Sicilian regional congressperson stated something similar:

> No, I wouldn't say so. This is the movement. Ours is a bottom-up movement, a civic movement, and it is right for every group to have their own regulations and to manage themselves according to their own organizational ideas. Were we to establish universally valid criteria to regulate activism we would simply become a party and we certainly don't want to go there. (Regional Councilman, Palermo, November 2013)

12 The M5S firmly refuses to use public funding to subsidize its political activities.

Principles of Delegation and Control over the Elected Members

A fundamental principle has regulated the inner life of the M5S since its origins: that of the connection between the electorate and the elected members, which is not supposed to be reduced to a *carte blanche* kind of delegation of power to which electors subscribe while voting – on the contrary, it has to be renewed day after day. Grillo has expressed his opposition against Article 67 in the Italian Constitution – the article that prohibits imperative mandates – more than once (see, for instance, Grillo 2013). On the contrary, he has spoken out in favour of the 'recall' institutions as a chance for the electors to control and sanction the elected representatives. In 2013 Gianroberto Casaleggio stated during an interview that 'elected members have to behave like spokespersons; it is their duty to act according to the electoral programme and to fulfil the obligations they have towards those who voted for them. Every electoral college should have the power to pass no-confidence motions against any Member of Parliament whenever they do not fulfil their obligations, and thus force them to resign; and this should be done through local referendums' (Casaleggio 2013).

Since, according to the Italian current legislation, it is not possible to force elected officials to follow their own electors' directions, in the Movimento 5 Stelle the principle of accountability is turned into a moral obligation for elected members to present themselves periodically before the activist assembly, report on their institutional activities and ask for new confidence motions. Whenever a no-confidence motion is passed against an elected member, they are obliged to resign:

> We [Sicilian regional council members] made a commitment when signing a document before presenting our candidacy. It is a commitment to visit every province every six months to discuss what we are doing: to describe what our political activities were during the previous months, to set guidelines for our political activities during the six months to come, and to listen to citizens' desiderata. (Regional Councilman, Palermo, November 2013)

All of this rarely implies factual discussions on the actions of elected members during elective assemblies. First of all, requests for confidence motions originate from reports written by elected members themselves, who are very unlikely to describe their own work in such a way that it could be questioned. Secondly, those who are supposed to pass no-confidence motions against elected members often lack the tools to evaluate what kind of work has been done in institutional contexts – something that is regulated by complex procedures. The lack of organizational units creating a connection between the 'party in public office' and the 'party on the ground' only increases the distance between the two, and the supremacy the former holds over the latter. Consequently, these periodic assemblies often result in self-celebratory rituals, which are certainly useful for strengthening the members' solidarity with one another, and also for delivering the active members' requests to the elected members – but which do not help improve the elected members' accountability.

Since 2013, the 163 M5S Members of Parliament have also experienced a similar accountability problem with the membership base of the movement. In this case, online communication tools – the webpage[13] on Beppe Grillo's blog where parliamentary activities are reported and the parliamentary Meetup[14] – have been judged to be unsatisfactory. These pages, although easily accessible to anyone and, indeed, well-frequented, can hardly be used as an effective bottom-up communication tool. This same drawback is often experienced by members of the movement when it comes to the blog beppegrillo.it: every post the leader writes receives hundreds, sometimes thousands, of comments; it is precisely this huge number of comments that prevents them from being in any way influential on the political choices of the movement. On the other hand, more sophisticated policy-making tools (such as the ones based on Liquidfeedback, or the 'operating system' that has recently been implemented on beppegrillo.it, only accessible to long-standing registered users[15]) are only addressed to the most critical activists:

> Simple tools that anyone can use in spite of their educational level, whether graduates or uneducated artisans, are bound to be user-friendly: the Internet is at everyone's disposal, everyone owns a smartphone or a tablet on which to access the internet. Therefore, social media is a widely accessible tool, but it also grants you very little decision-making power. You also have much more sophisticated tools such as Liquidfeedback or other such platforms, such as wiki, that are less accessible, since you need to have an higher level of proficiency to use them, and you are not just required to express your opinion; you are required to write down amendments to official deliberations, decrees, In this case it [the online tool] is more effective, but fewer people use it. (City Councilman, Monza, June 2012)

Therefore, the need to use offline methods of communication, in order to combine a wider participation of members and effective interactions between activists and elected representatives presents itself again. Meetings with Members of Parliament occur often in the same area in which they have been elected – actually, they usually occur much more often than they do in other more established parties. And yet, on these occasions, it is the way in which these meeting take place that counts, rather than the meetings themselves and their regularity. It is only when the assemblies with Members of Parliament take place after comprehensive preparatory work that the activists perceive them as truly satisfactory:

> We choose the themes that we deem fundamental for the place where we live. When we decide what these are, we work on them, we analyse issues and we try to

13 http://www.beppegrillo.it/movimento/parlamento [Accessed 30 April 2014].
14 http://www.meetup.com/Parlamento-5-Stelle [Accessed 30 April 2014].
15 http://sistemaoperativom5s.beppegrillo.it/ [Accessed 30 April 2014].

> work out proposals that we will later present before our Members of Parliament, and that they will publicly commit to turning into Acts of Parliament. ... So I went to Rome, I took this proposal to the Members of Parliament who were elected in the territories of Monza and Brianza ... We worked for four months, we held a very crowded public assembly with our Members of Parliament ... During the first part of the assembly four reports were read, which resulted from four months of working and reflecting on ... work-related issues, fiscal pressure, criminal infiltrations in our territory, education. ... We reversed the typical situation: Members of Parliament are not the ones who state what they want to do and which political course to follow; they are the ones who are being told what to do by assembly participants, otherwise no-confidence motions would be passed against them, because they have to do what they are told. (City Councilman, Monza, June 2012)

Conclusions

It is clear that the M5S has been able to pick up on a widespread need for participation that traditional actors in political life are no longer able to fulfil, and one that they are actually inclined to suppress. The M5S has done this thanks to an innovative organizational model and thanks to issues that are only innovative in an Italian context, since they echo what has been experienced for several decades by green and Left-libertarian parties in Germany and Northern Europe (Müller-Rommel 1989; Poguntke 1993).

Among the innovations, we certainly have to mention the interconnection between internet-based recruitment and communication tools (whose potential Grillo sensed well before other party leaders) and traditional modes of action based upon a widespread and visible presence on the ground. Moreover, the movement is essentially horizontally-structured, like green parties were at their origins: the activist assembly fulfils a major role in every kind of decision-making process in local groups, while delegation to elected members is strictly constrained.

The organizational model described above proved successful during the first years of the Movement, as it managed to engage thousands of people in politics – people from different social classes and those with heterogeneous ideological views – who had often been unable to access politics through traditional channels. This also disproves, at least partially, the widespread belief that the downfall of political activism is both irreversible and unstoppable. It still remains to be seen whether this model is flexible enough to adapt to the changes that the M5S has undergone and will undergo in the future. This is a dilemma that every 'movement party' experiences (Gunther and Diamond 2003; Kitschelt 2006): those organizational features that are typical of movements and parties in their genetic phases (fluidity, horizontality, minimized forms of delegation) are hardly sustainable when applied at supra-local level. The need for actions that have to be coordinated at supra-local level (developing shared programmes, planning campaigns, selecting candidates) inevitably requires the set-up of centralized and restricted organizational units. On the other hand, such organizational units may end up contradicting the very principles that the M5S is founded upon, as the interviews we conducted have shown on more than one occasion.

Up until now, Beppe Grillo's leadership has counterbalanced these organizational flaws (although they did create much tension: the leader's charismatic power, too, in the long run contradicts the idea of an organization that is not based upon hierarchical structures). If the M5S is to reinforce its electoral success in the future, the contradictions that are described above may turn out to be untenable; as a result, drastic organizational changes might happen with a move towards more traditional hierarchical structures or – as it seems more likely at the moment – towards a reinforcement of the personal and charismatic model.

References

Bardi, L. 2002. Italian Parties: Change and Functionality. In: P. Webb, D. Farrell and I. Holliday, eds. *Political Parties in Advanced Industrial Democracies*. Oxford: Oxford University Press, pp. 46–76.

Carta di Firenze. 2009. *Comuni a Cinque Stelle*. [online] Available at: http://www.beppegrillo.it/listeciviche/la-carta-di-firenze.html [Accessed 30 April 2014].

Casaleggio, G. 2013. Casaleggio: La democrazia va rifondata. Interviewed by S. Danna. *Il Club della Lettura – Il Corriere della Sera*, 23 June. [online] Available at: http://lettura.corriere.it/la-democrazia-va-rifondata/ [Accessed 30 April 2014].

Cento Bull, A. and Gilbert, M. 2001. *The Lega Nord and the Northern Question in Italian Politics*. Basingstoke: Palgrave.

Colloca, P. and Marangoni, F. 2013. Lo shock elettorale. In: P. Corbetta and E. Gualmini, eds. *Il partito di Grillo*. Bologna: Il Mulino, pp. 65–88.

Duverger, M. 1951. *Political Parties. Their Organization and Activity in the Modern State*. London: Routledge and Kegan & Paul.

Eliassen, K.A. and Svåsand, L. 1975. Formation of Mass Political Organizations: An analytical framework. *Scandinavian Political Studies*, 10(1), pp. 95–121.

Farrell, D. 1996. Campaign Strategies and Tactics. In: L. Le Duc, R.G. Niemi and P. Norris, eds. *Camparing Democracies, Elections and Voting in Global Perspective*. Thousand Oaks, CA: Sage, pp. 160–83.

Farrell, D. and Webb, P. 2000. Political Parties as Campaign Organisations. In: R.J. Dalton and M.P. Wattenberg, eds. *Parties without Partisans. Political Change in Advanced Industrial Democracies*. Oxford: Oxford University Press, pp. 102– 28.

Grillo, B. 2005. Incontriamoci: MeetUp. *Beppegrillo.it* [blog] 16 July. Available at: http://www.beppegrillo.it/2005/07/incontriamoci_m_1.html [Accessed 30 April 2014].

———. 2013. Circonvenzione di elettore. *Beppegrillo.it* [blog] 3 March. Available at: http://www.beppegrillo.it/2013/03/circonvenzione.html [Accessed 30 April 2014].
Gunther, L. and Diamond, R. 2003. Species of Political Parties. *Party Politics*, 9(2), pp. 167–99.
Hazan, R. and Rahat, G. 2010. *Democracy within Parties. Candidate Selection Methods and their Political Consequences*. Oxford: Oxford University Press.
Ignazi, P. 2004. Il puzzle dei partiti: più forti e più aperti ma meno attraenti e meno legittimi. *Rivista Italiana di Scienza Politica*, 35(3), pp. 325–46.
Katz, R.S. and Mair, P. 1993. The Evolution of Party Organizations in Europe: the Three Faces of Party Organization. *American Review of Politics*, 14(1), pp. 593–618.
———. 1995. Changing Models of Party Organization and Party Democracy: The Emergence of the Cartel Party. *Party Politics*, 1(1), pp. 5–28.
Kirchheimer, O. 1966. The Transformation of Western European Party Systems. In: J. La Palombara and M. Weiner, eds. *Political Parties and Political Development*. Princeton: Princeton University Press. pp. 177–200.
Kitschelt, H. 2006. *Movement parties*. In: R.S. Katz and W.J. Crotty, eds. *Handbook of Party Politics*. London: Sage. pp. 278–90.
Lanfrey, D. 2011. Il movimento dei grillini tra meetup, meta-organizzazione e democrazia del monitoraggio. In: L. Mosca and C. Vaccari, eds. *Nuovi media, nuova politica? Partecipazione e mobilitazione online da MoveOn al Movimento 5 stelle.* Milan: Angeli, pp. 143–66.
Merkl, H.P. and Lawson, K., eds. 1988. *When Parties Fail: Emerging Alternative Organizations*. Princeton: Princeton University Press.
Morlino, L. 2001. The Three Phases of Italian Parties. In: L. Diamond and L. Gunther, eds. *Political Parties and Democracies*. Baltimore: The Johns Hopkins University Press, pp. 109–42.
Müller-Rommel, F., eds. 1989. *New Politics in Western Europe: The rise and Success of Green Parties and Alternative Lists*. Boulder, CO: Westview Press.
Neumann, S. 1956. *Modern Political Parties. Approaches to Comparative Politics*. Chicago, IL: University of Chicago Press.
Panebianco, A. 1982. *Modelli di partito. Organizzazione e potere nei partiti politici*. Bologna: Il Mulino.
Passarelli, G. and Tuorto, D. 2012. *Lega & Padania. Storie e luoghi delle camicie verdi*. Bologna: Il Mulino.
Pinto, L. and Vignati, R. 2012. Il successo e i dilemmi del Movimento 5 Stelle. *Il Mulino*, 61(4), pp. 731–9.
Poguntke, T. 1993. *Alternative Politics. The German Green Party*. Edinburgh: Edinburg University Press.
Scarrow, S., Webb, P. and Farrell, D. 2000. From Social Integration to Electoral Contestation: The Changing Distribution of Power within Political Parties. In: R.J. Dalton and M.P. Wattenberg, eds. *Parties without Partisans. Political*

Change in Advanced Industrial Democracies. Oxford: Oxford University Press. pp. 129–53.

Van Biezen, I., Mair, P. and Poguntke, T. 2011. The Decline of Party Membership in Contemporary Europe. *European Journal of Political Research*, (51)1, pp. 24–56.

Vignati, R. 2013. Dalla Tv ai palasport, dal blog al Movimento In: P. Corbetta and E. Gualmini, eds. *Il partito di Grillo*. Bologna: Il Mulino, pp. 29–63.

Chapter 4
The Electoral Base: The 'Political Revolution' in Evolution

Andrea Pedrazzani and Luca Pinto

Introduction

The Five Star Movement (M5S) was the indisputable winner of the 2013 Italian general elections. Quite unexpectedly, the Movement won 25 per cent of the popular vote for the Chamber of Deputies and around 23 per cent for the Senate, thus obtaining only a few decimal points less than the most voted for party in that election, the Partito Democratico (PD). Such success, exceptional for a party competing for the first time in a national election, established the M5S as a prominent actor in contemporary Italian political life, driving many observers and commentators to speak of a true 'political revolution'. However, although a number of studies have focused on the Movement and its founding leader Beppe Grillo (Bordignon and Ceccarini 2013; Corbetta and Gualmini 2013; Natale and Biorcio 2013), its nature is still under question.

Several aspects hinder any simple definition of the M5S. Despite competing in elections in order to appoint representatives, Grillo's Movement defines itself as a 'non-party'. It has a written binding statute, which is however labelled as a 'non-statute'. It is organised as a network of hundreds of activist groups over the national territory, but these do not have any registered offices, with the only exception being the one hosting Grillo's website. Such ambiguity also pertains to the ideological profile of the Movement, as is demonstrated by the remarkable disagreement among both scholars and political observers in defining M5S's ideological position on several dimensions of political competition.[1] Because of its emphasis on environmental issues and participatory practices, the Movement has been appropriated to the family of left-libertarian parties that had some electoral success in the eighties. According to many observers, this has allowed the Movement to attract voters from the left side of the political spectrum, especially in the initial phase of its political life. However, not only does the M5S itself

1 A few weeks before the 2013 national elections, Italian political experts were asked to locate the M5S and other relevant parties on a set of policy domains, using 20-point scales (Di Virgilio et al. 2015). The results show a high level of disagreement among experts in locating Grillo's Movement and a policy profile that seems to escape from the classical left-right division.

refuse this classification, but many commentators have more recently highlighted common traits with neo-populist movements.

The purpose of this chapter is to make a further step towards understanding the M5S, and to try and shed some light on Grillo's Movement by looking at its electoral base. For this purpose, we use opinion poll data collected from March 2012 – two months before the first electoral exploits of the M5S in local elections – to March 2013 – one month after the landslide victory in the general elections. Our analysis reveals that the Movement's electoral base has evolved over time. At the beginning of the period under investigation, M5S voters were a rather distinct social group, somewhat similar to the electorate profile identified for left-libertarian parties. Indeed, the Movement was more successful among the categories traditionally attracted by programmatic themes such as environmentalism and libertarianism. Over time, however, the M5S electorate has become more similar to that of a catch-all party, succeeding in getting support from a rather heterogeneous base.

Our chapter proceeds as follows. In the next section we present the data and briefly trace the electoral history of Grillo's Movement in the period under investigation. In the third section we introduce some of the political formations to which the M5S has been compared, stressing the traits they share with the Movement. In the fourth section we describe the evolution of the Movements electoral base, taking into account a number of socio-demographic categories. Next, in the fifth section, we analyse how the political profile of M5S supporters has changed over time. Concluding remarks follow in the final section.

The Steps towards Success

In order to understand who the potential voters of the M5S are, what characteristics they have, and how the electoral support for Grillo's party has changed over time, we analyse survey data collected from March 2012 to March 2013. The opinion poll was jointly conducted by the research company Ipsos and the network Itanes (Italian National Election Studies), using computer assisted telephone interviews (CATI) in successive waves, with about 1,000 interviews made each week. The sample is representative of the Italian electorate in terms of sex, age and place of residence. During the 12 months from March 2012 to March 2013, a total of 49,822 interviews were conducted.[2] People in the sample were asked 'If new elections were held today, which party would you vote for?' About 65 per cent of the sample (32,588 people) indicated one party as their favourite option, while the remaining 35 per cent (17,234 people) did not answer the question.[3]

2 Interviews were not carried out during August 2012.

3 More precisely, among people who did not answer, 9 per cent refused to answer, 15 per cent said they were uncertain among more than one party on the list, and 11 per cent declared abstention, a blank vote or a spoilt vote.

We started our investigation when the M5S was already a well-established political formation presenting its own lists in local elections. Previously, Grillo had simply endorsed civic lists in local elections (2008) and various Five Star lists had appeared in a number of municipality ballots, without presenting a single recognisable label (2009). Only in the regional elections held in March 2010, a few months after the formal establishment of the M5S (October 2009), did the Movement run with a common label in five out of the 13 regions involved, achieving important successes in Emilia-Romagna (6 per cent) and Piedmont (4 per cent). One year later, in May 2011, council members from the M5S were elected in various municipalities – almost exclusively in Northern and Central Italy.

During the one-year period covered by our data, we can identify three key turning points in the political course of the M5S phenomenon, each corresponding to a major success for Grillo's party in an important electoral event. The first major event was the local elections held on the 6–7 May 2012, when the M5S presented its own candidates in about one hundred municipalities and was able, for the first time, to elect mayors in one important city (Parma) and other minor municipalities in Northern Italy. The second was the regional elections that took place in Sicily on the 28–29 October 2012, in which, although the M5S candidate for governor did not win, the Five Star list was the most voted for party. The third is the national elections that occurred on the 24–25 February 2013, when the Movement obtained over 8,700,000 votes and 25 per cent of consensus, thus becoming the second largest party in Italy.

The period under investigation can thus be divided into four phases. The first is the phase preceding the local elections held in May 2012. This is the period when, given the persisting economic crisis, Italian voters' positive assessment of the government started deteriorating, thus ending the initial 'honeymoon' between Mario Monti's technical cabinet and public opinion (Giannetti 2013). Appointed in November 2011 to tackle the economic crisis, Monti's government initially enjoyed a broad consensus both within and outside the parliament, as it was backed by all the main parties: the centre-left PD, the centre-right Popolo della Libertà (PDL), and the centrist Unione di Centro (UDC). Moreover, in early 2012 several Italian politicians were investigated for corruption. Among those investigated were the treasurer of the Lega Nord (LN) and some relatives of the party leader, Umberto Bossi. This context undoubtedly constituted a breeding ground for the unexpected success of the M5S in local elections.

The second phase spans from the local elections in May 2012 to the regional elections held in Sicily in October 2012. In this period, Grillo's party was able to successfully exploit (and stoke) the social discontent towards the austerity measures adopted by the government, the popular disaffection towards the traditional parties, and the widespread criticism towards the Euro, which was increasingly being seen as responsible for the economic crisis. In doing so, the M5S certainly took advantage of the visibility achieved after its positive performance in the 2012 local elections, and in particular after the appointment of Federico Pizzarotti as mayor of Parma, a mid-sized city in Emilia-Romagna. The growing popularity of the Movement led to its success in Sicily in late October 2012 (see Pedrazzani and Pinto 2013a).

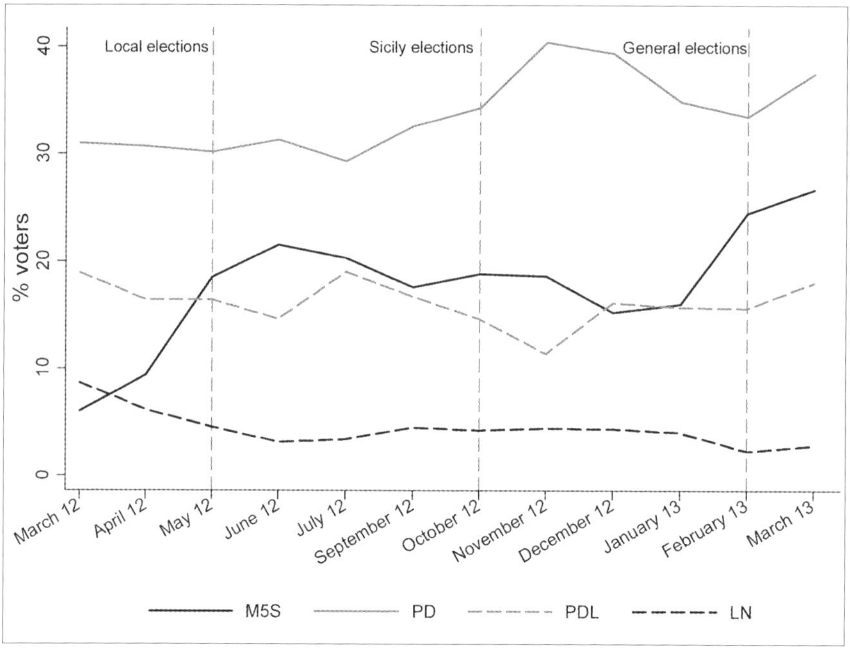

Figure 4.1 Voters' distribution by parties
Source: Itanes-Ipsos.

The third phase starts with the Sicilian election and ends with the campaign for the parliamentary elections in February 2013. A few weeks after the regional vote, the M5S set up online primaries to select candidates for the Italian parliament in the next general elections (Parlamentarie). At the same time, some organisational problems in the Movement emerged publicly as some M5S local leaders were expelled after criticising the lack of internal democracy. Then, Monti's resignation in late December and the necessity of holding early elections shifted public attention towards the electoral campaign, during which Grillo firmly excluded any future cooperation with other political forces. The strategy of 'isolation' was also pursued by the M5S in the fourth phase, after the national elections of February 2013. Following the national elections there were prolonged negotiations over the formation of the new government, during which the PD leader Pierluigi Bersani tried to get the support of the M5S, but Grillo firmly refused to participate in any coalition with other parties (see Di Virgilio et al. 2015).

Given this dramatic increase in popularity, how have the potential voters of the Movement evolved over time? On the whole, during the year from March 2012 to March 2013 the M5S more than tripled its consensus in national surveys. The upward trend of the M5S during the 2012–2013 period is displayed in Figure 4.1, where the potential electoral support for the Movement is reported on a monthly basis. In the period before the local elections held in May 2012, just 8.7 per cent of respondents declared that they would vote for Grillo's Movement: a percentage that, although not negligible, was only slightly higher than that of the LN and well below the support for the PD and the PDL. One year later, more than 27 per cent of voters declared their propensity to vote for the M5S, which by then had become the second most popular party after the PD.

Undeniably, the local elections in the Spring of 2012 gave a major boost to the popularity of the M5S: the potential electoral support for Grillo's party more than doubled after this event. In the months following the 2012 local elections, on average as many as one out of five voters stated that they would cast their vote for the Movement. The impressive performance of the M5S in the regional elections in Sicily consolidated the popularity of the party: the surveys show that, in the period between October 2012 and February 2013, the percentage of voters that were willing to support the Movement only slightly decreased (18.7 per cent). Another major surge in popular support for the M5S can be traced to after the 2013 national elections, when the M5S became the party with the greatest number of supporters in Italy. If in the elections the M5S won 25 per cent of the actual votes, the number of people who declared their willingness to vote for it after the elections was more than one out of every four (27.2 per cent).

A New Phenomenon?

Grillo and his supporters have repeatedly stressed the revolutionary and innovative nature of the M5S, which represents one of the strongest arguments of their electoral campaigns. Despite its novelty, however, the M5S shares common traits with other experiences already sketched in the literature and described as 'breaking points' in the tradition of Western European party politics. For a number of reasons – in particular, its emphasis on environmental issues and its refusal to organise the party along traditional hierarchical structures – the M5S resembles the parties of the green-wave, and more generally those belonging to the left-libertarian party family (Harmel 2002; Kitschelt 1988; Müller-Rommel 1989; Poguntke 1987a, 1987b, 1993). By contrast, the Movement's anti-establishment stance has similarities with those of neo-populist parties (Betz 1994; Ignazi 1992, 2003; Kitschelt and McGann 1995; Mény and Surel 2002; Taggart 1995, 2000).

Undoubtedly, Grillo's Movement shares common traits with both green-wave and new populist parties. Like green parties, it emphasises environmental issues, the adoption of participatory practices and the criticism of the 'old politics'. Indeed, the Five Star electoral programme pays primary attention to environmental protection, sustainable development, eco-friendly lifestyles and grassroots participation.[4] Moreover, Grillo has always refused to position himself and the Movement on

4 The five 'stars' of the Movement are: public water, transportation, development, internet connection and availability, and the environment.

the classic left-right axis of political competition, and the Five Star political agenda seems to draw more on the cultural revolution of the seventies and on post-materialistic issues (Bell 1973; Inglehart 1977). In addition, the Movement has a scarcely formalised organisation and promotes collective decision-making, stressing the importance of the *party on the ground* in driving the decisions of the *party in public office*. However, while German Greens were characterised by a high degree of internal democracy and the ban of any form of leadership (Müller-Rommel 1989; Poguntke 1987a, 1993), for the Movement the question of internal democracy still represents an open issue (see Chapter 2 in this volume).

If some programmatic elements suggest similarities between the M5S and green-wave parties, other characteristics recall those of new populist political formations. Not least, the rejection of the logic of the 'old politics' and of representative democracy, seen by M5S as corrupted and inefficient (Mény and Surel 2002; Taggart 2000). In its place, Grillo proposes a new concept of participation whereby the virtues of the 'ordinary people' are exalted vis-à-vis the self-referentiality and corruption of political elites. Furthermore, the M5S shares with populist parties a rather conservative approach towards immigration and a critical stance towards the process of European integration, together with a lack of appeal to a core constituency, and the adoption of catch-all strategies (Kirchheimer 1966; Katz and Mair 1995).

In the remainder of the chapter, we analyse the social and political traits of Five Star supporters, trying to identify the social segments in which the Movement is more likely to attract voters. This helps us to understand the degree to which the M5S electoral base resembles that of the above mentioned party types. Moreover, the analysis allows us to trace changes in the electoral support for the Movement over time. In particular, we examine the socio-demographic traits and political preferences of M5S potential voters, identified as those respondents who in the Ipsos-Itanes opinion polls declared their intention to vote for the Movement in the next elections.

The Socio-Demographic Profile of the M5S Electoral Base

The socio-demographic traits examined in this section are; gender, age, geopolitical area, size of the city of residence, level of education, profession and working status. For each of these categories, Table 4.1 shows the percentage of respondents who declared their intention to vote for the M5S (the total N on which the percentage has been computed is reported in parentheses).[5] In order to capture the evolution over time in the M5S electoral base, we computed the percentage of potential Five Star voters in each of the four phases that we broke up the period under investigation into. A comparison between the percentage of potential M5S

5 We thank Prof. Paolo Segatti and the Dipartimento di Scienze Politiche e Sociali of the Università di Milano for allowing us to use the Ipsos data presented throughout this chapter. Data are available thanks to a grant of the Fondazione Cariplo, year 2012–2013.

voters in a certain category and the percentage of potential M5S voters in the entire sample allows us to identify the segments where support for Grillo's Movement is higher than the overall mean.[6] In order to facilitate a clear interpretation of the results, in the last column of Table 4.1 we reported the index of variation between phase 4 and phase 1, which has been calculated setting the value of phase 1 as equal to 100.[7]

Table 4.1 Socio-demographic characteristics of potential M5S voters

	Phase 1		Phase 2		Phase 3		Phase 4		Variation
	% M5S	(N)	% M5S	(N)	% M5S	(N)	% M5S	(N)	(4/1)
Gender									
Men	10.7	(2,054)	22.8	(6,610)	21.7	(5,383)	26.7	(1,791)	250
Women	6.4	(1,912)	16.8	(6,585)	15.4	(5,744)	27.7	(2,021)	*436*
Age									
18–24	7.0	(351)	22.5	(1,041)	24.4	(734)	41.0	(259)	*585*
25–34	11.2	(523)	26.7	(1,607)	26.2	(1,080)	35.6	(438)	*318*
35–44	13.4	(667)	28.5	(2,144)	25.8	(1,760)	36.7	(635)	274
45–54	12.8	(682)	24.6	(2,370)	24.2	(2,204)	29.5	(719)	230
55–64	5.9	(702)	14.3	(2,469)	12.2	(2,186)	19.4	(722)	*332*
65 +	2.7	(1,041)	6.5	(3,564)	5.6	(3,163)	9.2	(1,039)	*336*
Geo-political area									
North-west	9.3	(1,016)	21.3	(3,372)	16.8	(2,928)	26.7	(985)	287
North-east	10.5	(456)	21.9	(1,476)	20.0	(1,276)	25.6	(437)	244

continued ...

6 The results presented and discussed in this chapter are based on bivariate analyses. Indeed, some bivariate relationships might be affected by other variables. For instance, the age of respondents could affect their level of education, and therefore alter the relationship between this variable and voting choice. If we found the M5S to be under-represented among lowly educated people, this could depend on the fact that many aged people are lowly educated and aged people can be particularly reluctant to vote for Grillo's Movement. In this case, the relationship between education and vote for the M5S would be spurious due to the effect of age. To check for such spurious effects, in a multivariate analysis we regressed respondents' voting choice on education including the relevant antecedent variables (gender, age, geopolitical area and city size) as control variables. We did the same using profession and working status as dependent variables. Based on the regression results, we then calculated the 'adjusted percentage' of potential M5S voters in each social category, a percentage which is thus computed after controlling for the antecedent variables (Graubard and Korn, 1999). The results, which are available upon request, are however almost the same.

7 For example, an index of variation of 250 for men implies that, from early 2012 to March 2013, the percentage of men supporting the M5S increased two and a half times. Italicised values of the index indicate increases higher than the average growth calculated for the entire sample (311).

Table 4.1 *concluded*

	Phase 1		Phase 2		Phase 3		Phase 4		Variation
	% M5S	(N)	% M5S	(N)	% M5S	(N)	% M5S	(N)	(4/1)
Red Belt	10.7	(703)	18.4	(2,301)	15.6	(1,972)	23.8	(691)	222
Centre	8.5	(563)	20.2	(1,996)	19.1	(1,545)	26.4	(560)	*312*
South	6.6	(1,228)	19.0	(4,050)	21.6	(3,406)	30.7	(1,139)	465
City size									
up to 10k residents	7.9	(1,179)	20.9	(3,926)	18.3	(3,384)	25.3	(1,171)	*320*
10k – 30k	9.4	(935)	19.9	(3,187)	18.3	(2,692)	25.5	(917)	272
30k – 100k	10.0	(856)	19.6	(2,924)	20.9	(2,388)	33.8	(839)	*340*
100k – 250k	10.4	(348)	19.2	(1,097)	16.0	(924)	19.2	(315)	185
over 250k	7.1	(648)	19.3	(2,061)	18.6	(1,739)	28.4	(570)	*401*
Education									
Low	6.8	(947)	16.7	(3,180)	16.7	(2,589)	26.9	(917)	*395*
Medium	10.2	(2,099)	22.7	(7,093)	20.8	(6,061)	27.1	(2,073)	266
High	9.9	(920)	21.4	(2,922)	17.4	(2,477)	28.3	(822)	286
Profession									
Retired	3.1	(1,330)	8.5	(4,363)	6.7	(3,963)	10.7	(1,279)	*347*
Housewife	5.9	(424)	12.9	(1,402)	18.8	(1,207)	31.9	(456)	*545*
Student	9.3	(283)	21.2	(859)	23.4	(614)	38.4	(195)	*412*
Unemployed	9.7	(362)	25.6	(1,258)	25.5	(1,132)	39.7	(396)	*411*
Executive	6.1	(93)	22.1	(190)	25.1	(188)	33.7	(59)	*557*
Teacher/ Professor	9.8	(165)	15.1	(620)	12.0	(461)	19.5	(149)	199
White collar	13.3	(607)	28.2	(2,031)	23.8	(1,609)	27.0	(583)	203
Worker/farmer	14.7	(323)	27.8	(1,096)	23.0	(850)	37.4	(313)	254
Entrepreneur/ Professional	6.9	(255)	25.2	(851)	28.1	(732)	32.8	(249)	*475*
Craftsman/ Retailer	12.7	(110)	25.4	(441)	26.9	(340)	33.6	(125)	265
Working status									
Not working	5.6	(2,397)	14.0	(7,875)	14.2	(6,908)	23.5	(2,323)	*423*
Temporary worker	6.2	(188)	24.5	(617)	21.4	(414)	34.8	(145)	*561*
Self-employed	11.4	(386)	25.7	(1,375)	27.6	(1,166)	33.1	(396)	290
Regular worker	14.0	(995)	27.2	(3,328)	22.6	(2,639)	29.8	(946)	213
Total	8.7	(3,966)	20.0	(13,195)	18.7	(11,127)	27.2	(3,812)	311

Notes: Among professions, the 'other' category is not displayed. The index of variation is calculated between phase 4 and phase 1 setting the value of phase 1 equal to 100. Phase 1: before 2012 local elections; Phase 2: between 2012 local elections and 2012 Sicilian regional elections; Phase 3: between 2012 Sicilian regional elections and 2013 National elections; Phase 4: after 2013 National elections.
Source: Itanes-Ipsos.

Gender, Age and Territorial Distribution

As our data shows, before the local elections held in May 2012, the M5S was a more attractive voting option for men than for women. In early 2012, when those willing to vote for the Movement were 8.7 per cent of the entire population, 10.7 per cent of male respondents declared their intention to vote for Grillo's party, while just 6.4 per cent of female respondents declared the same intention. Such a difference in voting intentions, which persisted until the 2013 general elections, might be attributed to the digital divide existing between men and women in Italy (Sartori 2006). In fact, the intensive use of the internet has been documented as one of the main characterising traits of initial Five Star supporters (Bordignon and Ceccarini 2013; see also Chapter 6 in this volume). However, the relationship between gender and support for the M5S also holds when controlling for the use of the internet. Moreover, after the 2012 local elections, the percentage of female voters indicating their intention to vote for Grillo's party increased more than four times, whereas the percentage of male voters declaring the same grew by two and a half times. As a result, after the parliamentary elections that took place in February 2013 the initial imbalance between gender groups had disappeared.

The M5S has been described as a movement originally supported by young voters, a typical trait of the green-wave parties of the eighties. Once again, the reason of this success was attributed to the importance of the internet as an organisational instrument for Grillo's party (Lanfrey 2011). Another reason is that the M5S seems particularly appealing for people who are interested in politics but do not sympathise with traditional Italian parties. In fact, our data shows that in early 2012, before its first electoral exploit, the M5S tended to attract more support from younger as opposed to older age cohorts, although this did not hold for the youngest category of voters (18–24). Before the 2012 local elections, when the support for the M5S was 8.7 per cent in the entire electorate, the M5S seemed particularly attractive for the central and relatively young cohorts, as more than 10 per cent of the electors from the 25–34, 35–44 and 45–54 age categories declared their intention to vote for it. Support for the Movement was extremely low among the aged: among those who were 65 or older, less than three respondents out of 100 said they were ready to cast their vote for the M5S in the next elections. The support for the M5S was also limited among the youngest voters, as just 7 per cent of the people between 18 and 24 were potential Five Star electors.

However, the support among voters under the age of 25 rose dramatically from March 2012 to March 2013: the percentage of under-25s ready to vote for the M5S grew by almost six times, while the support for the M5S in the entire electorate has increased by slightly more than three times. As a result, after the 2013 elections the under-25s became the age group with the highest propensity to support the Movement: as many as 40 per cent of the youngest electors declared their intention to vote for Grillo's party. This is evident in Figure 4.2, which shows the difference from the overall mean in the percentage of Five Star voters before the 2012 local elections and after the 2013 general elections for each age cohort.

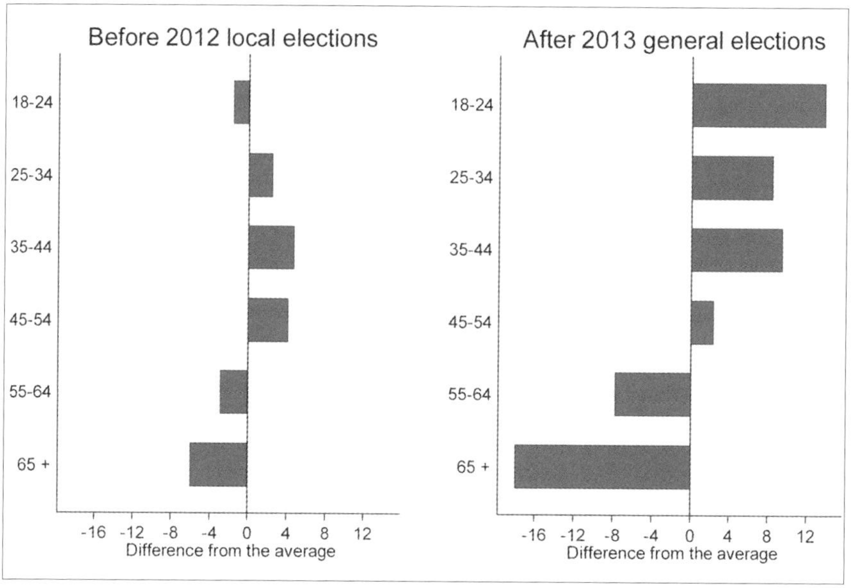

Figure 4.2 Differences from the average percentage of M5S voters before the 2012 local elections and after the 2013 general election. By age cohort

Source: Itanes-Ipsos.

The Movement's popularity amongst the youngest cohort expanded especially due to its success in the 2012 Spring elections, after which the consensus for the Movement more than tripled in this age group. As for the other age cohorts, the M5S has consolidated and strengthened its support over time in the central age groups (35–44 and 45–54), as well as among the relatively young (25–34). The main difficulties for the M5S concern the oldest cohorts, and especially the over-65s, among whom Grillo's party has only slightly more than 10 per cent of support. Summing up, after the 2013 elections the M5S can be described as a party that is electorally strong among the young and central age cohorts. The over-65s are instead unlikely to sympathise with the M5S, as the Movement represents only the third most popular option in this cohort, following the PD and the PDL.

Another way to interpret the relationship between age and support for the M5S is in terms of political generation, i.e. a cohort of individuals who have developed their political attitudes as a consequence of a set of shared post-adolescent socialisation experiences (Mannheim 1928; De Martini 1992; Bettin Lattes 1999). According to the previous analysis, the M5S message is particularly attractive for those born after 1969, and turned 18 when the traditional ideological references that had been shaping Italian politics since the end of the Second World War were gradually disappearing. The oldest among them witnessed the fall of the Berlin wall, the Tangentopoli judicial inquiries and Silvio Berlusconi's entrance into the political arena. Many of them were unconcerned with politics and quite hostile towards parties, while being well disposed toward the message of Silvio Berlusconi, who contrasted state bureaucracy with the model of private enterprise (Corbetta 2002, p. 110). The youngest became voters in the middle of the 'Berlusconism' era, an extremely turbulent phase of Italian political life characterised by the transformation of the main political forces into new parties, and the early termination of both left-wing and right-wing governments. It comes therefore as no surprise, that during this period mainstream parties did not appear as attractive options for new voters. By contrast, the M5S gathers scarce support in the political generations of those born before 1959. The oldest among them saw the phase of postwar reconstruction, a phase during which Italian mass parties enjoyed their moment of maximum leverage, while the 'generation of '68' shaped their political views during a phase characterised by a clear polarisation between left and right. And are therefore less likely to be attracted by the anti-systemic stance and the blurred political position of the M5S.

As for the territorial distribution, Table 4.1 shows that before the 2012 local elections potential Five Star voters were mainly concentrated in the northern part of Italy.[8] Whilst the average support for Grillo's movement was still 8.7 per cent over the entire national territory, in early 2012 more than one out of ten respondents indicated the M5S as their favourite voting option in the north-east (especially in Trentino-South Tyrol and Veneto) and in the 'Red Belt' (most of all in Emilia-Romagna and Marche). At that time, the M5S also gathered percentages higher than 10 in Liguria, the region where the leader Beppe Grillo was born and still lives (see Figure 4.3). The area where the M5S initially had the lowest success was Southern Italy, where it gained just 6.6 per cent in opinion polls.

Thenceforward, the Movement has been able both to consolidate its consensus in the Northern regions and to broaden its electoral base in the rest of Italy: during the 2012–2013 period the support for the M5S grew by more than four and a half times in the South, and by more than three times in the Centre. This result is particularly impressive considering that the literature on voting behaviour in Italy has identified territorial areas as being strongly characterised by persistent political cultures, and hence as having longstanding relationships with specific political parties. In particular, the PD is deep-rooted in the 'Red Belt', just like its forerunners PCI, PDS and DS were. The legacy of the former Democrazia Cristiana (DC) has instead been inherited by the LN, which is well-established in the north-east, and by Berlusconi's PDL, which has a strong basis in the south and in the north-west (Diamanti 2009).

In territorial terms, the local elections held in May 2012 represented the main turning point in the electoral history of the Movement, as they gave Grillo's party

8 North-west: Aosta Valley, Piedmont, Lombardy, Liguria. North-east: Veneto, Trentino-South Tyrol, Friuli-Venezia Giulia. Red Belt: Emilia-Romagna, Tuscany, Marche, Umbria. Centre: Abruzzo, Lazio, Molise, Sardinia. South: Campania, Apulia, Basilicata, Calabria, Sicily.

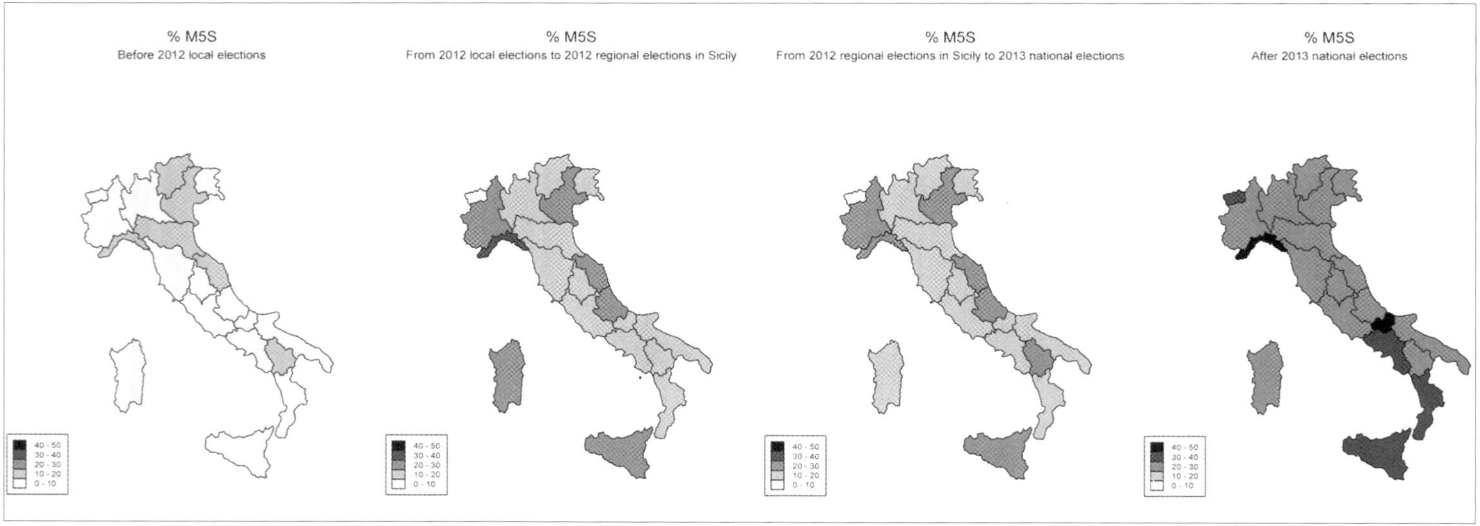

Figure 4.3 Territorial distribution of M5S voters
Source: Itanes-Ipsos.

a truly nationwide visibility. After that, the support for the M5S among voters rose by more than 10 percentage points in almost all Italian regions, and especially in the South, where Five Star sympathisers almost tripled. The growth of the Movement in Southern Italy was further boosted by the unexpected success of the M5S in the regional elections in Sicily in late October 2012, after which almost 30 per cent of Sicilian respondents indicated their intention to vote for it.

After the 2013 general elections, the South remains the area with the highest potential electoral base for the M5s, as almost 30 per cent of voters declared that they are ready to vote for the Movement in the next elections, against a national mean of 27.2 per cent. Support for the M5S is particularly high in Campania, Calabria and Sicily. The level of consensus for the Movement is close to the general mean in the North-west, the North-east and the Centre, while more than 40 per cent of the electorate in Liguria, Grillo's stronghold, are potential Five Star voters. The regions of the 'Red Belt', and Tuscany in particular, instead represent the geopolitical areas which the M5S has found relatively hard to penetrate: a well-established political culture and the persisting political links with the main party of the left (formerly the Communists, now the PD) probably makes voters in the 'red regions' more reluctant to support the M5S than voters in the rest of Italy. However, even in these areas up to 24 per cent of respondents declare themselves willing to vote for the M5S in the next elections. In summary, the distribution of the M5S's potential electoral base seems quite balanced over the Italian territory, with particularly high support in the South and in Liguria: this makes the M5S probably the only truly 'national' party in Italy.[9]

In terms of the respondents' place of residence, at its origins the M5S was sometimes interpreted as a phenomenon with a specifically urban nature, as it was associated with people with relatively high levels of education and familiarity with the internet. According to others, the Movement was instead rooted in small towns: from the beginning, the M5S refused any partisan references, and the first electoral lists that were linked to Grillo's name were presented as civic lists, a typical form of competition in small municipalities. As reported in Table 4.1, our data tells a rather different story. In early 2012, the M5S enjoyed its greatest support neither in the largest cities (with resident populations of more than 250,000), nor in the smallest urban centres (with populations of less than 10,000). On the contrary, at that time Grillo's Movement had relatively greater support in medium-small cities (with populations between 10,000 and 30,000), medium-sized cities (between 30,000 and 100,000), and medium-large cities (between 100,000 and 250,000). As in the case of the geopolitical areas, following the electoral boom in the 2012 local elections, the M5S was able to broaden its consensus over the entire territory. After the 2013 national elections, support for Grillo's party is above the overall mean in the largest urban centres (28.4 per cent) and especially in cities of medium

9 As our data shows, potential PD voters are over-represented in the 'Red Belt' and in the Centre, but considerably under-represented in the South. Potential PDL voters are instead over-represented in the South, but under-represented in the 'Red Belt'.

size (33.8 per cent). The only category where the support for M5S is significantly lower than the general mean is in cities with populations between 100,000 and 250,000, where about one respondent out of every five declares her/his intention to vote for the Movement. On the whole, during the 2012–2013 period the M5S was able to increase its consensus, especially in small towns and medium cities where its potential voters have more than tripled, and most of all in the largest urban centres, where the party was initially weaker. In large Southern cities like Naples, Palermo and Catania, support for the M5S has risen by more than four times.

Education, Profession and Working Status

At the time of its origination, the M5S was often described as a movement particularly appreciated by well informed and rather highly educated people. This is because the vote for Grillo's Movement was initially understood as a 'vote of opinion' (see Parisi and Pasquino 1977), a choice based on the evaluation of policy proposals and made outside the traditional left-right scheme. A predominance of well-educated people among the M5S voters would also assimilate the Five Star electoral base with the electorate of green parties, whose supporters had levels of education above the average. As Table 4.1 shows, initially the M5S did indeed have scarce levels of attractiveness for the lowly educated (6.8 per cent against an overall mean of 8.7 per cent), while having greater success among highly educated people (9.9 per cent) and those with a medium level of education (10.2 per cent).[10] Thereafter, the Movement has progressively increased its ability to attract lowly educated voters: during the 2012–2013 period, support for Grillo's party grew by about four times among the lowly educated, but by less than three times among the highly educated (less than the average increase). As a result, after the 2013 elections Five Star sympathisers were represented almost equally in the three education categories. The propensity to vote for the M5S is close to the general 27.2 per cent in all levels of education, indicating, again, a 'normalisation' of the Movement's electorate.

An analysis of respondents' professional category and working status can undoubtedly add greater precision to the definition of the socio-demographic profile of those who are ready to vote for the Movement. As previously noted, Grillo's party has been assimilated to political formations such as left-libertarian parties or new populist movements, each of which is characterised by a particular electoral base defined in terms of professional categories. The typical voters for the green parties of the eighties were mostly people employed in the state bureaucracy

---

10 Low education: primary education or less; Medium education: high school; High education: Bachelor's degree or more. In terms of level of education, in early 2012 the M5S was somewhat similar to Italian left and centre-left parties like the Sinistra, Ecologia e Libertà (SEL) and the PD, whose electoral basis is weaker among the lowly educated and stronger among the highly educated. On the contrary, electoral support for right and centre-right parties like the LN and the PDL is greater among lowly educated voters and lower among the highly educated.

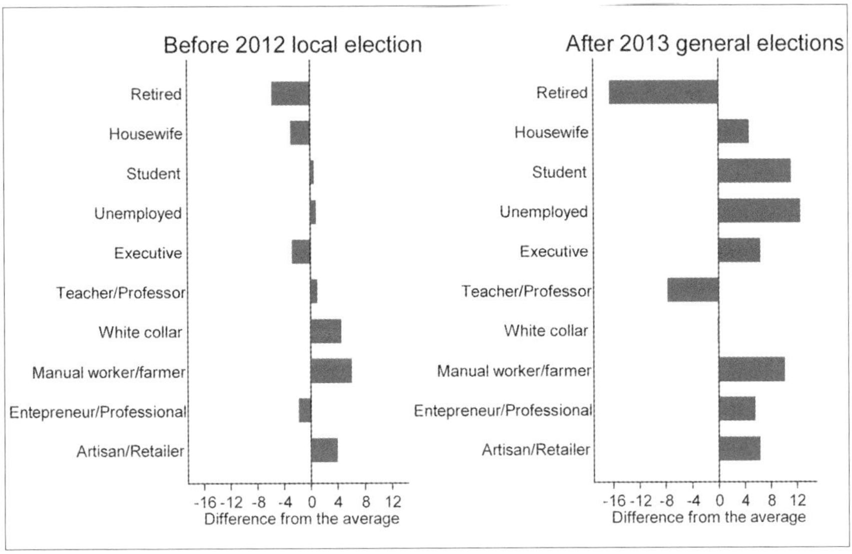

Figure 4.4 Differences from the average percentage of M5S voters before the 2012 local elections and after the 2013 general election. By professional category

Source: Itanes-Ipsos.

and in the service sector, as well as students and the unemployed with high levels of education. These individuals were far from factories and places of production and developed post-materialist values (Poguntke 1987b). Instead, new populist movements have a rather heterogeneous electoral base, which places them closer to the definition of a catch-all party. The literature has, however, highlighted the remarkable attractiveness of new populism for those working in the private sector, where individuals are more likely to become critical toward the state and its bureaucracy as well as of trade unions and corporatist agreements (Taggart 1995).

As our data shows, currently the professional categories and working statuses of potential M5S voters are similar to the electoral base of new populist movements and catch-all parties. In terms of voters' profession, since the beginning of our investigation period Grillo's party has had a rather heterogeneous base. Before the 2012 local elections, the Five Star Movement was particularly popular among employees (white-collar workers, blue-collar workers and farmers) and in small businesses (craftsmen and retailers): roughly one out of seven respondents in these professional groups declared themselves ready to vote for the Movement in the next elections. The M5S also had some success among students, teachers and the unemployed, although the percentage of Five Star supporters in these categories was not far from the overall mean of 8.7 per cent. At that time, the M5S seemed particularly unappealing for the retired and for housewives (see Figure 4.4). Since the 2012 local elections, the M5S has been able to consolidate its popularity among small businesses and among workers and farmers: after the parliamentary elections held in February 2013, more than one-third of respondents in these categories indicated their intention to vote for the Movement, while 27.2 per cent of all respondents did the same. Moreover, support for Grillo's party has increased by more than four times amongst students and the unemployed, among whom the M5S is currently the first party, with just under 40 per cent consensus. At the same time, the Movement has achieved growing popularity in the categories in which it was originally under-represented. This is the case for executives, professionals and entrepreneurs, as well as for housewives, where the M5S has increased its support by roughly five times. In these groups, after the 2013 elections about one in three respondents declared their intention to vote for the Movement. However, by contrast, the M5S seems to have partially lost its grip on white collar workers.

Generally speaking, then, the M5S has expanded over time in those categories where it was initially weak, considerably increasing the heterogeneity and the inter-class nature of its electoral base. Only two groups seem to be somehow impenetrable for Grillo's movement: teaching personnel and retired people. Teachers and professors represent the occupational category where the M5S has grown least, since its consensus in this category has 'just' doubled in the 2012–2013 period. The category where Grillo's party has always had the lowest success is that of retired people, with just 11 per cent of potential retired voters willing to vote for the Movement after the 2013 general elections.

The heterogeneity of the Five Star electorate is also evident if we look at respondents' working status. While in early 2012 the Movement was particularly successful among regular workers and the self-employed, over time the popularity of the M5S rapidly increased among those not working and especially among temporary workers. This seems to indicate the Movement's ability to attract the social categories at the margins of the labour market, and have therefore probably been most negatively affected by the economic crisis. As a result, after the 2013 elections the M5S became the most popular party among those who are self-employed or have temporary contracts, as one-third of respondents in these categories declared themselves ready to vote for the Movement. At the same time, Grillo's party is the favourite voting option for as many as 30 per cent of regular workers, while its consensus is lower among those not working, due to the aversion that the retired have for the M5S.

Summing up, the socio-demographic features of the electoral base of the M5S indicate a growing heterogeneity. While in the early days the party displayed some aspects resembling those of the left-libertarian parties, in 2013, for several of the social traits considered (gender, age, territory, education, profession and working status) it seems hard to identify a clear link with some reference constituencies. Is this growing heterogeneity also reflected in the political preferences of M5S voters? We now turn our attention to this aspect of the puzzle.

The Political Profile of the M5S Electoral Base

In this section we sketch the political profile of Five Star voters by employing two main indicators: the M5S voters' distribution according to the coalition they voted for in the previous general elections held in 2008, and the distribution of left-right self-placement scores. An initial way to trace individual political preferences relies on the analysis of respondents' past voting choice.[11] Respondents were asked to indicate which coalition they had voted for in the 2008 national elections, where they had four main possibilities: the Sinistra Arcobaleno, composed of minor left-wing lists, a centre-left coalition comprising the PD and the Italia dei Valori (IDV), a centrist coalition led by the UDC, and a centre-right electoral alliance formed by the PDL and the LN plus minor parties.[12] Previous analyses performed with the Goodman methodology (Goodman 1953, 1959), and conducted immediately after the M5S's electoral exploits in the 2012 local elections showed that the initial electoral base of the Movement was mainly composed by former voters of left-wing parties (Colloca and Marangoni 2013). Our findings partially confirm these results. As Figure 4.5 illustrates, before the local election of May 2012 more than half of Five Star electors stated that they had voted for the left or centre-left coalition in 2008, while only 27.6 per cent declared that they had chosen Berlusconi's centre-right coalition. However, the picture has largely changed over time.

If we consider the Five Star electoral base during the final run towards the national elections of February 2013, those who declared that they had voted for the centre-right coalition exceed those who voted for the left or centre-left coalition (42.1 per cent against 38.8 per cent). Moreover, the percentage of M5S voters who formerly supported Berlusconi's coalition is greater than the percentage of those coming from the PD-led coalition. Finally, it should be noted that throughout the 2012–2013 period about 13.5 per cent of Five Star voters declared themselves to come from the 'no vote' area. This figure, which is higher than the one registered for the entire electorate (6.3 per cent), seems to confirm the widespread view that the M5S gathers support from the vast audience of people 'disappointed' by politics, and thus choose not to vote in the previous election. This ability to mobilise citizens who have previously expressed their disaffection toward the ruling parties by refusing to vote is a distinctive feature of the M5S, and in this way the Movement has similarities with the political formations defined by Taggart (1995, p. 43) as 'neo-populist'.

However, there are valid reasons to believe that the Five Star electoral base consists largely of those disappointed by the conduct of 'their' party, and not just with politics in general. On the left side, the PD has probably paid in terms of its consensus for its support of Monti's technical government, which is less popular

11 This strategy presents some problems which are mainly related to the memory of the respondents and their reluctance to declare socially reprehensible behaviour, such as failure to turnout.

12 This question was not asked after the general elections held in February 2013.

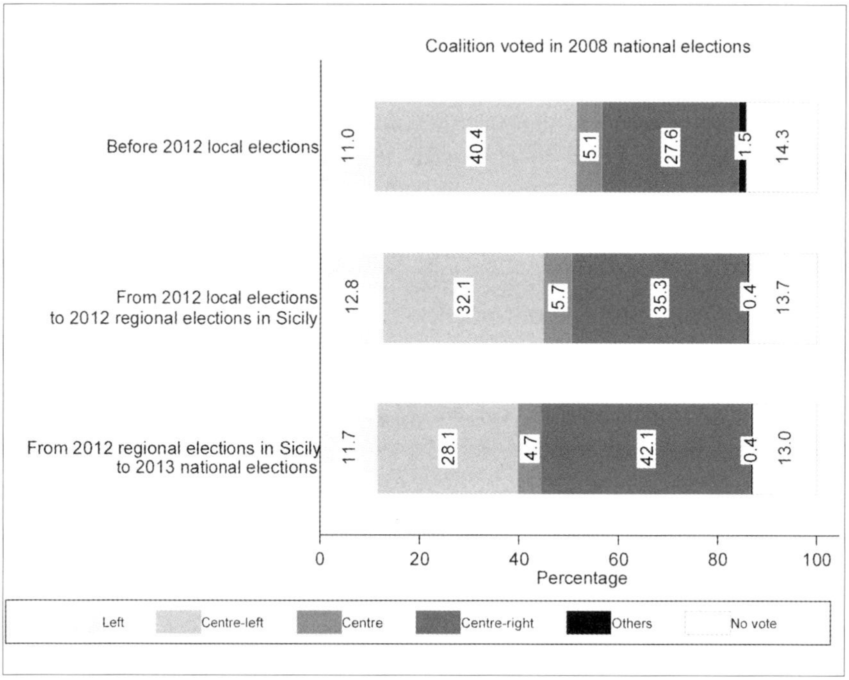

Figure 4.5 M5S voters' distribution according to coalition voted in 2008 general elections
Source: Itanes-Ipsos.

among M5S voters than it is in the rest of the electorate.[13] The IDV, the former junior partner of the PD in the centre-left coalition, could have been 'punished' for its ambiguous nature that stems from being a protest party that is, at the same time well institutionally established. Finally, the leftist political project of the Sinistra Arcobaleno ended immediately after the 2008 elections because the coalition failed to reach the threshold required in order for it to elect representatives to the parliament, leaving its voters without a clear reference point. On the right side, the support for Monti's cabinet – although less committed than that expressed by the PD (Pedrazzani and Pinto 2013b) – is almost certainly mainly responsible of the stream of voters moving towards the M5S. Moreover, the PDL saw a long internal struggle for leadership, while the LN had been shaken by a series of corruption scandals that finally led to the marginalisation of its founder and historic leader Bossi.

13 A mean-comparison test shows that the means in the two groups are significantly different (4.22 versus 5.57, $t = 24.41$, d.f. = 16,189, $p < 0.01$). The popularity of Monti's government is measured on a 10-point scale.

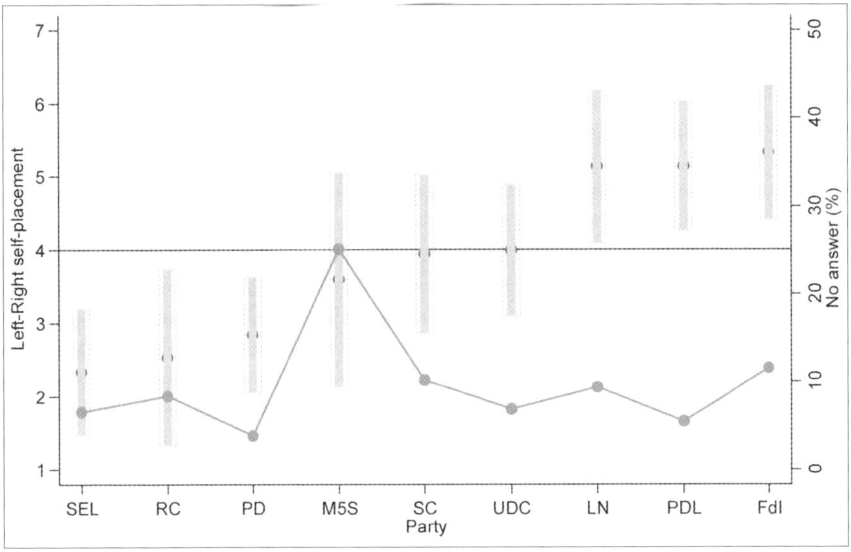

Figure 4.6 Mean of left-right self-placement by party

Notes: The average positions of parties and the associated standard deviations were calculated over the entire 2012–2013 period. Grey bars: Mean +/− 1 SD.
Source: Itanes-Ipsos.

Mass surveys offer a more robust way to study party positions on the left-right scale than simply looking at previous vote choices. Respondents were asked to locate themselves on a seven-point left-right scale ranging from extreme left to extreme right. Individual responses were then aggregated according to the party indicated as the favourite voting option, thus obtaining party average locations based on voters' preferences. According to Mair (2001, p. 15), this methodology 'is believed to come closer to tapping into the core ideological identity of the parties, and the electorates, involved'. For this reason, it has been widely used by scholars interested in party systems and party system polarisation (Sani and Sartori 1983).

Figure 4.6 gives three pieces of information for each of the main parties that participated in the 2013 national elections: the mean of individual left-right positions of that party's voters, the dispersion from the average (measured with the standard deviation), and the percentage of 'no answer' registered on the left-right scale. As far as the first point is concerned, the figure shows that the position of the M5S derived from its own voters is quite centrist, closer to the UDC and Monti's Scelta Civica (SC) than to the PD. In this sense, there is an almost perfect agreement between the positions obtained aggregating voters' preferences and the ones based on expert judgments (Di Virgilio et al. 2015).[14] Remarkably, the

14 The two measures are almost perfectly correlated ($r = 0.99$, $p < 0.01$).

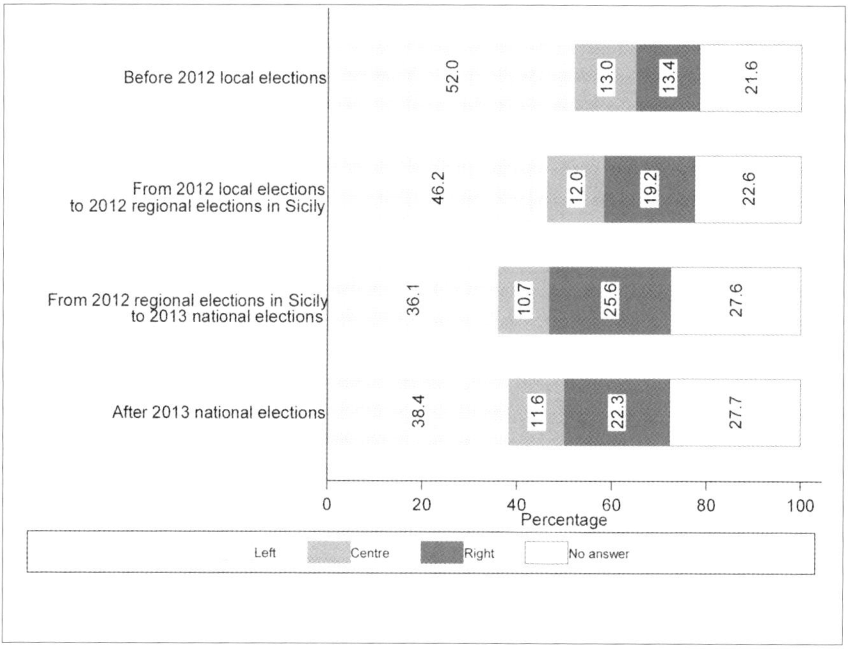

Figure 4.7 M5S voters' distribution of left-right self-placement
Source: Itanes-Ipsos

centrist position of Grillo's Movement is not the expression of an ideologically cohesive group of moderate voters, as is the case for UDC or SC, but results from the aggregation of opposite preferences. According to Figure 4.6, in fact, the M5S shows the highest dispersion around the average, ranging from left to centre-right positions. Conversely, for the three main left-wing formations – SEL, Rivoluzione Civile (RC) and the PD – the distribution of voters' self-placements is clustered in a range of values below the central horizontal line, while for the three right-wing parties – LN, PDL and the Fratelli d'Italia (FdI) – it is grouped in an area above the central line. Finally, the broken line that crosses Figure 4.6 shows that the M5S displays the highest level of 'no answer' on the left-right placements: one out four among Five Star voters refused to locate themselves in this ideological domain.

In Figure 4.7 we show the distribution of individual self-placements among M5S voters in the four time stages which we broke up the period under investigation into. Remarkably, before the 2012 local elections the distribution was skewed to the left side of the political space: more than half of Five Star voters expressed preferences ranging from extreme left to centre left (52 per cent), and the rest was divided between respondents who refused to be placed along the left-right dimension (21.6 per cent), centre voters (13 per cent) and right-wing voters (13.4 per cent). This suggests that in the initial phase most M5S voters more or less shared common beliefs, and some identifiable collective identity. Over time, however, the electoral base of the Movement has become much more heterogeneous: after the 2013 national elections, the percentage of left-wing voters in the M5S was just 38.4 per cent; right-wing voters almost doubled, increasing to 22.3 per cent; and people who refuse to be placed along left-right divide reached 27.7 per cent. Thus, starting from the electoral success of the 2012 local elections, Grillo's party has been able to mobilise an increasing number of voters against a 'common enemy' – the 'old' parties – at the expense of internal cohesion.

In conclusion, the growing ideological heterogeneity in the M5S electorate between 2012 and 2013 is consistent with what we found regarding the socio-demographic composition of the Five Star electoral base. The Movement's ability to attract voters from across most of the ideological space parallels its great skill in gaining electoral support in a variety of socio-demographic categories. The increasing popularity of the Movement in social sectors typically oriented towards right-wing positions, means that today it is more difficult to place the M5S on the left-right axis than it was in 2012. Moreover, the large number of M5S voters who refuse to be placed along left-right dimension, together with the high levels of dispersion in the distribution of their political preferences, reveal Five Star voters' increasing refusal to interpret the left-right axis as a significant source of collective identity.

Conclusions

Investigating party electoral bases can be extremely useful for gaining a deeper understanding of the nature of parties and their role in the political system. Knowing who the electoral supporters of a party are can reveal precious information regarding its strategies, and give hints on the future moves of that party inside and outside institutions. The main evidence emerging from our journey into the Five Star electorate is that Grillo's Movement is a party in continuous evolution. One electoral success after another, the M5S has evolved from a political formation supported by a quite identifiable group of voters into a party able to attract supporters from a wide array of social categories. This necessarily translates into an increased level of ideological heterogeneity in the Five Star electoral base (on this point, also see the concluding chapter of this volume).

In its early days, the M5S electorate was quite similar to those supporting the left-libertarian parties that formed across Europe in the eighties, of whom the German Greens are the most studied example. Thanks to its political platform, which is centred around the preservation of the environment and the common goods and the promotion of grassroots participation, the Movement was initially able to attract some of the social categories that are usually associated with the new left: young people, mid- and highly-educated white-collar workers and students. For the most part, these groups tend to be ideologically oriented towards the left and were predominant among Five Star voters before the electoral success in the 2012 local elections. Over time, as the economic crisis persisted and the popularity of mainstream parties has increasingly eroded, the M5S has come to adopt new-populism style anti-establishment positions in order to broaden its electoral base.

However, although the 'generalist' campaign strategy adopted by the M5S might resemble those of populist parties, some elements clearly differentiate the Movement from them. Like neo-populist political formations, Grillo's party rejects the logic of representation and 'old politics', and instead emphasises the virtues of the 'ordinary people'. Nevertheless, the Movement neither refers to a community defined in ethno-cultural terms, nor does it promote, at least officially, strong leadership and plebiscitary democracy. On the contrary, the Five Star idea of democracy is based on the active participation of the citizens in political life, as well as on the use of the internet, which is presumed to enable ordinary citizens to control and guide those in power.

Regardless of its similarities and differences to other political bodies, Grillo's anti-system stance has led to a relevant change in the composition of the Five Star electorate, which has gradually become more heterogeneous. Indeed, after the 2013 national elections the Movement's electoral base is much larger but less clearly defined in both socio-demographic and political terms. Currently, the Movement is successful among various categories of voters, many of which probably hold contrasting interests and values (see Chapter 9 in this volume). For instance, the M5S is particularly attractive to blue collar workers and to entrepreneurs and executives, as it is to students and to housewives. Several social groups have 'jumped on the Five Star bandwagon', moving the M5S to the right of the political space. The catch-all strategy employed by the Movement seems to be leading to a blurred party identity swinging between two heads that look in different directions.

References

Bell, D. 1973. *The Coming of Post-Industrial Society: A Venture in Social Forecasting*. New York: Basic Books.

Bettin Lattes, G. 1999. Sul concetto di generazione politica. *Rivista Italiana di Scienza Politica*, 29(1), pp. 23–53.

Betz, H.-G. 1994. *Radical Right Wing Populism in Western Europe*. Basingstoke: Macmillan.

Bordignon, F. and Ceccarini, L. 2013. Five Stars and a Cricket. Beppe Grillo Shakes Italian Politics. *South European Society and Politics*, 18(4), pp. 427–49.

Colloca, P. and Marangoni, F. 2013. Lo shock elettorale. In: P. Corbetta and E. Gualmini, eds. *Il partito di Grillo*. Bologna: Il Mulino, pp. 65–88.

Corbetta, P. 2002. Le generazioni politiche. In: M. Caciagli and P. Corbetta, eds. *Le ragioni dell'elettore*. Bologna: Il Mulino, pp. 79–111.

Corbetta, P. and Gualmini, E., eds. 2013. *Il partito di Grillo*. Bologna: Il Mulino.

De Martini, J.R. 1992. Generational Relationships and Social Movement Participation. *Sociological Inquiry*, 62, pp. 450–63.

Diamanti, I. 2009. *Mappe dell'Italia politica. Bianco, rosso, verde, azzurro ... e tricolore*. Bologna: Il Mulino.

Di Virgilio, A., Giannetti, D., Pedrazzani, A. and Pinto, L. 2015. Party Competition in the 2013 Italian Elections: Evidence from an Expert Survey. *Government and Opposition*, 50(1), pp. 65–89.

Giannetti, D. 2013. Mario Monti's Technocratic Government. In: A. Di Virgilio and C.M. Radaelli, eds. *Italian Politics. Technocrats in Office*, 28. New York and Oxford: Berghahn Journals, pp. 133–52.

Goodman, L.A. 1953. Ecological Regression and Behaviour of Individuals. *American Sociological Review*, 6, pp. 663–4.

———. 1959. Some Alternatives in Ecological Correlation. *American Journal of Sociology*, 64, pp. 610–25.

Graubard, B.I. and Korn, E.L. 1999. Predictive Margins with Survey Data. *Biometrics*, 55(2), pp. 652–9.

Harmel, R. 2002. Party Organisational Change. Competing Explanations? In: K.R. Luther and F. Müller-Rommel, eds. *Political Parties in the New Europe: Political and Analytical Challenges*. Oxford: Oxford University Press, pp. 119–42.

Ignazi, P. 1992. The Silent Counter-Revolution: Hypotheses on the Emergence of Extreme Right Parties in Europe. *European Journal of Political Research*, 22(1–2), pp. 3–34.

———. 2003. *Extreme Right Parties in Western Europe*. Oxford: Oxford University Press.

Inglehart, R. 1977. *The Silent Revolution: Changing Values and Political Styles among Western Publics*. Princeton, NJ: Princeton University Press.

Katz, R. and Mair, P. 1995. Changing Models of Party Organisation and Party Democracy. *Party politics*, 1(1), pp. 5–28.

Kirchheimer, O. 1966. The Transformation of Western European Party Systems. In: J. La Palombara and M. Weiner, eds. *Political Parties and Political Development*. Princeton, NJ: Princeton University Press, pp. 177–99.

Kitschelt, H. 1988. Left-Libertarian Parties: Explaining Innovation in Competitive Party Systems. *World Politics*, 40(2), pp. 194–234.

Kitschelt, H. and McGann, A. 1995. *The Radical Right in Western Europe: A Comparative Analysis*. Ann Arbor: University of Michigan Press.

Lanfrey, D. 2011. Il MoVimento dei grillini tra meetup, meta-organizzazione e democrazia del monitoraggio. In: L. Mosca and C. Vaccari, eds. *Nuovi media, nuova politica? Partecipazione e mobilitazione online da MoveOn al MoVimento 5 stelle*. Milan: Franco Angeli, pp. 143–66.

Mair, P. 2001. Searching for the Positions of Political Actors. A Review Of Approaches and a Critical Evaluation of Expert Surveys. In: M. Laver, ed. *Estimating the policy positions of political actors*. London: Routledge, pp. 10–30.

Mannheim, K. 1928. The Problem of Generations. In: K. Mannheim, ed., 1952. *Essays on the Sociology of Knowledge*. London: Routledge and Kegan Paul, pp. 276–320.
Meny, Y. and Surel, Y., eds. 2002. *Democracies and the Populist Challenge*. London: Palgrave Macmillan.
Müller-Rommel, F. 1989. The German Greens in the 1980s: Short-Term Cyclical Protest or Indicator of Transformation? *Political Studies*, 37(1), pp. 114–22.
Natale, P. and Biorcio, R. 2013. *Politica a 5 stelle. Idee, storia e strategie del movimento di Grillo*. Milan: Feltrinelli.
Parisi, A.M.L. and Pasquino, G. 1977. Relazioni partiti-elettori e tipi di voto. In: A.M.L. Parisi and G. Pasquino, eds. *Continuità e mutamento elettorale in Italia*. Bologna: Il Mulino, pp. 215–49.
Pedrazzani, A. and Pinto, L. 2013a. Gli elettori del Movimento 5 stelle. In: P. Corbetta and E. Gualmini, eds. *Il partito di Grillo*. Bologna: Il Mulino, pp. 89–122.
———. 2013b. The Work of Parliament in the Year of the Technocratic Government. In: A. Di Virgilio and C.M. Radaelli, eds. 2013. *Italian Politics. Technocrats in Office*, 28. New York and Oxford: Berghahn Journals, pp. 153–72.
Poguntke, T., 1987a. New Politics and Party Systems: The Emergence of a New Type of Party? *West European Politics*, 10(1), pp. 76–88.
———. 1987b. The Organisation of a Participatory Party: The German Greens. *European Journal of Political Research*, 15(6), pp. 609–33.
———. 1993. *Alternative Politics: The German Green Party*. Edinburgh: Edinburgh University Press.
Sani, G. and Sartori, G. 1983. Polarisation, Fragmentation and Competition in Western Democracies. In: H. Daalder and P. Mair, eds. *Western European Party Systems*. London: Sage, pp. 307–40.
Sartori, L. 2006. *Il divario digitale. Internet e le nuove disuguaglianze sociali*. Bologna: Il Mulino.
Taggart, P. 1995. New Populist Parties in Western Europe. *West European Politics*, 18(1), pp. 34–51.
———. 2000. *Populism*. Philadelphia: Open University Press.

Chapter 5
From 'Citizens' to Members of Parliament: The Elected Representatives in the Parliamentary Arena

Luca Pinto and Andrea Pedrazzani

Introduction

The Five Star Movement's (M5S) astonishing success in the 2013 general election, which saw the Movement secure as many as 109 deputies and 54 senators, has moved the M5S off the streets and into the parliamentary arena. Although Five Star representatives constitute the second largest group in the Chamber of Deputies and the third largest group in the Senate, the attitudes of the Movement towards parliamentarism remain critical. Representative democracy, and parliamentary politics in particular, have long been the target of criticism from its founder and leader Beppe Grillo. Even before the birth of the Movement, Grillo – who did not run as a candidate – had repeatedly attacked, in his speeches, the extreme bureaucratism characterising parliamentary procedures, as opposed to more direct forms of democracy. Moreover, during its electoral campaign the M5S frequently depicted the Italian parliament as a self-referential and inconclusive 'talking shop', where, despite their apparent differences, traditional political parties colluded with each other in perpetuating their own power and corruption. Similarly, elected members of parliament (MPs) were accused of being more interested in retaining office and their pay cheques, than in serving on behalf of voters. How the M5S reconcile these criticisms of the rules and practices of parliamentary politics with their obligation to operate in the parliamentary arena, is therefore an intriguing puzzle.

A first clue as to how to solve this puzzle comes from Grillo himself, who has eloquently stated that M5S will 'open Italian parliament like a can of tuna'. These words vividly express the will to renew the relationship between parties and their elected members, thus seeming to imply the need for a rebalancing of the roles of the three faces that characterise party organisations; the *party on the ground*, the *party in central office* and the *party in public office* (Katz and Mair 1994). In order to achieve this goal and establish a more direct link with voters, the M5S have designed some very peculiar internal rules and procedures, whereby parliamentary leadership is collective and rotating, and elected representatives are bound by decisions taken by party activists outside the parliament. Furthermore,

Grillo has introduced primary elections, thus opening the parliament to legislators belonging to previously unrepresented social categories. These legislators refuse the title of 'honourable' usually attributed to deputies and senators, opting instead to call themselves simply 'citizens'. Are these elements enough to characterise a radically different pattern of behaviour for the M5S in the legislative arena?

In this chapter we provide an answer to this question by carefully analysing the innovations introduced by the Movement and their impact on the relationship between Five Star representatives and their party. Focusing on the Chamber of Deputies, we investigate the organisation of the M5S's legislative party, the candidate selection procedures and the profile of the elected representatives. Moreover, we assess how these elements affect a set of legislative behaviour indicators, such as; rebel votes, bill initiative, parliamentary questioning and amendatory activity. This enables us not only to compare the M5S's legislative party with other parliamentary groups, but also to gleam important information on how the Movement's legislators interpret their own roles. Thus, we also provide an initial evaluation of whether these new parliamentarians are becoming socialised to the rules and practices of parliamentary politics and moving from 'citizens' to true members of Parliament.

The chapter proceeds as follows. First, starting from the analysis of the M5S legislative statute we briefly illustrate the relationships between the *party in public office* with both the *party on the ground* and the *party in central office*. Next, we focus on candidate selection procedures. In the fourth section, we sketch a profile of the Five Star representatives, analysing their socio-demographic characteristics, as well as the political background of the parliamentary elite. In sections five, six and seven we concentrate on four crucial indicators of legislative behaviour: legislative voting, bill introduction, parliamentary questioning and amendatory activity. Concluding remarks follow in the final section.

Organisation of the M5S Legislative Group

Contemporary parties are characterised by three different but complementary faces: the *party on the ground*, the *party in central office*, and finally, the *party in public office* (Katz and Mair 1994). Central to the first face (the *party on the ground*) are the local branches of the party and the activities of its members. The second face is the central organisation of the party, namely the national bodies and offices, and the professional staff who logistically support them. Finally, the third face includes the elected representatives at each level (European, national, regional, provincial, municipal) and the public organisation that supports their work. The elected members have at their disposal autonomous organisations provided by the institutions in which they operate, which support – and in certain cases compete with – those offered by their own party. The study of the relationship and balance between these faces has allowed scholars to better understand party organisational change by tracing the evolution that has transformed mass parties, strongly linked to their social base, into cartel parties, which conversely lack a reference electorate and mainly aim to divide up political positions and public resources (Harmel and Janda 1994; Harmel 2002; Katz and Mair 1995).

Starting from the seminal work of Katz and Mair (1994), several studies have pointed out that the *party on the ground* has been gradually declining, while the other two faces have been strengthening. This process has been coupled with the atomisation of party electoral bases and an increasing role of party leaders, to the extent that leadership now controls much of the decision-making power at the expense of party activists and simple members (Poguntke and Webb 2005). At the same time, the progressive decline in party membership has been compensated for by the expansion of central organisation, making parties increasingly dependent on public resources (Katz and Mair 1992; Mair and van Biezen 2001; Scarrow 2000). In recent years the balance of power between the three faces has further changed, as power is shifting from the *party in central office* to the *party in public office* (Katz 2002). Elected representatives are now more autonomous from their parties: parliamentarians are less constrained by what central organisations decide, and, in turn, parties are less able to exert control over them. Moreover, an increasing number of representatives are also party officials: this overlapping is an additional sign of the dominance of the *party in public office* over the other two faces of party organisation. According to Bardi and Morlino (1994) and Bardi, Ignazi and Massari (2007), Italian parties also underwent the evolution described above, especially after the earthquake that shook the party system during the 1990s. However, the M5S, at least apparently, seems to have escaped this trend by setting up a party organisation aimed at re-balancing the roles of party members, leaders and elected representatives.

The M5S is organised around two pillars: Grillo's blog and the 'meet-up' platform. The former represents the central level of the M5S organisation (the *party in central office*). Launched in 2005, it has served both as an instrument of communication for Grillo and as a virtual space where ordinary people can interact. The 'meetup' platform has instead been used to organise activists in local groups, and hence constitutes the local branch of the party organisation (the *party on the ground*).[1] In other words, the organisational structure of the Movement features a central level controlled mainly by Grillo and his professional staff (for the maintenance of the website and political communication),[2] and a local level consisting of partially autonomous and self-organising micro-groups of activists engaged in a wide range of activities (Lanfrey 2011, p. 146). In this framework, the web represents not only a fundamental organisational resource for the M5S,

1 On the organisation at local level, see Chapter 3 in this volume.

2 In political communication, an important role is played by the Casaleggio Associati, a private marketing company owned by Gianroberto Casaleggio, the co-founder of the M5S. The Casaleggio Associati is responsible for the design and maintenance of the blog and, more recently, the '5 Star Platform'. On the role of Casaleggio and his relations with Beppe Grillo, see the first chapter in this volume.

but also an instrument for realising the democratic ideal often invoked by Grillo in his public speeches: a democracy founded on the participation of active citizens in the guidance and control of the State (on this point, see Chapter 6 in this volume). The web can thus be employed as a means for controlling and guiding elected representatives (*the party in public office*), as well as for encouraging grassroots participation in circulating new ideas and policy programmes (Ceccarini and Bordignon 2013).

These principles were translated into a legislative statute that aspires to reconcile the three faces of party organization in the parliamentary arena. The internal rules of the Five Star parliamentary groups are rather unique in the Italian party system, although some of them seem to come close to the peculiar experience of the German Green Party (Poguntke 1987, 1993). In any case, despite the emphasis placed by Grillo on the importance of the role of the *party on the ground*, a careful analysis of the legislative party organisation reveals that the Movement's members and activists influence over their representatives encounters legal and technical limits. By contrast, a number of provisions illuminate the strong degree of authority exorcised by Grillo and his staff over the members of the Five Star legislative groups.

Leadership

The M5S parliamentary leadership differs greatly from those of traditional legislative parties in two main elements: its collective nature and its rotation. In order to limit the formal power of the *party in public office*, the M5S's parliamentary party has resorted to forms of collective leadership inspired by the principle of rotation, on the basis of what had already been done by the German Greens in the past (Poguntke 1993, pp. 144–6). Both in the Chamber and in the Senate, the leadership group is composed of a president and four deputy presidents. According to the statute, the president is elected every year and is the legal representative of the parliamentary group in all registered offices. The first deputy president acts as the chair of the group, and is therefore the only one to have formal political powers. The second deputy president assists the first deputy-president, taking her position after three months, at which time another second deputy president is elected. Finally, the remaining two deputy presidents have coordination functions and hold office for one year, with the possibility of reappointment.

The president and the four deputy presidents, together with the treasurer and the secretary, form the 'directive committee'. These positions are reserved only for elected representatives. However, external members can be appointed as managing director or audit manager of the group. Despite the existence of a directive committee, the true heart of the M5S's parliamentary party is the 'assembly', composed of all Five Star deputies and senators. The assembly meets once a month and has the following main responsibilities: to elect the members of the directive committee, to establish the general guidelines on the use of the financial resources of the legislative group, and to decide the political line of the party.[3] Decisions are taken by majority voting under open roll call and are binding for all members.

The connections between the *party on the ground* and the *party in central office* are guaranteed by two other relevant provisions contained in the statute. First, in its decisions the M5S assembly must take into account the instructions provided by M5S members through the web. For this purpose, the Movement has implemented a technological platform to give citizens an active role in shaping political decisions, thus following the experience of the German Pirate Party. In particular, Grillo has recently launched the '5 Star Platform', an integrated system that allows 'certified' M5S members (i.e. those who registered on the Movements website before June 2013, around 50,000 people) to discuss the bills proposed by Five Star MPs.[4] Second, the statute provides for the existence of a 'communication group' to ensure the accuracy and the effectiveness of communication. There is no equivalent of this organism in any of the other parties: in fact, its members are appointed directly by Grillo and are not chosen from among the elected representatives, but hired by the parliamentary group. Moreover, their office is not subject to any mandatory term, which differentiates them from members of the directive committee. These characteristics seem to give the communication group a rather autonomous role from the parliamentary group. Therefore, there are good reasons for believing that this communication group could serve as an instrument for the *party in central office* to instruct M5S representatives about what to say in public and, presumably, how to operate in the legislative arena.[5]

Imperative Mandate

'Imperative mandate' means that those who are elected to be part of the parliament are directly accountable to their voters and have a duty to comply with their will, and that if they fail to do so their powers may be revoked. Regarding this topic, the M5S's principles clash with legal and technical constraints. According to their statute, Five Star legislators are bound by the decisions taken by majority vote in the M5S assembly, and thus must follow the instructions provided by the Movement's members on the web. However, in its attempt to guaranty the freedom and independence of MPs, Article 67 of the Italian Constitution explicitly

---

3 The assembly takes decisions regarding three important aspects of parliamentary works: legislative voting (which includes how MPs should vote on the floor), bill proposal and the allocation of positions in committees.

4 The 5 Star Platform was officially launched in October 2013, but it is still under development.

5 The current communication managers of the M5S are Nicola Biondo, for the Chamber of Deputies, and Claudio Messora, for the Senate. The first is a free-lance journalist, who has written several articles for the left-wing newspaper *L'Unità*. The second is a former consultant of the Casaleggio Associati. Both are responsible for public relations and the general political coordination of the two groups.

forbids the imperative mandate. In any case, despite the development of the above mentioned 5 Star Platform, the efforts to establish a direct link with voters remains at the level of a mere declaration of political will: in October 2013, the 5 Star Platform contained only one bill proposal ready for discussion.

Transparency and Openness

The statute of the M5S legislative group recognises the web as the main instrument for informing party members and citizens about the activity of the parliamentary party. According to the statute, the Five Star parliamentary groups must submit both their whole decision process and the resulting compromises reached in the sessions of the M5S assembly, to public scrutiny. Only in exceptional circumstances, and through a majority vote, can the assembly exclude the web broadcasting.[6] This emphasis on openness and transparency in public proceedings is coherent with the general principle of democratic power and could constitute a general improvement in the quality of representative democracy.[7] Nevertheless, this rule also reflects the political position of the Movement, based on their distaste for the 'politics of compromise' and a general rejection of the logic of the 'old politics', which are seen as corrupted and inefficient.

Parliamentary Allowance

The M5S political manifesto generically reports that the salary of Five Star representatives will be aligned to the national average (according to ISTAT, 1,400 euro net per month). During the electoral campaign, Grillo declared that MPs would receive no more than 2,500 euro net per month. Accordingly, the 'code of conduct' for M5S parliamentarians asserts that the parliamentary allowance is limited to 5,000 euro gross per month (more or less 50 per cent of the entire gross salary), while what remains unclaimed must be returned to the State. This behaviour recalls the conduct followed by the German Greens (Poguntke 1993, p. 145), whose (partial) refusal of parliamentary benefits represented a sign of their rejection of 'vicarious politics'. The underlying idea is to minimize the distance between the political elite and common citizens by closing the gap between the politicians' salary and the average salary in the population. However, this rule can be also interpreted as representing a form of delegitimisation of the political elites, described by the M5S as a clique.

Of course, Five Star representatives have no legal obligation to return the money they get. This has generated a series of tensions between M5S legislators,

6 In November 2013, during a debate on a number of irregularities committed by two M5S senators, the communication manager of the group asked the assembly to exclude the web broadcasting because he feared that it could bring negative feedback to the Movement.

7 Following the M5S, other parties, such as the Partito Democratico (PD), started to broadcast the meetings of their governing boards.

party members and Grillo himself, who has threatened of expulsion those who do not return the money. Finally, a compromise has been reached. The wage of an Italian MP actually comes from several sources and the allowance is only one of them. According to the statute, the Movement's representatives have the right to keep all the so called 'ancillary components' of an MPs salary (more or less 7,000 euro net per month), provided that they present a detailed financial statement of all the expenses.[8]

Selection of M5S Representatives

Procedures for the selection of candidates are particularly relevant because they are often assumed to have an influence on how representatives behave in parliament and carry out their duty in general (Carey and Shugart 1995; Katz 2001; Rahat and Hazan 2001; Shomer 2009). In particular, when candidates are selected by a democratic mechanism – such as primary elections – it is expected that legislators seeking re-election, will emphasise their personal reputation in order to distinguish themselves from competitors within their own party. Conversely, when party leaders exercise a strong degree of control over candidates' access to party labels, and have the last word on ballot ranks in electoral lists, the incentives to cultivate personal reputation in the legislative arena are minimised. In this case, legislators will behave in a party-centred manner, 'emphasizing their loyalty to their party as well as accentuating their conformity with the party's ideological stance and beliefs' (Shomer 2009, p. 946). Variations in candidate selection procedures, therefore, configure different types of legislative behaviour and lead to a different relation between the *party on the ground* and the *party in central* and *public office*.

The Five Star Movement is the first political party in Italy (according to Grillo, the first in the world) to have selected its representatives through web primaries (parlamentarie). In order to understand the impact of candidate selection process on the relationship between M5S legislators and their party, we rely on the theoretical framework developed by Rahat and Hazan (2001). The authors classify candidate selection mechanisms by evaluating their degree of inclusiveness/exclusiveness in four dimensions. The first dimension, *candidacy*, ranges from an inclusive pole in which all citizens can become candidates, to an exclusive one where only party members with certain characteristics can present their candidacy. The second dimension, *selectorate*, spans from rules enabling the entire electorate to select candidates to rules that only allow party leaders the authority to determine the party's list. The third dimension, *decentralisation*, distinguishes the methods in which candidates are chosen by local branches of the party from centralised

8 In the period June-October 2013, the M5S declared that it had returned more than 2.5 million euros to the state. According to M5S declarations, the money has been paid into a fund for small and medium enterprises. The amount of money returned by elected representatives of the M5S is detailed in the web site www.tirendiconto.it.

national-level procedures. The fourth dimension, *voting*, differentiates methods that use voting from those that use an appointment system to determine party lists. Methods characterised by scarce restrictions to potential candidates, an inclusive selectorate, a decentralised selection, and the adoption of voting procedures, should promote more personalised behaviour. By contrast, rules that allow limitations to candidacy and entrust a small and centralised selectorate to appoint candidates should induce party-centred behaviour.

According to the rules of the M5S parlamentarie, candidates are chosen from among party members who have the following requirements: a minimum of 25 years of age (i.e., the constitutional requirement for the passive electorate in the Chamber of Deputies), no criminal conviction, have not already served in any political institutions for two electoral mandates, have not been a member of other parties, live in the electoral district where the candidature is presented, have already competed in municipal or regional elections in a list certified with the Five Star logo without being elected. Therefore, only party members satisfying very stringent requirements could present their candidature. Candidate lists were proposed at the local level, but they required Grillo's approval to be valid. Like candidates, voters had to be party members; however, only those registered on the Movement's website before September 2012 were eligible to vote. The voting process was very simple: in each electoral district, after having evaluated candidates' curricula, each voter could cast three preferences. According to the M5S website, around 95,000 votes were cast for 1,400 candidates, configuring quite a small selectorate of just around 32,000 voters. The M5S parlamentarie were then characterised by a rather exclusive selection process, revealing again an imbalance in the relationship between the three faces of party organisation in favour of the *party in central office*.

This statement can be better appreciated by comparing the M5S's experience with that of other parties. In the wake of the initiative sponsored by the Movement, two other parties – the Partito Democratico (PD) and Sinistra, Ecologia e Libertà (SEL) – also launched their own primaries to select candidates for the parliament. For both parties, all members and citizens claiming to be supporters of PD or SEL could present their candidatures, which were then examined and approved exclusively by local branches of the parties. As far as the selectorate is concerned, more than three million voters were eligible to vote.[9] However, although generally adopting more inclusive rules in comparison with M5S, the PD and SEL reserved a small portion of high-ranked list positions (10 per cent of all candidates) for prominent figures directly appointed by party leadership. The results of this strategy can be observed in Table 5.1: only 67 and 51 per cent of PD and SEL representatives were selected by primaries with voting procedures.

9 The selectorate was composed of party members and those voters who participated in the primary election to choose the leader of the center-left coalition in November 2012.

Profile of M5S Representatives

The political and institutional earthquake that occurred in the early 1990s led to the collapse of the so called First Italian Republic and marked a significant discontinuity in the composition of the Italian parliament. In particular, two of the parties emerging from the decomposition of the old Italian party system after the 1992 corruption scandals – Forza Italia (FI) and Lega Nord (LN) – introduced a new political elite into the parliament: many FI representatives were businessmen and managers from Silvio Berlusconi's companies, while the LN recruited several young local activists from middle class professions such as craftsmen, small-business people, self-employed professionals and farmers. However, the novelty represented by these new political forces quickly disappeared and progressively the parliamentary elite reacquired its traditional profile (Cotta and Verzichelli 2007). Like before 1994, a full time occupation in parties and trade unions or a professional career as a lawyer, journalist, teacher or doctor still represents a typical background for most members of the Italian parliament. Moreover, Italian MPs usually experience an articulated process of political socialisation characterised by a series of party appointments at the local and national level and the participation in local elective bodies (Verzichelli 1998; Zucchini 2001).

Table 5.1 Profile of the members of the Chamber of Deputies

	M5S	LN	FDI	PD	PDL	SCPI	SEL	IND.	Total
Gender									
Female	**34.0**	0.0	11.1	37.5	27.1	21.3	27.0	18.2	31.3
Male	**66.0**	100.0	88.9	62.5	72.9	78.7	73.0	81.8	68.7
Age									
25–34	***56.6***	15.0	0.0	10.9	3.1	0.0	8.1	22.7	16.8
35–44	***43.4***	35.0	22.2	27.7	19.8	12.8	40.5	18.2	28.4
45–54	**0.0**	30.0	55.6	33.8	43.8	38.3	27.0	22.7	29.5
55–54	**0.0**	10.0	11.1	23.6	22.9	31.9	21.6	31.8	19.7
65 +	**0.0**	10.0	11.1	4.1	10.4	17.0	2.7	4.6	5.6
Education									
Lower	**0.9**	0.0	0.0	0.7	2.1	0.0	5.4	0.0	1.1
Intermediate	***32.1***	55.0	22.2	30.0	22.9	17.0	27.0	18.2	28.4
Higher	**67.0**	45.0	77.8	69.3	75.0	83.0	67.6	81.8	70.5
Profession									
Architect	**0.9**	0.0	11.1	1.0	1.0	0.0	2.7	0.0	1.1
Lawyer	**2.8**	5.0	11.1	12.6	21.9	6.4	2.7	27.3	11.6
Housekeeper	**0.9**	0.0	0.0	0.0	0.0	0.0	0.0	4.6	0.3
Business consultant	**0.0**	15.0	11.1	3.1	4.2	2.1	0.0	0.0	2.9
Retailer	**1.9**	5.0	0.0	0.3	0.0	0.0	2.7	0.0	0.8
Public official	**0.9**	0.0	11.1	4.8	7.3	10.6	2.7	9.1	4.9

continued ...

Table 5.1 *concluded*

	M5S	LN	FDI	PD	PDL	SC	SEL	IND.	Total
Unemployed	***6.6***	0.0	0.0	0.3	0.0	0.0	0.0	0.0	1.3
Pharmacist	**0.0**	0.0	0.0	0.0	2.1	0.0	0.0	0.0	0.3
Party official/ Local administrator	**0.0**	15.0	0.0	13.7	5.2	2.1	32.4	4.6	9.8
Journalist	**0.9**	0.0	11.1	6.5	11.5	6.4	13.5	9.1	6.7
White collar	*37.7*	10.0	22.2	19.5	3.1	4.3	21.6	9.1	18.4
Entrepreneur/ Executive	**3.8**	25.0	11.1	6.8	27.1	34.0	2.7	13.6	12.1
Engineer	*5.7*	0.0	0.0	1.0	0.0	0.0	2.7	9.1	1.9
Teacher/Professor	**7.6**	5.0	0.0	16.0	4.2	17.0	2.7	0.0	11.0
Self-employed	***9.4***	15.0	0.0	5.1	6.3	4.3	2.7	4.6	6.0
Magistrate	**0.0**	0.0	0.0	0.3	0.0	2.1	0.0	0.0	0.3
Doctor	**2.8**	0.0	0.0	2.4	5.2	6.4	0.0	4.6	3.0
Soldier/Policeman	**0.0**	0.0	11.1	0.0	0.0	4.3	0.0	0.0	0.5
Worker/Craftsman/ Farmer	*4.7*	5.0	0.0	1.0	0.0	0.0	0.0	4.6	1.6
Trade unionist	**0.0**	0.0	0.0	2.7	1.0	0.0	5.4	0.0	1.8
Student	***13.2***	0.0	0.0	2.7	0.0	0.0	5.4	0.0	3.8
Previous Parliamentary Experience									
Newcomer	***100.0***	45.0	11.1	62.5	12.5	87.2	78.4	63.6	62.7
Up to 2 legislatures	**0.0**	40.0	66.7	30.7	60.4	6.4	21.6	22.7	28.3
Up to 4 legislatures	**0.0**	10.0	11.1	6.8	25.0	6.4	0.0	13.6	8.4
More than 4 legislatures	**0.0**	5.0	11.1	0.0	2.1	0.0	0.0	0.0	0.6
Previous Local Experience									
No	***99.1***	20.0	22.2	43.3	55.2	78.7	64.9	45.5	57.5
Yes	**0.9**	80.0	77.8	56.7	44.8	21.3	35.1	54.6	42.5
Candidate selection									
Appointment	**0.0**	100.0	100.0	32.8	100.0	100.0	48.6	100.0	48.9
Voting (Primaries)	***100.0***	0.0	0.0	67.2	0.0	0.0	51.4	0.0	51.1
(N)	**106**	20	9	293	96	47	37	22	630
Total	**100.0**	100.0	100.0	100.0	100.0	100.0	100.0	100.0	100.0

Notes: Data are updated to November 2013. The categories overrepresented in the M5S are in italics. Acronyms: M5S: Five Star Movement; LN: Northern League; FDI: Brothers of Italy; PD: Democratic Party; PDL: People of Freedom; SCPI: Civic Choice; SEL: Left, Ecology and Freedom; IND.: Independents.

Source: www.camera.it; www.openparlamento.it.

In this scenario, the emergence of the M5S in the Italian parliament has certainly been a factor of discontinuity. According to Table 5.1, in fact, most of the categories that previously constituted a frequent professional background for MPs are underrepresented among the M5S ranks: lawyers are 2.8 per cent among Five Star deputies (11.6 per cent in the entire Chamber), journalists are less than

1 per cent (6.7), teachers and university professors are 7.6 per cent (11.0) and finally doctors are 2.8 per cent (3.0). The difference with the other parliamentary groups also emerges from looking at the percentages of MPs having a full time occupation within a party or a trade union organisation: while about 16 per cent of PD legislators have declared to be either a party official or a trade unionist, nobody has done the same in the M5S. The situation is the same if we consider previous experiences in local bodies: only one Five Star representative declared that he had been elected in a local council in the past. On the one hand, these figures depend on the M5S's party organisation, which is young, not fully institutionalised and lacks any formal body besides a central level which is dominated by Grillo himself; on the other hand, they also suggest a different pattern of political socialisation for the Movement's legislators and activists (Passarelli, Tronconi and Tuorto 2013).

In accordance with the populist concept of participation proposed by Grillo – whereby the virtues of the 'ordinary people' are exalted vis-à-vis the self-referentiality and corruption of political elites – members of the M5S parliamentary group where chosen from among non-professional politicians. Breaking from the past, the Movement has opened the Chamber of Deputies to previously underrepresented categories. The most noticeable are the unemployed and students, who respectively constitute 6.6 per cent (1.3 per cent in the entire Chamber) and 13.2 per cent (3.8) of M5S deputies. This means that almost one out of five of Five Star representatives come from a non-productive professional category, a figure that exceeds that of any other party. The remaining Five Star MPs are engineers (5.7 per cent), self-employed (9.4) or workers, craftsmen or farmers (4.7). However, the vast bulk of M5S legislators belong to the professional category of white collar workers (37.7 per cent), twice the number recorded in the entire Chamber of Deputies. Finally, in order to complete the profile of the Movement's legislators, it should be noted that, excluding the LN, high school graduates (*intermediate education*) are more common in the Five Star group than in other parties (32.1 vs 28.4 per cent registered in the entire Chamber), while university graduates (*higher education*) are slightly underrepresented (67.0 vs 70.5 per cent).

The reasons behind this peculiar composition need to be further investigated. In fact, this profile could depend specifically on the nature of M5S's message – which could have mainly attracted activists coming from specific sectors of society – or be the result of other factors, such as age or candidate selection procedures. On the one hand, as shown by Table 5.1, M5S legislators are all grouped in the youngest age cohorts (25–44). This is an effect of the rules governing the parlamentarie, which force over-40s candidates to be automatically moved onto the Senate lists, in which the age to elected is constitutionally fixed at 40 or more. As a consequence, the age of M5S legislators in the Chamber is strongly skewed to the right of the distribution. This could therefore affect other variables. In particular, the overrepresentation of students and the unemployed could be the product of this peculiar age distribution.[10]

10 At the end of 2013 the registered unemployment rate for under-35-year-olds in Italy was around 20 per cent, almost twice that registered in the whole population.

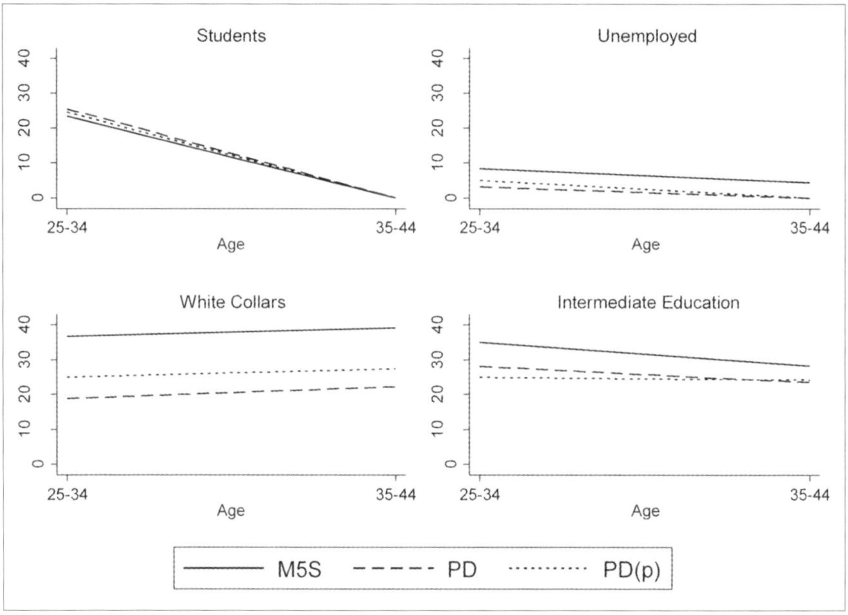

Figure 5.1 M5S and PD legislators by age cohort
Source: www.camera.it.

On the other hand, the selection process itself could have influenced the legislators' profile. Primary elections, in fact, can give previously underrepresented categories a higher chance of entering parliament in comparison with methods based exclusively on leaders appointment.

In order to understand the role of age, we compare the profile of M5S and PD legislators in two professional categories strongly affected by this variable: students and the unemployed.[11] Figure 5.1 shows that, considering only the 25–34 and 35–44 age cohorts, there are no differences among the percentages of students in the two parliamentary groups. However, diversity remains when the unemployed are taken into account. Similarly, in order to assess the role played by selection procedures, we compare M5S representatives with the PD legislators who were selected through primaries. Controlling for both age and candidate selection process, white collar workers, like the unemployed, continue to be overrepresented among the M5S ranks. The same occurs for legislators with intermediate education. Therefore, it can be concluded that the peculiar profile of M5S representatives emerging from our analysis seems genuinely to derive from

11 We compare M5S with PD only – and not with all the other party groups – not only because the latter is the major party in the Chamber, but, more specifically, because it is the only one to include both students and the unemployed among its ranks.

the participation model proposed by Grillo, explicitly aimed at mobilising common citizens and promoting the destabilization of the political elites in contrast to the logic of the 'old politics'.[12]

Legislative Voting, Party Unity and Discipline

After examining the profile of Five Star representatives, we now turn to their behaviour in the legislative arena. More precisely, in the remainder of this chapter we concentrate on four indicators of parliamentary behaviour: legislative voting, bill introduction, questioning and amendatory activity. This will allow us to compare the behaviour of M5S members with that of legislators from other parliamentary parties. Our aim is twofold. First, we intend to shed some light on how the Movement's members interpret their role as parliamentarians. Second, we try to understand the degree to which these new parliamentarians are becoming socialised to the rules and practices of parliamentary politics.

Legislative voting is one of the fundamental indicators of the functioning of a parliamentary party group. It is, in fact, a crucial phase in representative democracies, since it represents the main instrument legislators and parties have to express their preferences and to demonstrate their support for the government. Moreover, from a normative point of view, legislative voting is crucial for the accountability of individual and collective actors, and is therefore essential in the political representation process (Carey 2009). In particular, legislators' voting behaviour reveals information about the degree of unity in party groups. Unity, understood as the capacity to act in unison in legislative voting (Sieberer 2006), is a crucial asset for both party leaders and backbenchers: first, voting as a cohesive bloc enables the achievement of party policy goals; second, party unity allows parties from both the majority and the opposition to build a coherent and reliable party label (Cox and McCubbins 1993; Aldrich 1995). Unity can be the product of shared preferences, and in this case it is usually referred to as cohesion. Yet, even like-minded individuals often disagree on something. In this situation, unity is sustained by discipline. The threat of sanctions for rebel behaviour reduces the autonomy of the single members of the group and makes defection a politically costly option (Bowler, Farrell and Katz 1999; Hazan 2006). Indeed, it has been argued that the key to understanding individuals propensity to challenge party leaders and break unity, lies in the balance of resources between legislators and the party to which they belong (Curini, Marangoni and Tronconi 2011).

12 This is further demonstrated by the fact that, while almost none of the M5S representatives had a previous political experience, almost one out of five of the PD legislators selected by primaries had worked as a party official or a trade unionist (18.3 per cent) and more than two thirds had previous experience in a local body (71.6 per cent). Therefore, unlike M5S primaries, PD primaries have mainly benefited party officials or local administrators.

In the previous sections, we described the organisation of Grillo's party and some relevant characteristics of its parliamentary group. Our analysis has sketched a peculiar relationship between the faces of the party organisation. On the one hand, a number of elements in the organisation of the legislative group – rotating leadership, imperative mandate, representatives limited control over personal allowances – are all designed to strongly curtail the autonomy and resources of the members of the *party in public office*. On the other hand, the candidate selection procedures, although aimed at empowering the *party on the ground*, were conducted in a rather exclusive way, granting a significant degree of control to the *party in central office*. Finally, the novelty of the M5S political experience and the composition of its parliamentary group (whose members are 'common citizens' lacking previous political experience) seems to place elected representatives in a rather weak position vis-à-vis the *party in central office*. This peculiar distribution of resources, strongly unbalanced in favour of Grillo and his staff, suggests the existence of very few incentives for Five Star MPs to break party unity in legislative voting.

In order to empirically evaluate this statement, we collected data on the legislative behaviour of individual legislators in the 2,418 roll-call votes cast from February to November 2013. In particular, for each MP we counted the number of 'rebel votes', that is, the number of times a legislator voted against the majority of her party. Then, we built a simple statistical model in which the dependent variable is how many rebel votes an MP cast, and the independent variables of interest are a set of dummies indicating legislators' party. As highlighted in the literature, legislators are expected to conform less to party discipline when, in order to achieve re-election, they exploit their personal resources more than those provided by their party (Curini, Marangoni and Tronconi 2011). For this reason, we included a number of control variables identifying personal characteristics that can influence individual propensity to break party unity: education, profession, previous parliamentary experience, previous experience in elected local bodies, candidate selection procedures (appointment vs voting) and government membership (minister or junior minister vs simple member of the Chamber).[13]

Figure 5.2 summarises the results of our model. Dots represent the average difference in the expected number of rebel votes between M5S legislators, which is our reference category, and MPs from other parliamentary groups. Vertical bars correspond to 95 per cent confidence intervals, i.e. the range of values in which the true number of expected rebel votes is included. When the bars are either above or below the zero line (the reference category) the differences are statistically significant – that is, there is a reasonable probability that an association between

13 Since our dependent variable is a count, we use a count model, and in particular a negative binomial regression model. This model assumes a probability distribution that yields predictions that are also counts. Other modelling strategies, such as linear regression, may produce biased and nonsensical results such as negative or fractional counts (Long 1997). We exclude independents in the mixed group from our analysis.

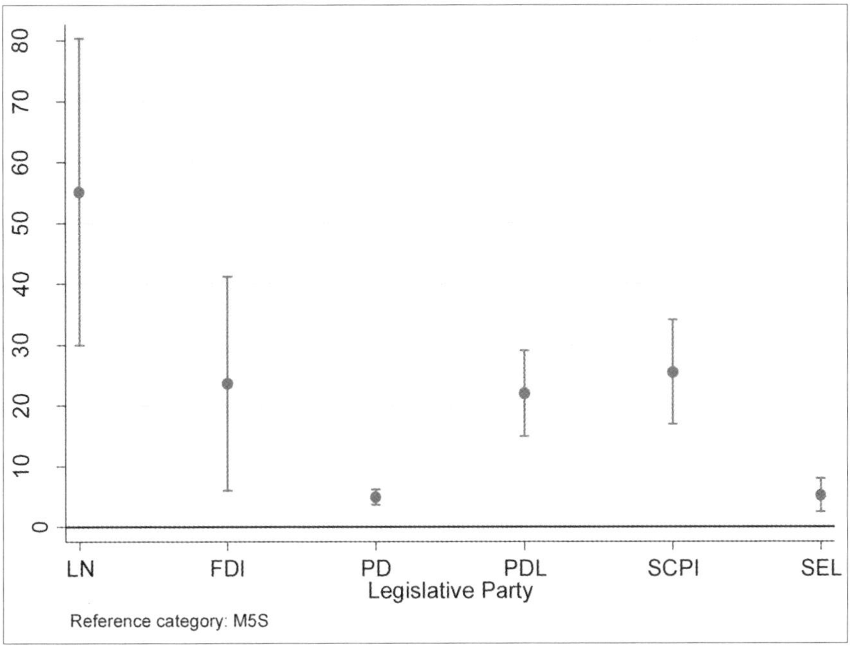

Figure 5.2 Effect of legislative party on the number of rebel votes with 95 per cent CIs

party groups and the amount of rebel votes exists. By contrast, if the bars cross the zero line the effect of party group might be due to chance only. As we can see from Figure 5.2, keeping everything else constant (the level of education, profession, etc.), legislators of all the parliamentary groups in the Chamber are more likely to cast a higher number of rebel votes than M5S members. In particular, PD and SEL legislators are expected to cast on average about 5 rebel votes more than Five Star MPs; for FDI, PDL and SCPI the number of rebel votes is comprised between 20 and 30, while for the LN it was more than 50. This means that differences are not only significant but also have a substantive impact. Thus, we can conclude that, holding individual incentives constant, the characteristics of the M5S legislative group make MPs less likely to challenge the party line and break discipline in legislative voting in comparison with other parliamentary parties. This is probably due to a distribution of resources between Grillo and M5S representatives that is skewed toward the former.

In fact, in the M5S ranks breaking party discipline is not only less likely, but also more hazardous than in other parties. The proof of this are the expulsions of MPs from the M5S, promoted by Grillo and voted on by party activists through web ballots. First, Senator Marino Mastrangeli was expelled in April 2013; his participation in numerous TV programmes was considered to violate the rules of procedures of the M5S parliamentary group, which emphasize the centralisation of the process of communication, thus limiting the exposition of its members. A few months later, Senator Adele Gambaro was expelled as a consequence of her criticism of Grillo's communication and political strategy. In reaction to these expulsions, two other senators, Paola De Pin and Fabiola Antinori, decided to leave the party. Antinori explained her defection by declaring that she no longer recognised the initial setup of the Movement, which, according to her: 'has become just that personal party so criticised by Grillo, with a feudal system of loyalty that repels or expels those who disagree, who are not aligned'. Similar words were expressed by four other senators, who were expelled in February 2014 because they were accused of 'colluding with the enemy' (the Partito Democratico). This generated a new cascade of defections that saw another five senators leave the parliamentary group, reducing it to 41 members. Three members of the Chamber also decided to leave the Movement and to move to the mixed group, following similar disagreements with the leadership.[14] These expulsions and defections mean that the M5S has experienced more change in its core members in the first phase of the legislature than any other party.

Bill Initiative, Co-Sponsorship and the Content of Legislation

According to the literature on parliamentary behaviour, bill proposals are used by MPs as an instrument for both affecting legislative agenda, and for communicating with voters. Analysing West European parliaments, Mattson (1995) argued that most of the time bills are submitted to parliament by individual legislators as a way of attracting media attention and communicating with their own electorate, thus showing their voters (and their party) what they are doing for them. Remarkably, legislators may be willing to table bills even when knowing that their actual chances of success are scarce. For these reasons, bill initiation has often been considered as an activity through which MPs cultivate their personal reputation at the expense of the party label (Crisp et al. 2004; Shomer 2009).[15] The introduction of bills can thus be interpreted through the lens of the relationship between the *party in central office* and the *party in public office*.

As we have already seen, the M5S legislative group is organised in such a way as to reduce the autonomy and the resources of its members, therefore limiting

14 The senators expelled in February 2014 are Lorenzo Battista, Fabrizio Bocchino, Francesco Campanella and Luis Alberto Orellana. A few days later, another five senators left the group: Alessandra Bencini, Laura Bignami, Monica Casaletto, Maria Mussini and Maurizio Romani. The three defectors from the Chamber of Deputies were Alessandro Furnari, Vincenzo Labriola and Adrano Zaccagnini.

15 In Mayhew's (1974) seminal contribution on legislative behaviour, representatives engage in three types of electorally oriented activities: advertising, credit claiming and position taking.

the individual incentives to cultivate personalised behaviour. This could have potential consequences for Five Star representatives' legislative initiative. Indeed, in the first nine months of the XVII legislature Five Star deputies have introduced a disproportionately low number of bills to parliament, compared to the size of the M5S legislative group in the Chamber. According to Table 5.2, whilst the Movement controls 16.8 per cent of parliamentary seats, its members have submitted 119 bills – that is, just 6.8 per cent of the total 1,750 private member bills introduced to parliament in the period under investigation. As displayed by the second column of Table 5.2, other parliamentary party groups (PD, SCPI, SEL) present some discrepancy between their share of seats and their share of sponsored bills, but the disproportionality is undoubtedly higher for the M5S. The contrast is stark if we consider one of the other main opposition parties, the LN, whose share of sponsored bills is more than three times its share of its seats. On average, each Five Star MP has proposed one bill as first signatory, while MPs belonging to the PD, the SCPI and the SEL have proposed more than two bills each. In the same period, each PDL member has introduced on average more than three bills, and each deputy from the LN has submitted more than nine bills.

Table 5.2 Legislative initiative and co-sponsorship

Parl. Group	First-signature Bills		MPs		Sponsored or co-sponsored bills	Bills sponsored alone	Rate of alone-sponsoring
	N	%	N	%	N	N	%
M5S	**119**	**6.8**	**106**	**16.8**	**137**	**114**	**83.2**
LN	177	10.1	20	3.2	196	171	87.2
FDI	52	3.0	9	1.4	58	52	89.7
PD	749	42.8	293	46.5	785	643	81.9
PDL	326	18.6	96	15.2	369	319	86.4
SCPI	102	5.8	47	7.5	176	80	45.5
SEL	78	4.5	37	5.9	126	71	56.3
IND.	147	8.4	22	3.5	206	140	68.0
Total	1,750	100.0	630	100.0	2,053	1,590	78.5

Notes: Data are updated to November 2013. *Number (or percentage) of first-signature bills*: For each party, it is the number (or percentage) of bills whose first signatory is an MP from that party. *Number of sponsored or co-sponsored bills*: For each party, it is the number of bills where either the first signatory is an MP from that party, or among the co-signatories there is (at least) one MP from that party. *Bills sponsored alone*: Bills whose signatory and co-signatories are all from the same party. *Rate of alone-sponsoring*: For each party, it is the percentage of bills sponsored alone by that party on the total of bills sponsored or co-sponsored by that party's MPs. The total rate of alone-sponsoring is calculated excluding the independents in the Mixed group.
Source: www.camera.it.

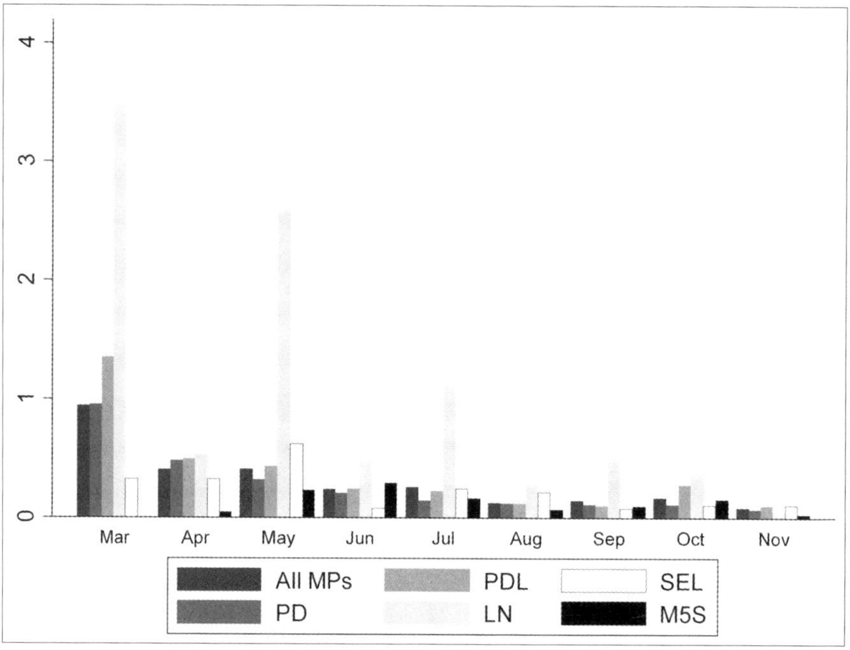

Figure 5.3 Monthly average number of bills introduced by MPs

The M5S is the parliamentary group with the lowest use of legislative initiative. This result is strongly dependent on the relatively low number of bills introduced by Five Star members in the first months of the legislature, when, in contrast, MPs from the other groups presented a huge quantity of legislative proposals. Figure 5.3 displays the average number of bills presented monthly by MPs in the period under investigation. Generally speaking, the legislative initiative is not constant over time: the bulk of proposals are submitted to the Chamber in the first months after the elections and in the following months the quantity of bills introduced settles down. As Figure 5.3 shows, this holds for all parliamentary party groups with the only exception being the M5S. In the case of the Five Star parliamentary group, bill introduction activity was null at the beginning and increased in the following months: no bills were submitted by M5S members in March and only five were initiated in April, while thenceforth roughly 20 bills were presented on average by Five Star MPs. Five Star members' behaviour contrasts not only with the behaviour of LN members, whose monthly average initiative is by far the most intense in the Chamber, but also with the behaviour of other opposition deputies such as those from SEL, whose average initiatives are almost always higher than those of M5S members.

Overall, the data on bill introduction indicates a lower level of activism amongst M5S members compared to their colleagues in the Chamber, which could depend on the relatively scarce resources at the Five Star representatives' disposal. However,

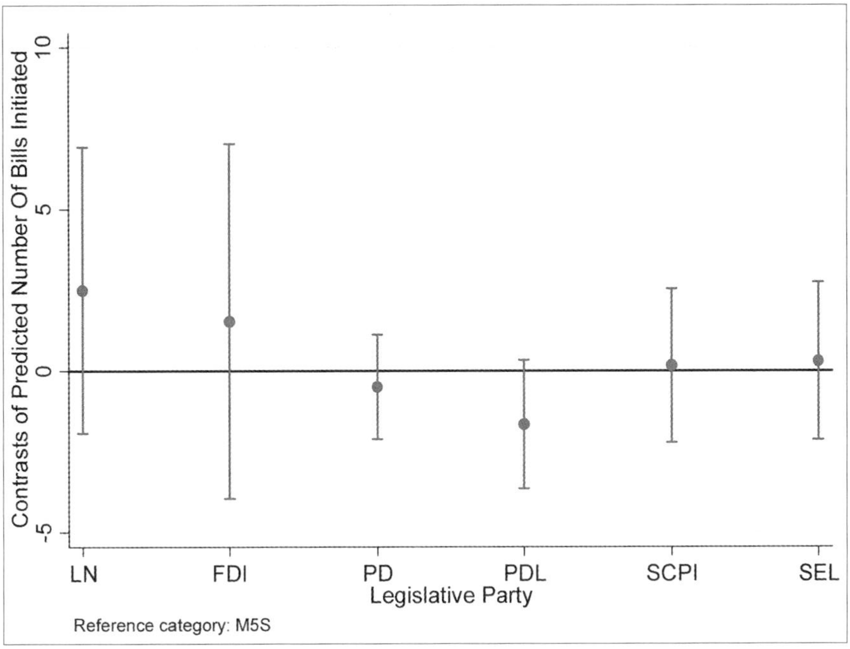

Figure 5.4 Effect of legislative party on the number of bills initiated with 95 per cent CIs

our time-series analysis suggests that the explanation could lie in M5S members' lack of parliamentary experience. Five Star deputies are all newcomers to the parliament, and hence in spring 2013 they were absolutely unfamiliar with parliamentary practices and proceedings, which resulted in negligible legislative activity in the period immediately after the general elections. Indeed, the trend in legislative initiatives shows that from June onwards the figures for the Five Star members are not notably different from those of MPs from other parliamentary groups (except for the LN). In order to ascertain if the scarce use of legislative initiative of M5S legislators is caused by their lack of parliamentary experience, rather than their lack of resources vis-à-vis the party in central office, we built a simple statistical model similar to the one applied in the preceding section. This time the dependent variable is how many bills an MP introduced, while, as independent variables, we use previous parliamentary experience plus the same set of covariates related to individual resources described above. Figure 5.4 shows that, once seniority and other individual factors are accounted for, the differences in legislative initiative between M5S and other groups disappears, as is illustrated by the vertical bars, which this time cross the zero line for every parliamentary group. This implies that belonging to the Five Star legislative group does not have a negative impact on bill introduction. By contrast, it is the lack of parliamentary experience that mostly determines the lower levels of activism of M5S members compared to other legislators: taking all the other factors as constant, an MP with experience of up to four legislatures is expected to introduce a number of bills 7 times higher than that of a newcomer.

Turning now to bill co-sponsorship (Fowler 2006), columns 6 and 7 of Table 5.2 report the number of sponsored or co-sponsored bills, and the number of bills sponsored by each party separately. For the M5S, the former is computed as the number of bills in which the name of a Five Star member appears either as the first signatory, or among the co-signatories. The latter is instead the number of bills in which among the signatory and co-signatories there are only Five Star members. In other words, the number of sponsored or co-sponsored bills takes into account the pieces of legislation that the M5S has proposed jointly with other parliamentary party groups, while the number of bills sponsored separately indicates only the proposals submitted by Five Star members without the collaboration of other MPs. Taking into account its share of legislative seats, the M5S is the parliamentary group with the lowest value in terms of these two indicators: on average, the Movement's representatives present both the lowest quantity of sponsored or co-sponsored legislation, and the lowest number of bills proposed alone.

What is more important, however, is the legislation proposed by the M5S together with other parliamentary groups. Throughout the first nine months of the XVII legislature, 23 bills were jointly proposed by Five Star MPs and MPs from other parties. As displayed in the last column of the table, about 83 per cent of the legislation proposed by M5S members carries the signature of just M5S members, while the remaining 17 per cent was introduced jointly with other groups. The rate of separate sponsoring by the M5S is higher than the overall rate calculated for the whole parliamentary party group (78.5 per cent excluding the Mixed group), implying that – as far as legislative initiative is concerned – Five Star members are less likely to co-operate with MPs from other groups than the average member of the Italian Chamber. More precisely, M5S members are less likely than PD, SCPI and SEL legislators to present bills jointly with others. At the same time, Five Star MPs are more likely than PDL, LN, and FDI MPs to act jointly with other parties when proposing legislation.

Among the 23 bills that the M5S has proposed jointly with other parliamentary groups, more than half (14) are bills widely supported in the Chamber, being introduced with the involvement of parties from both the majority and the opposition. Among these, there are actions against mafia, the ban of neo-fascist electoral lists, and measures of social assistance like subsidies for young families, food aid, and protection of children, the epileptic and the disabled. Six bills were proposed by Five Star members jointly with members from the majority: two with the PD, two with the PDL, one with SC, and one with all three government parties. Whilst three bills contained the signatures of the M5S and other opposition groups: the SEL in one case (the ratification of a UN treaty regulating arms trade) and minor groups in the other two cases.

Let us now turn to the content of the legislation introduced by Five Star members. Based on the programme of the Movement and on Grillo's speeches, one could expect M5S legislation to emphasise environmental themes, the protection of common natural resources and the promotion of new technologies. Indeed, the 'five stars' of the Movement are; the safeguarding of public water, environmental protection, the promotion of public transport, the fostering of technological connectivity, and sustainable development. To understand the degree to which such expectations are grounded in reality, we classified the content of the bills introduced in the first nine months of the XVII legislature using the categories of the Comparative Agendas Project (CAP). More precisely, we assigned each private member bill introduced to parliament during the March–November 2013 period to one of the 21 policy sectors laid out in the codebook relating to Italy.[16]

Table 5.3 The content of legislation

CAP Topic	All parl. groups		M5S	
	N	%	N	%
Agriculture	114	6.5	**11**	**9.2**
Banking, Finance, and Domestic Commerce	148	8.5	**11**	**9.2**
Civil Rights, Minority Issues, and Civil Liberties	89	5.1	**2**	**1.7**
Community Development and Housing Issues	38	2.2	**2**	**1.7**
Culture Policy Issues	77	4.4	**8**	**6.7**
Defense	49	2.8	**2**	**1.7**
Domestic Macroeconomic Issues	65	3.7	**5**	**4.2**
Education	67	3.8	**8**	**6.7**
Energy	12	0.7		**0.0**
Environment	84	4.8	**5**	**4.2**
Foreign Trade	9	0.5		**0.0**
Government Operations	240	13.7	**16**	**13.5**
Health	131	7.5	**10**	**8.4**
Immigration Issues	60	3.4	**4**	**3.4**
International Affairs and Foreign Aid	20	1.1		**0.0**
Labour, Employment	108	6.2	**8**	**6.7**
Law and Crime	227	13.0	**15**	**12.6**
Public Lands and Water Management	40	2.3	**5**	**4.2**
Social Welfare	92	5.3	**3**	**2.5**
Space, Science, Technology and Communications	8	0.5	**1**	**0.8**
Transportation	72	4.1	**3**	**2.5**
Total	1,750	100.0	**119**	**100.0**

Notes: Data are updated to November 2013.
Source: www.camera.it.

16 Each category, or major topic, is in turn divided into subcategories, making a total of over two hundred minor topics. The classificatory scheme of the Comparative Agendas Project was drawn up to study how attention towards different political issues varies, and how such oscillations affect policy. The scheme is used to analyse the policy content of various kinds of agendas, including party manifestos, government programmes and legislative production (see Borghetto and Carammia 2010).

As Table 5.3 shows, the legislation introduced by Five Star members does not indicate a particular concern, at least in purely quantitative terms, with the categories dealing with environment, transport and new technologies. The percentage of bills presented by the Movement's representatives in these categories is not higher than the overall mean. Probably, M5S's environmental sensitivity is to be found in the bills dealing with 'Agriculture' and 'Public lands and water management', whose presence among the Five Star proposals is larger than in the legislation proposed by all parliamentary groups together (9.5 against 6.5 per cent, and 4.2 against 2.3 per cent, respectively). For the rest, about one-eighth of the Five Star legislative initiatives fall into the 'Government operations' category, dealing with the functioning of the state and institutional issues, and another one-eighth concerns 'Law and crime'. Roughly 9 per cent of the proposals made by M5S members are about the regulation of the 'Banking, finance and domestic commerce' sector. In these respects, the M5S does not behave differently from the rest of the parliamentary party groups. Among Five Star bills, more attention than the overall mean is given to issues relating to education and culture (6.7 per cent each), while social welfare issues receive relatively lower attention (2.5 per cent).

Parliamentary Questions and Amendments

Until now we have focused our attention on two forms of parliamentary behaviour: rebellion and bill introduction. In this section, we consider two other types of legislative activity: amendatory activity and parliamentary questioning. These procedures are crucial for individual representatives and their relevance is commonly acknowledged in legislative studies. Similarly to bill proposals, amendments and questions are important not only for the formal functions indicated by parliamentary standing orders, but most of all because they are used by individual representatives for self-promotion and expressive purposes. However, these two types of activity are also strongly linked to the divide between government and opposition.

According to Mattson (1995), amendments are often introduced not just as a means of affecting legislation, but also as instruments for promoting legislators' re-appointment and re-election. In addition, a large proportion of amendments are presented for merely obstructionist purposes by opposition parties (see Capano and Vignati 2008 on the Italian case). Similarly, parliamentary questions are not simply one of the institutional means that legislative assemblies have developed, and used especially by opposition parties, to oversee cabinet ministers and their bureaucracy. Oral and written questions can be considered as signalling activities, through which representatives communicate with other political actors inside and outside parliament (Wiberg 1995). Questioning offers important publicity and self-promotion opportunities to the questioners, thus

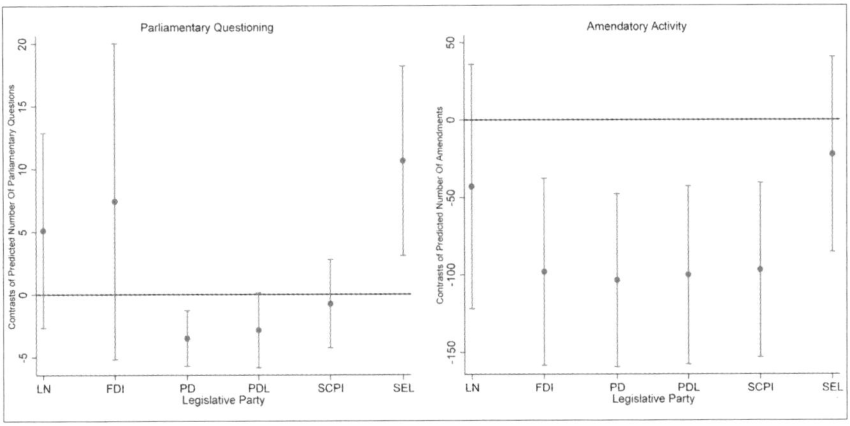

Figure 5.5 Effect of legislative party on the number of parliamentary questions and amendments with 95 per cent CIS

being part of an MP's re-selection and re-election strategies (Martin 2011; Rasch 2011). Therefore, the analysis of amendatory activity and parliamentary questioning is useful for a better understanding of the relationship between elected representatives and their party.

In order to analyse M5S legislators' behaviour, imitating our approach to rebel votes and bill initiative, we regress the number of parliamentary questions and amendments introduced by each legislator on the legislative party to which she belongs, plus the usual series of covariates indicating individual characteristics variously related to self-promotion incentives (candidate selection procedures, previous parliamentary experience, previous local experience, seniority, etc.). Results are shown in Figure 5.5. In the first panel, we can see that on average, once all other factors are accounted for, a Five Star deputy is more likely to introduce a higher number of questions than an MP belonging to the PD, which is the main governing party (the grey dot corresponding to this party is below the black line representing M5S, which is our reference category). By contrast, there are no significant differences with the other opposition parties, with SEL constituting the main exception. In the second panel we can appreciate that the Movement's legislators are expected to introduce more amendments than the other parties in the assembly. Analogously to what we have found for parliamentary questioning, this difference does not hold for two of the main parties in the opposition, LN and SEL, since the vertical bars cross the black line corresponding to the reference category. Thus on the whole, our analysis suggests that it is the division between government and opposition that mainly drives parliamentary questioning and amendments activity, supporting the idea that (particularly in the case of amendments activity) these activities are mainly conducted merely for obstructionist purposes.

Conclusions

The M5S is as a scarcely formalised organisation that promotes collective decision-making. These traits appear to have given rise to internal rules of procedures that stress the importance of the *party on the ground* in driving the decisions of the *party in public office*. However, the picture emerging from our analysis is quite different. On the one hand, we found that the organization of the legislative group is designed to strongly limit the autonomy of Five Star legislators in favour of Grillo and his staff. On the other hand, the candidate selection rules, although intended to empower the *party on the ground*, were conducted in a rather exclusive way, allowing for a significant degree of control to be exercised by the *party in central office*. Finally, the composition of the M5S group, characterised by, 'common citizens' lacking any previous political experience, seems to favour a strong dependence of the elected members on the guidance of their leadership. As a consequence, the relationships M5S legislators have with their party does not seem to be so different from that observed in 'traditional' political formations. This is further confirmed by our analysis of four types of legislative behaviour which are considered to be indicators of legislators' autonomy vis-à-vis their party in cultivating a relationship with their own voters. The examination of individual behaviour in legislative voting, bill introduction, parliamentary questioning and amendatory activity shows that, in fact, Five Star representatives either present a more accentuated party-centred attitude in comparison with legislators belonging to other groups, or do not show any significant difference from legislators belonging to other groups.

These results suggest that the revolutionary zest and impetus which Grillo harnessed during the M5S ascension to parliament, has soon petered out. Excluding a series of unconventional and entertaining public demonstrations (as discussed in Chapter 7 in this volume), the Movement's representatives seem to have quickly become socialised to the rules and practices of the parliament, to the extent that they are now almost indistinguishable from other MPs in many of their activities. Furthermore, they show an overall level of conformity to their party's stances similar to that observed in other legislative groups, suggesting therefore, that behind the rhetoric of direct democracy hides, in reality, a hierarchical organization in which the decision-making power is centralized in the leadership of Grillo, at the expense of party activists and simple members. However, it must be underlined (and this is the good news for all the M5S voters and sympathizers) that in this way the party seems to be able to perform quite well, as it at least approaches the performance of more experienced parties in crucial parliamentary activities, in particular, in interpreting its own role of opposition.

References

Aldrich, J.H. 1995. *Why Parties? The Origin and Transformation of Political Parties in America*. Chicago: University of Chicago Press.

Bardi, L., Ignazi, P. and Massari, O., eds. 2007. *I partiti italiani. Iscritti, dirigenti, eletti*. Milan: Università Bocconi Editore.

Bardi, L. and Morlino, L. 1994. Italy: Tracing the Roots of the Great Transformation. In: R. Katz and P. Mair, eds. *How Parties Organize. Adaptation and Change in Party Organizations in Western Democracies*. London: Sage, pp. 242–77.

Borghetto, E. and Carammia, M. 2010. L'analisi comparata delle agende politiche: il 'Comparative Agendas Project'. *Rivista italiana di scienza politica*, 40(2), pp. 301–16.

Bowler, S., Farrell, D. and Katz, R.S. 1999. Party Cohesion, Party Discipline, and Parliaments. In: S. Bowler, D. Farrell and R.S. Katz, eds. *Party Discipline and Parliamentary Government*. Columbus: Ohio State University Press, pp. 3–22.

Capano, G. and Vignati, R. 2008. Casting Light on the Black Hole of the Amendatory Process in Italy. *South European Society and Politics*, 13(1), pp. 35–59.

Carey, J.M. 2009. *Legislative Voting and Accountability*. Cambridge: Cambridge University Press.

Carey, J.M. and Shugart, M.S. 1995. Incentives to Cultivate a Personal Vote: A Rank Ordering of Electoral Formulas. *Electoral Studies*, 14(4), pp. 417–39.

Ceccarini, L. and Bordignon, F. 2013. Five Stars and a Cricket. Beppe Grillo Shakes Italian Politics. *South European Society and Politics*, 18(4), pp. 427–49.

Cotta, M. and Verzichelli, L. 2007. *Political institutions in Italy*. Oxford: Oxford University Press.

Cox, G.W. and McCubbins, M.D. 1993. *Legislative Leviathan. Party Government in the House*. Berkeley: University of California Press.

Crisp, B.F., Escobar-Lemon, M.C., Jones, B.S., Jones, M.P. and Taylor-Robinson, M.M. 2004. Electoral Incentives and Legislative Representation in Six Presidential Democracies. *Journal of Politics*, 66(3), pp. 823–46.

Curini, L., Marangoni, F. and Tronconi, F. 2011. Rebels With a Cause – But Which One? Defections from Legislative Party Unity in Italy and Their Individual and Institutional Determinants. *Rivista Italiana di Scienza Politica*, 41(3), pp. 385–409.

Fowler, J.H. 2006. Connecting the Congress: A Study of Cosponsorship Networks. *Political Analysis*, 14(4), pp. 456–87.

Harmel, R. 2002. Party Organisational Change. Competing Explanations? In: K.R. Luther and F. Müller-Rommel, eds. *Political Parties in the New Europe: Political and Analytical Challenges*. Oxford: Oxford University Press, pp. 119–42.

Harmel, R. and Janda, K. 1994. An Integrated Theory of Party Goals and Party Change. *Journal of Theoretical Politics*, 6(3), pp. 259–88.

Hazan, R. 2006. Does Cohesion Equal Discipline? Towards a Conceptual Delineation. In R. Hazan, ed. *Cohesion and Discipline in Legislatures*. London: Routledge.

Katz, R. 2001. The Problem of Candidate Selection and Models of Party Democracy. *Party Politics*, 7(3), pp. 277–96.

———. The Internal Life of Parties. In: K.R. Luther and F. Muller-Rommel, eds. *Political Parties in the New Europe*. Oxford: Oxford University Press, pp. 87–118.

Katz, R. and Mair P. 1995. Changing Models of Party Organisation and Party Democracy. *Party politics*, 1(1), pp. 5–28.

Katz, R. and Mair P., eds. 1992. *Party Organization 1960–1990. A Data Handbook*. London: Sage.

———. 1994. *How Parties Organize. Adaptation and Change in Party Organizations in Western Democracies*. London: Sage.

Lanfrey, D. 2011. Il MoVimento dei grillini tra meetup, meta-organizzazione e democrazia del monitoraggio. In: L. Mosca and C. Vaccari, eds. *Nuovi media, nuova politica? Partecipazione e mobilitazione online da MoveOn al MoVimento 5 stelle*. Milan: Franco Angeli, pp. 143–66.

Long, S.J. 1997. *Regression Models for Categorical and Limited Dependent Variables*. London: Sage.

Mair, P. and van Biezen, I. 2001. Party Membership in Twenty European Democracies. *Party Politics*, 7(1), pp. 5–21.

Martin, S. 2011. Using Parliamentary Questions to Measure Constituency Focus: An Application to the Irish Case. *Political Studies*, 59(2), pp. 472–88.

Mattson, I. 1995. Private Members' Initiative and Amendments. In: H. Döring, ed. *Parliaments and Majority Rule in Western Europe*. New York: St Martin's Press, pp. 448–87.

Mayhew, D. 1974. *Congress: The Electoral Connection*. New Haven, CT: Yale University Press.

Passarelli, G., Tronconi, F., and Tuorto, D. 2013. Dentro il Movimento: organizzazione, attivisti e programmi. In: P. Corbetta and E. Gualmini, eds. *Il partito di Grillo*. Bologna: Il Mulino, pp. 89–122.

Poguntke, T., 1987. The Organisation of a Participatory Party: The German Greens. *European Journal of Political Research*, 15(6), pp. 609–33.

———. 1993. *Alternative politics: The German Green Party*. Edinburgh: Edinburgh University Press.

Poguntke, T. and Webb, P., eds. 2005. *The Presidentialization of Politics. A Comparative Study of Modern Democracies*. Oxford: Oxford University Press.

Rahat, G. and Hazan, R.Y. 2001. Candidate Selection Methods: An Analytical Framework. *Party Politics*, 7(3), pp. 297–322.

Rasch, B.E. 2011. Behavioural Consequences of Restrictions on Plenary Access: Parliamentary Questions in the Norwegian Storting. *The Journal of Legislative Studies*, 17(3), pp. 382–93.

Scarrow, S. 2000. Parties Without Members? Party Organization in a Changing Electoral Environment. In: D.J. Russel and M.P. Wattenberg, eds. *Parties Without Partisans: Political Change in Advanced Industrial Democracies*. Oxford: Oxford University Press, pp. 79–101.

Shomer, Y. 2009. Candidate Selection Procedures, Seniority, and Vote-Seeking Behaviour. *Comparative Political Studies*, 42(7), pp. 945–70.

Sieberer, U. 2006. Party Unity in Parliamentary Democracies: A Comparative Analysis. *Journal of Legislative Studies*, 12(2), pp. 150–78.

Verzichelli, L. 1998. Parliamentary elites in transition. *European Journal of Political Research*, 34(1), pp. 121–50.

Wiberg, M. 1995. Parliamentary Questioning: Control by Communication? In: H. Döring, ed. *Parliaments and Majority Rule in Western Europe*. New York: St Martin's Press, pp. 179–222.

Zucchini, F. 2001. Arena elettorale, arena parlamentare e arena legislativa. In: G. Capano and M. Giuliani, eds. *Il processo legislativo in Italia: continuità e mutamento*. Bologna: Il Mulino, Bologna, pp. 57–84.

Chapter 6

An Internet-Fuelled Party? The Movimento 5 Stelle and the Web

Lorenzo Mosca, Cristian Vaccari and Augusto Valeriani[1]

Introduction

Since its founding and throughout all its developmental stages, the Movimento Cinque Stelle (M5S) has been characterised, among Italian parties, by its reliance on the Web as a tool for organisation, decision-making, communication, and identity-building. In this chapter, we analyse three dimensions of the Web's role for the M5S against the backdrop of international theoretical debates and empirical research on digital politics. First, we discuss the narratives that Beppe Grillo and his chief consultant, Gianroberto Casaleggio, have employed to talk about the democratic role of the Internet against some real-world examples of whether and how the M5S upholds democratic principles in its operations. Secondly, we investigate how the Web was employed to select candidates for the 2013 general elections. Thirdly, we assess how M5S voters use the Internet to inform themselves about and participate in politics. Our purpose, therefore, is to conduct empirical scrutiny on how the M5S has used the Internet as a rhetorical device, as an organisational platform, and as a tool for campaign communication and engagement.

In the first section, we analyse the ways in which a hyperbolic narrative of the Web as an inherently transparent, democratic, and accountability-enhancing technology has been cultivated by the leaders of the movement. This narrative has become a crucial component of the collective identity of M5S members and an important rhetorical device with which the party pursues legitimacy when addressing outsiders. We investigate whether and how the M5S leadership's rhetoric about the Internet and democracy compares with the empirical reality of how the Internet is employed in the movement's communication and organisation.

With respect to the M5S's use of the Web for internal decision-making, we evaluate the process of online candidate selection for the 2013 Italian general

1 In accordance with Italian academic conventions, we specify that the introductory and concluding sections were written collectively by all three authors, whereas Augusto Valeriani wrote the section on the Internet as ideology, Lorenzo Mosca the one on the online primaries, and Cristian Vaccari the one about the use of the Internet in campaign communication.

elections. This web-based primary election (dubbed 'parlamentarie' by Grillo) saw participation by a limited group of registered members, and it was criticised by the mass media and by other parties for lacking transparency and inclusiveness. By contrast, the M5S's elite and its members celebrated the event as an important example of direct democracy, as opposed to the top-down procedures to select candidates adopted by most other Italian parties.

Finally, we address the role of the Internet in the participatory repertoires of its supporters, particularly in regard to Web 2.0 platforms and against the backdrop of a population heavily dependent on television for political news and less digitally connected than in most other Western democracies. On the basis of survey data, we show that M5S voters make intense use of the Internet for political purposes, much more so than the rest of the population. However, data also suggest that television and newspapers are still the main sources of political information for M5S voters, just as they are for all Italians. The Internet is used by Grillo and his staff not only to communicate with his supporters directly but also to reach other voters indirectly through coverage by the mainstream media, which often report posts made on his blog by the M5S's leader and elected officials.

An Internet-Fuelled Ideology

The M5S has an unofficial anthem, frequently played at public events. It was also chosen as the soundtrack for several of the self-made YouTube videos prepared by militants running for the primary elections to select candidates for the 2013 general elections. The text is as follows:

> There is a leaderless and ownerless movement/ You can find it by searching for the word 'non-association'/ A network of directly-connected people/ We are the web multitude, live now on our webcams/ … / everybody counts as one, everybody counts as one, everybody counts as one.

Far from being merely the M5S's preferred organisational tool, the Internet is an intrinsic part of the movement's identity, with supporters describing themselves as a 'web multitude' and identifying a close link between a vision of a 'streamed', 'open' and 'direct' democracy and the relational *milieu* enabled by the Web.

However, even in the few verses quoted above, contradictions emerge between this linguistically constructed self-representation and the reality on the Web and on the ground. First, it is hard to define the M5S as 'leaderless', considering the influence of Beppe Grillo on all decision-making processes. Secondly, far from being 'ownerless', M5S is a registered entity and its brand name and logo are owned exclusively by Grillo (on these points, see Chapters 1 and 2 in this volume).

Both linguists (e.g. Chomsky 2004; Lakoff 2004) and political scientists (e.g. Edelman 1988; Entman 1993) have considered language to be a form of political action and a fundamental means for political actors to re-create reality. According to Edelman (1988), it is by linguistically evoking values, symbols and myths that political actors strategically re-frame issues, events and phenomena by fitting them into a narrative compatible with an audience's ideology.

In this section we discuss various inconsistencies between what may be described as the 'mystique' of the Web as a panacea for contemporary 'corrupted' democracy – a narrative mainly developed by Beppe Grillo and Gianroberto Casaleggio – and the praxis of the M5S in regard to internal democracy and dissent management. By analysing a selection of speeches, writings and videos produced by Casaleggio and Grillo, and by stressing marked inconsistencies between such narratives and the M5S's organisational and operational praxis, we aim to detect some of the core elements of the M5S's ideology as linguistically developed by its leaders.

We start our analysis with specific reference to Casaleggio's rhetoric concerning the nexus between the Internet and democracy. Casaleggio is, with Grillo, the co-founder of the M5S. A seasoned tech-entrepreneur, he currently runs Casaleggio Associati, a consulting firm specialising in web strategies and managing Grillo's blog. Moreover, Casaleggio Associati hosts 'La cosa' (The Thing), the official M5S web television channel, and it owns the platform used by the movement to manage the overall 'parlamentarie' process and which has recently been expanded to become the 'M5S operational system'.

Before presenting Casaleggio's notion of 'web democracy' and examining its coherence with the M5S's praxis, it might be argued that the adoption of a copyrighted logo and the employment of privately-owned platforms conflict with the conception of the Internet as the realm of a new knowledge economy based on free sharing and open source collaboration. Although Casaleggio often cites (see Grillo 2013d) Lawrence Lessig – the most popular advocate of a radical overhaul of copyright laws – among his web theorists of reference (together with Steven Johnson, Malcolm Gladwell and Howard Rheingold), he has exclusive control over all the M5S's web infrastructures.

Based, among other things, on the theories of the above-mentioned 'web gurus', Casaleggio has described (see Grillo, 2013d) his vision of the implications of the Internet for political institutions and democracy thus:

> The kind of direct democracy that has been made possible by the web is not only applicable to public consultation but also places the citizen at the center of society. The current political and social organizations will be dismantled and some may even disappear altogether. Representative democracy, in other words by proxy, will become totally meaningless.[2]

---

2 Beppe Grillo's blog has an English version where almost all posts (originally in Italian) are translated. The quality of translation is generally poor, but we have decided to present the original quotes instead of editing them.

Casaleggio's vision of 'Internet democracy' appears to be consistent with the narrative developed by globally recognised 'web prophets'. However, a couple web-videos produced by Casaleggio Associati may help in understanding why we use the term 'mystique' to denote the approach to the Internet that Casaleggio has pushed, top-down, into the M5S symbolic repertoire. 'Prometheus – the media revolution' and 'Gaia – the future of politics' are two short videos posted on YouTube respectively in 2007 and 2008 and which predict the future of the world. Although presented as 'experimental' products describing only potential – and not necessarily desired – scenarios, both videos, which went viral online, contain all the elements of a science-fiction novel: a global war in 2040, a battle between Good and Evil, a post-apocalyptic society created by a community of enlightened people rebuilding a new world of direct democracy, a future where 'man becomes God', mainly by embracing an Internet revolution.

As stressed by Natale and Ballatore (2014), cyber-utopianism and the idea of the Internet as a force liberating contemporary socio-political systems from all constraints, combined with the M5S's close identification with the Web, have been crucial in representing the movement as a disruptive entity not comparable with any other political actor. As Natale and Ballatore write (ibid., p. 111), 'technological novelties and achievements are represented as the carriers of a quasi-pastoral message of faith in progress and modernity'. Within this frame, the debate on Internet technology is shifted to a transcendental dimension, and the political actor represented as embodying such technology assumes the function of re-moralising corrupted national politics.

We now consider the contradictions between this Internet-fuelled ideology and the M5S's praxis in its management of dissent among elected members, militants and web-users. When mentioning the transformative power of the Internet, Casaleggio (see Grillo 2013d, original emphasis) frequently refers to the emergence of networked organisations and bottom-up deliberative processes destined to replace pyramidal structures and command-and-control management:

> The selection must be done '*from the bottom-up*', in other words by the citizens who must nominate the most suitable candidates whose background and abilities are well known. It should be noted that the concept of leadership is foreign to direct democracy. The direct democracy movements actually reject the idea of having a leader.

Accordingly, we should expect to find that disagreement expressed by elected members with Grillo's statements, as well as with the M5S's general positions, is managed through bottom-up, inclusive discussions and decision-making. Moreover, Casaleggio frequently describes the nature of the communicative and deliberative processes enabled by the Internet as necessarily transparent and disintermediated, because broadcast and closely-controlled unilateral messages are replaced by multidirectional, open and frank conversations. Again, this proclaimed vision should result in the open management of the M5S's online platforms, and specifically of Grillo's blog, which should constitute a conversational milieu in which disagreement and dissent are highly tolerated if not encouraged.

We start with a brief analysis of dissent management among elected members. Between March 2012 and December 2013, nine M5S militants,[3] elected to either municipal and regional councils or to the national parliament, were expelled from the movement. Federica Salsi, elected to the Bologna city council, was expelled because of her participation, despite Grillo's general instruction to avoid television appearances, in a political talk show in October 2012. In most cases however, the expulsion process began, or was accelerated, after a public expression of criticism of Grillo's or Casaleggio's influence over the movement: Giovanni Favia, elected to the regional council of Emilia-Romagna, was deceitfully – he alleged – recorded by a journalist in September 2012 while denouncing Casaleggio's authoritarianism and the lack of internal democracy within the M5S. Grillo's reaction on the blog (Grillo 2012b) was as follows:

> We have a battle, we have a war from here to the elections. As long as the ones waging war are the newspapers, the TV stations, the real enemy are OK. But I don't want any more internal fighting. If there's someone that reckons that I'm not democratic, that Casaleggio is hanging onto the money, that I'm dishonest, well let them take their things and get out. Let them go away. Let them leave the MoVement. Let them exit from the MoVement.

After this public disavowal, Grillo exercised his personal property rights on the M5S logo and name to expel Salsi and Favia. He had his lawyer send them a letter cautioning them against further use of his 'personal property'.

While in these cases Grillo acted unilaterally without any formal decision by M5S members, a different process was used for the expulsion of the MP Adele Gambaro in June 2013. While commenting on television on the unsatisfactory M5S results in municipal elections held on 10 June in four Sicilian cities, Gambaro expressed her disagreement with Grillo's communication strategy. Again, the first reaction to such public criticism came from Grillo's blog (Grillo 2013b), and it sounded like a banishment:

> Senator Adele Gambaro made false declarations regarding myself and specifically my view of National Parliament. In this way she has damaged my reputation and the 5Stars Movement. As a consequence I urge her to leave immediately the M5S.

Just three days later, the coordinators of the M5S in parliament convened an assembly of M5S MPs to discuss the case. The announcement of the meeting

3 Valentino Tavolazzi, Sandra Poppi, Fabrizio Biolé, Giovanni Favia, Federica Salsi, Raffaella Pirini, Marino Mastrangeli, Antonio Venturino, Adele Gambaro (see Antonucci 2013).

(see Grillo 2013c) omitted mention of Grillo's call for Gambaro's resignation. It merely made vague reference to requests 'from the Web" urging her expulsion. Moreover, the same statement also declared that the Web would 'have the final word' on ratification of the expulsion. The MPs assembly was initially announced as a web-streamed event, but it was eventually held on 17 June as a closed-doors meeting which resulted in the senator's expulsion (79 MPs voted in favour, 42 against and 9 abstained). As the final step in the process, on 19 June, all the 48,292 users registered with the M5S platform were asked to ratify the decision: 19,780 voted (a 41 per cent turnout) and 66 per cent of them approved the expulsion. Such a process can hardly be described as bottom-up.

Thus, whilst great use is made of the rhetoric of the Web as an equaliser of hierarchies in the management of dissent among elected members, one observes strong intervention by Grillo, who acts either as exclusive controller or as the initiator of top-down processes. His action is implicitly justified with references to the M5S's 'sake' and 'reputation', or even to a 'battle' against an enemy that in some circumstances assumes the guise of the mainstream media and in others of the entire established political system. Within this emergency frame, some of the elements crucial for the M5S's self-presentation as a web-fuelled entity – i.e. the online streaming of deliberative processes – can be circumvented without being explicitly questioned; and Grillo, consistently with the narrative common in populist leaderships (Mudde, 2004), appears as a responsible father, personally intervening in order to protect the good name of his people.

Corbetta (2013) has used the term 'web populism' to denote the specific qualities of Grillo's charismatic leadership. He argues that the M5S strategy, while contending that political power must be restored to the people, leverages the Internet to strengthen the personal power of Grillo. By identifying the 'people' with the opinions expressed online, and specifically on personally-owned platforms, the leader can present himself as simply the interpreter of the general will of his people. Grillo thus acts, de facto, as a re-intermediator in a process that is nonetheless described as entirely dis-intermediated.

Grillo's blog has emerged as the core of this process. This highly centralised pattern can per se be described as contradicting Casaleggio's praise for online disintermediated communication. The M5S leaders have frequently rebutted such criticisms by arguing that the posts on the blog are only the starting-points of chains of comments and conversations. However, even if this vague idea of centralised disintermediation is accepted, other contradictions emerge when one considers how comments posted by users are managed, and specifically those expressing disagreement. In this regard, it is interesting to note that, when Grillo (2013a) explained his interpretation of an allegedly increased level of criticism in comments after the M5S's success in the general elections, he drew on the jargon of online communities to describe the posters of those messages as 'trolls':

> Obviously someone is paying them to create spam from morning to night. These squirts of digital shit can be sorted into a few major categories.

By describing dissenters as trolls, Grillo exploits Web culture to implicitly gain censorship authority over the debate: according to the ethics of online communities, 'flames' (i.e. deliberately provocative comments) can be legitimately deleted by the administrators for the sake of the conversation.

To gain better understanding of these dynamics, we analysed[4] the content of a random sample of comments removed from the blog between 19 September and 10 November 2013. We found that the presence of hate-speech and vulgarity could hardly be described as the sole rationale for the removals. Some offensive comments were left visible while others were removed; and the same applies to those expressing criticism of the M5S and Grillo's positions. However, it should be noted that the majority of the removed comments contained some sort of criticism, even if presented in calm and polite terms. For example, a deleted comment on Grillo's post (2013e) describing an upgrade of the existing platform as the 'M5S operational system'[5] (the long-awaited online tool to unleash a fully developed M5S online direct democracy) read as follows:

> Why come out now with such a vague post? Right now that, after Berlusconi's back turn, the M5S was gaining credibility? Are we going or not to develop this platform? If this is the case, well, fantastic, up with democracy and participation. If this is not the case, it is fine anyway: those willing to participate will have to make more effort. But, arguing that we are going to develop something new and then coming out saying that, with the existing site, we already have what we need, well, to me sound like a jest.

The principles of transparency and disintermediation are thus clearly contradicted. By deleting comments, the blog's administrators (Casaleggio Associati staff) deliberately mediate and influence the discussion. Secondly, apart from Grillo's post describing the alleged 'aggression of the trolls', the process of removal is devoid of transparency, for there is no code defining legitimate versus banned behaviour.

As Dal Lago (2013) has written, it seems that disagreement within the stream of comments is tolerated provided that it does not assume the nature of 'massive dissent'; if it does, the administrators intervene to rebalance the situation by removing critical comments. Dal Lago (ibid.), adapting a concept introduced by political theorist Carl Schmitt, defines this strategy as *complexio oppositorum*, that is, a situation where opposite views and interpretations are not channelled into a

4 Andrea Guerrieri, an Italian blogger, has developed a system (available at: http://nocensura.eusoft.net) that periodically crawls Grillo's blog to keep track of comment removals. While we cannot test the accuracy of the system, and consequently prefer not to present any quantitative data, we used the archive of removed comments to analyse their content qualitatively and compare them with those left on the blog.

5 It should be acknowledged that a more developed version of 'the operational system' went online on 28 October 2013.

discursive process conducive to mediation but are simply put together and, in this way, neutralised.

To conclude, as also argued by Bordignon and Ceccarini, whilst the M5S still enjoys flexibility at local level where – also through online mobilisation – various independent initiatives are pursued, the nature of the movement's organisation at the national level 'makes elected members subordinate to non-appealable sanctions (expulsions) from the central node of the membership network, which is in Grillo's hands' (2013a, p. 12). Accordingly, what we have described as an 'Internet-fuelled ideology' becomes crucial in managing this contradiction by attributing to the Web positive intrinsic properties that are, mainly through the linguistic re-creation of the reality performed by the leaders, transferred to the 'web multitude' (the M5S), protecting it from criticism regardless of praxis on the ground.

M5S Online Primaries: Rules, Inclusiveness, and Participation

M5S organised the 'parlamentarie' between 3 and 6 December 2012. In emulation of the American political system, primary elections had already been held by Italian political parties in the past (especially the Partito Democratico). Nonetheless, it was the first time that an election to select parliamentary candidates took place entirely online. The parlamentarie provide an interesting case study to test the M5S's claims concerning direct democracy and the Internet as an instrument with which to put such claims into practice. This online election was the first of a series of similar efforts (i.e. selecting the movement's candidates for the Presidency of the Republic) to engage members in its decision-making.

Before we describe the rules and outcomes of the voting procedure, we should first discuss why the M5S used primary elections to select its representatives in the national parliament. Officially, the elections were called for two main reasons: first, to circumvent the electoral law ('porcellum') based on blocked lists which prevented voters from expressing their preferences on individual candidates but only for political parties; secondly, to give the M5S's members an opportunity to take part in an event crucial for the life of the movement.

Official declarations aside, the reasons for organising primary elections can vary from expressive to instrumental, although one often finds a mix of these two possible motivations. The reason for primaries consists mostly in their effect of mobilising and galvanising supporters, because these procedures involve active members and sympathisers in the internal life of a party or a coalition. An important aspect of primary elections (as for all kinds of elections – see Pizzorno 1987) concerns their ritual dimension: that is, calling upon people to confirm their support for a party. In those cases, the final outcome of primary elections can be taken for granted. This has been the case of many primary elections held by the Partito Democratico in Italy, which have simply ratified choices already made clear in advance (Valbruzzi 2005; Gelli and Bolgherini 2011; Pasquino and Valbruzzi 2013).

The purposes of primaries are more instrumental when they are called to resolve conflicts within different factions within parties or parties within coalitions. In this case, candidates' characteristics can bring to ballot 'unusual suspects' able to widen the party's electoral appeal. Primaries can also be seen as a good ways to raise funds. The Italian Partito Democratico asked participants in its primary elections to pay up to 2 euros to finance their organisation: a choice whose outcome becomes clear if one considers that participants in the primaries held to select the party's secretary and the centre-left coalition's leader numbered 4.3 million in 2005, 3.5 million in 2007, and 3.1 million in 2009 and 2012 (Sandri et al. 2013).

Another important aspect of organising primaries concerns media coverage, resonance and visibility in public discourse. Primaries can become media events because they contradict the widely-held assumption that citizens are detached from political parties and politics. The mass media seek to make sense of this spectacle by interviewing participants and exploring their motivations. Above all, however, primary elections suit the media logic particularly well because they can be easily covered through journalistic frames recalling the horse-race metaphor. Primaries are more attractive to the mass media than traditional party congresses because they allow the development of a narrative anticipating the official electoral campaign and its crucial events (i.e. live debates among candidates on television).

The M5S's primaries were conducted online and free of charge in order to distinguish the movement from the Partito Democratico, which first imported this type of consultation into Italy (see Figure 6.1). In what follows we provide evidence that the main aim of the M5S's parlamentarie was to attract media coverage. Moreover, because the M5S is not organised as a traditional political party, the primaries could serve to give popular legitimacy to unknown candidates who would represent the movement in the campaign and later in parliament.

In order to explain the M5S's primaries, the rules and inclusiveness of the electoral process will now be briefly discussed. First to be noted is that, although the movement's members, sympathisers and voters tend to use the Internet more than does the average population (see pp. 142–7), an election held only online cannot be really considered inclusive if one considers the fact that in 2012 only six in every ten Italians had Internet access.

Moreover, wide participation in the parlamentarie was prevented by a series of barriers erected by Grillo and his staff in their definition of the active and passive electorates.[6] The active electorate was defined as Italians aged over 18 who had joined the movement and sent a digital copy of their ID to the staff managing the blog before 30 September 2012. Voters could express up to three preferences for candidates in their electoral district. The passive electorate was defined as former candidates of the movement aged over 25 who had already participated in local elections without being elected. According to the electoral system, the 1,486 candidates were allocated to 31 electoral districts (27 in Italy and 4 abroad). Candidates presented themselves to voters by publishing a curriculum vitae on

6 See Movimento Cinque Stelle (2013a).

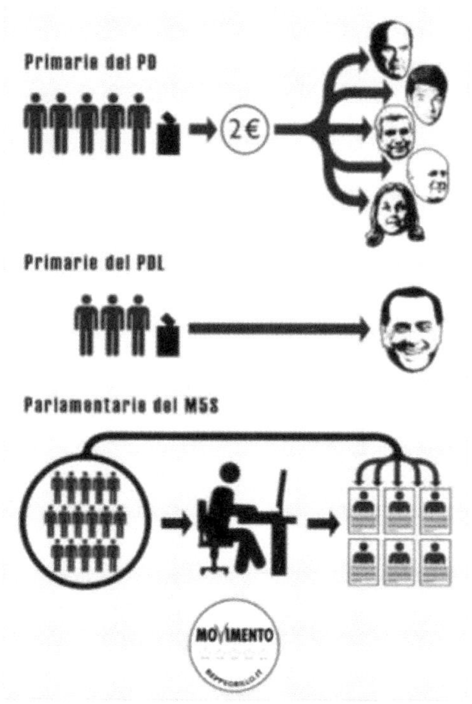

Figure 6.1 A poster calling for M5S primaries

the movement's website, where they could also post links to their profiles on social networks and a short video presentation on YouTube. In order to run for the primary elections, they had to subscribe to a code of conduct drawn up by Grillo and Casaleggio. This is an important issue because formal references to violation of the code were later made when dissidents were expelled. The code of conduct defines an MP's monthly gross salary (5,000 euro, which is substantially less than the allowance that Italian MPs receive from the state), and it obliges MPs to repay the difference to the state, to report monthly expenses connected to parliamentary activities, and to resign in the case of a conviction. Moreover, it sets rules on how registered members can introduce parliamentary bills and on the expulsion of those violating the code itself (see Movimento Cinque Stelle 2013b).

Procedural aspects of the online primaries also shaped the electoral process. Online voting was only possible for registered users during working days, and mainly during working hours (Monday 10 a.m.–5 p.m.; Tuesday 10 a.m.–9 p.m.; Wednesday 10 a.m.–5 p.m.; Thursday 10 a.m.–8 p.m.).[7] According to the staff of

7 The voting procedure was subject to a series of technical problems: no user with an email account on gmail.com received the message from the staff inviting them to vote, while

Grillo's blog, this limitation was necessary so that they could check the correctness of voting procedures in real time and avoid hacker attacks.

As regards transparency, the entire electoral process was administered by the staff managing Grillo's blog. No forms of external control were possible, which means that data could easily have been manipulated. Only after reiterated pressure from M5S's members and journalists did Grillo disclose the overall number of participants in the parlamentarie.[8] However, data on votes received by individual candidates have never been made public, and they could only be retrieved for the purposes of our research because they had been leaked by voters and candidates able to access the results of their electoral district.

Candidates' Selection

The outcomes of online primaries can be judged on the basis of, among other things, the number of participants and by comparing the characteristics of elected and unelected candidates. According to official data published by the organisers, just under two-thirds of those entitled to vote (31,612) took part in the election: 20,252. Overall, preferences given by voters amounted to 57,272 (as opposed to a potential number of up to 60,756).[9] Turnout figures were similar – although generally decreasing – in other online consultations organised by Grillo and his staff in the following months (see Figure 6.2). While parlamentarie and 'quirinarie' (online elections to select the movement's candidates for the Presidency of the Republic) involved around 60% of potential voters, turnout in subsequent votes concerning expulsions and specific policies (immigration and electoral reform) decreased to 30–40 per cent with only a few exceptions.[10]

Interestingly, the final outcome of parlamentarie – that is, candidates' selection and placement on the closed lists of the party – is only partially related to the number of votes gained by individual candidates. According to the rules established in advance on composition of the lists in each electoral district, candidates for the lower chamber should have been selected, firstly by giving priority to their age (from 25 to 39), and secondly according to their ranking in terms of votes. Hence the age factor has been considered more important than the number of preferences

---

some users regularly registered on the blog complained that they had not been recognised by the online system, which meant that they could not log in and vote. Others stated they could even vote twice or more.

8 On 6 December, after the primaries had concluded, Grillo simply stated on his blog (Grillo 2012a) that 'votes were around 95,000'. The lack of information on the exact number of participants induced groups of activists to count votes at the district level and make them available through a Facebook group. On 18 December, Grillo provided real data on the overall number of participants in the election.

9 See Grillo (2012c).

10 However, the number of those entitled to vote on the blog has increased over time to reach 85,408 users.

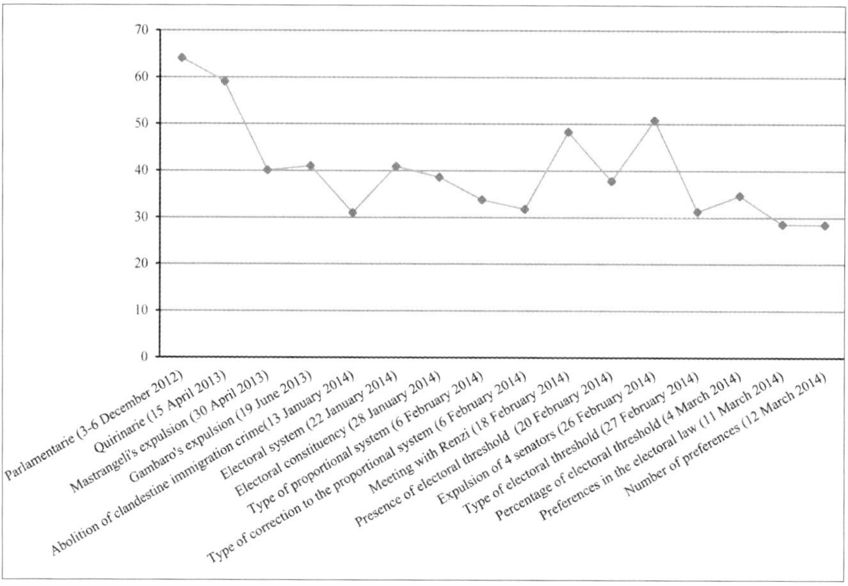

Figure 6.2 Voter turnout in the M5S's online consultations (percentages)
Source: Grillo's blog.

obtained by each candidate. In some districts, this has meant excluding candidates gaining more votes but aged over 40. While this distortion (excluding candidates from the lists because of their age although they obtained more preferences) did not affect those running for the Senate because the Constitution states that candidates to this chamber must be over 40 years of age, candidates elected to the lower chamber must be over 25, but the Constitution does not set a maximum age limit. The M5S's rules have resulted in a clear penalisation of candidates aged over 40 because the number of seats available in the Senate (315 overall) is half that in the lower chamber (630 overall). Accordingly, the M5S elected 54 senators and 109 deputies.

The effect of these rules are well exemplified by the case of one district (Liguria) where, instead of selecting the second, the third, and the fourth most voted candidates (all aged over 40) to run for the lower chamber, the fifth, the ninth, and the tenth were put on the list because they were under 40. Selecting candidates for the lower chamber regardless of age and considering only their ranking based on votes would have translated into a different composition of the parliamentary group. According to our records, almost one-sixth of the most voted candidates (N = 25) do not overlap with those currently sitting in the lower chamber. If we consider the socio-demographic characteristics of those gaining more votes and compare them with the group of deputies, we notice that average age increases from 32.6 to 35.7 years, while, if we look at gender, the percentage of female increases from 33.9 per cent to 40.4 per cent. Education level does not change significantly.

The preferences gained in primary elections by each current MP belonging to the M5S averaged around 130 (Table 6.1), with minimal differences between senators and deputies. The figures range from a minimum of 28 votes for senators (Basilicata district) and 22 for deputies (Europe district) to a maximum of 381 votes for senators (Lombardy 2 district) and 602 for deputies (Lombardy 1 district). The low number of votes gained by winning candidates is clearly related to the strict rules set for definition of the active electorate. Grillo's decision not to communicate the votes gained by each candidate in all districts was probably due to a desire to hide the low participation in the primary election and the limited popular legitimation of the winners. From this point of view, we can conclude that the parlamentarie were characterised by parochialism, in that they involved only restricted circles of activists.

Table 6.1 Average number of votes per candidate in the parlamentarie

Elected representatives	Average votes	Min–Max	N	S.D.
Deputies	132.7	22–602	109	84.7
Senators	131.3	28–381	54	71.4
TOTAL	132.2	22–602	163	80.3

In what follows we compare the characteristics of the M5S's elected representatives (N = 163) with those of all candidates for the online primaries who were not elected (N = 1,323). As data on the votes gained by each candidate in online primaries are not available, the only way to evaluate the outcome of the selection process is to consider their position in the electoral lists, which depended – at least partially (since, as we have illustrated, this requisite was biased by giving priority to the young age of deputies) – on the votes obtained by each candidate. Because the votes gained by the M5S in the 2013 general elections were quite homogeneously distributed among the various areas of the country (Bordignon and Ceccarini 2013b), and because candidates were elected in each constituency according to their position in the party lists, we consider the election of candidates to parliament as a proxy with which to distinguish the winners and losers of the online primaries.

The Outcomes of the Online Primaries

Comparison between elected and non-elected candidates shows differences concerning gender, age and education: there were more women and younger people among MPs. In fact, only 9.7 per cent of non-elected candidates were female, while this percentage increased to 38 per cent among the 163 M5S MPs. On comparing age cohorts of MPs and non-elected candidates, we found relevant differences (Table 6.2). Considering average values, while the average age of unelected candidates was 43 years, the average age of MPs was 37 (33 for deputies and 46 for senators). On comparing the education of MPs and non-elected representatives, we found that around two-thirds of MPs had a university degree as opposed to 44 per cent among unelected candidates.

Table 6.2 Age cohorts of candidates (percentages)

Age	Non-elected candidates	MPs	Total
Under 29	7.2	19.6	8.5
30–39	29.8	47.2	31.7
40–49	39.9	25.2	38.3
50–59	18.4	7.4	17.2
Over 60	4.7	0.6	4.3
	100.0	100.0	100.0
N	(1323)	(163)	(1486)

In terms of occupation, 30.1 per cent of all candidates were either self-employed professionals or freelancers, 28.1 per cent were office employees, 17.7 per cent were public employees or administrative officials, 7.4 per cent entrepreneurs and 5.9 manual workers, while 9.3 per cent did not work (retired, housewives, unemployed, and students). MPs were more likely than candidates to be unemployed and students (this was probably related to their young age), and less likely to be manual workers, entrepreneurs, and self-employed (see Figure 6.3).

Besides socio-demographic characteristics, we also gathered data on two aspects that are particularly important for the M5S because they represent the core of its political activity: candidates' presence on social media and their involvement in the M5S's Meetup groups.

Considering social networking sites, Facebook was the most popular platform, being used by almost 75 per cent of the candidates, followed by YouTube, to which about 40 per cent uploaded their videos, Twitter (used by 39 per cent), and the professional social network LinkedIn (28 per cent). Candidates' popularity on the various social networks was rather limited: the average candidate had 648 friends or fans on Facebook, 95 contacts on LinkedIn, and 50 followers on Twitter, whereas the mean number of views of their YouTube videos was 800. These results indicate that, except for some special cases, among the candidates in these consultations there was not a significant portion of 'digital opinion leaders' able to influence many other people through social media. Compared to unelected candidates, however, the winners of the parlamentarie tended to be more present

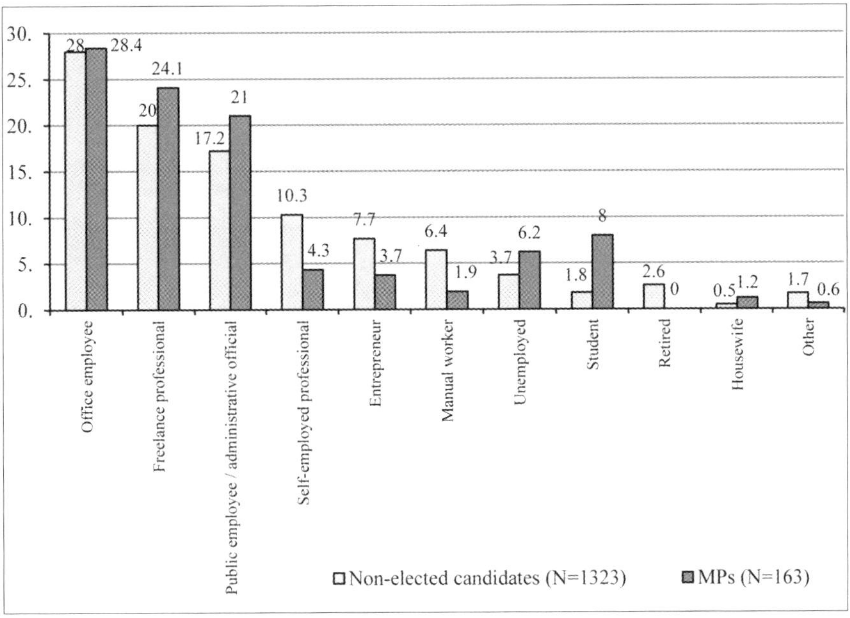

Figure 6.3 Occupation of candidates in the M5S's primary elections (percentages)

and more popular on social networking platforms: the percentages of presence rise to 89 per cent (Facebook), 74 per cent (YouTube), 63 per cent (Twitter) and 39 per cent (LinkedIn). Significant differences also emerged when comparing the popularity of elected and unelected candidates on the same platforms: the average number of friends or fans on Facebook was 955 among the former (vs 601 among the latter), the video views on YouTube 1,345 (vs 660), the contacts on LinkedIn 72 (vs 99), and the followers on Twitter 100 (vs 39).

After the parliamentarie, their winners did not make significant use of social media for campaigning in the general election. We monitored the candidates in the three months until Election Day and found that only a few new profiles were opened after the primaries (+4 per cent). As regards their popularity, the increase was on average very limited (around 100 new contacts on each platform). This is not surprising because the electoral law – based on blocked lists – does not provide any incentive for individual candidates to campaign on their own.

According to our records (see Figure 6.4), membership in Meetup groups seems to explain – at least partially – the performance of candidates in the primaries. The most successful ones were those who had played a leading role within the groups. Compared to unelected candidates, MPs were more involved in Meetups (69.8 per cent versus 39.5 per cent) and half of them (34.4 per cent) held positions of responsibility in such groups (founder, organiser, co-organiser, assistant organiser).

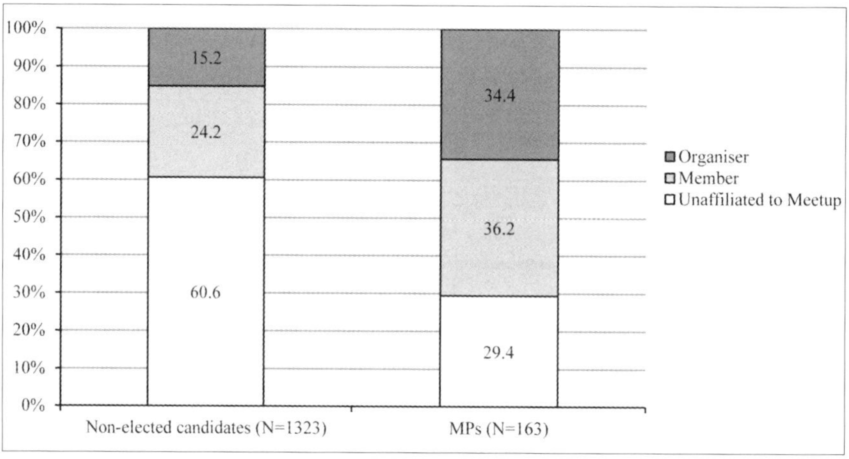

Figure 6.4 Candidates' involvement in Meetup groups (percentages)

M5S Voters and the Internet: A Continuing Elective Affinity

As we have shown so far, the Web is a central, though by no means uncontested, rhetorical symbol and organisational tool for the M5S. We now assess how M5S supporters use the Internet for campaign communication and participation. In an earlier study based on survey data collected between March and July 2012 (Mosca and Vaccari 2013), we showed that citizens who stated that they intended to vote for the M5S at that time were substantially more likely than the rest of the voting-age population to be frequent Internet users, to rely on the Web for political information, to visit party and candidate websites, and to discuss politics online. On the basis of this evidence, we concluded that, even after the substantial growth in popularity enjoyed by the movement in the first half of 2012 and which expanded its electoral base way beyond the Internet enthusiasts that initially fuelled it, the M5S's electorate was still distinctive from the rest of the Italian population with respect to its media choices and engagement with political communication through the Web. The movement's electoral base was still relatively more likely to engage in 'postmodern' (Norris, 2000) styles of election campaigning, where a mixture of tools both 'newer' (such as digital media and voter targeting) and 'older' (such as grassroots campaigning, leafleting, and canvassing) are employed on top of mass-media electioneering, and citizens' participation is more encouraged than it is in the television-centred style that has dominated Italian politics for about two decades (Grandi and Vaccari 2009).

In this section, we assess whether these tendencies were consolidated during the course of M5S's first national campaign. The 2013 elections are a particularly probing test for two main reasons: first, the high-stakes nature and uncertainty of the vote amid the M5S's novelty, which may have enhanced citizens' interest and engagement; secondly, the particular media environment that characterises general elections in Italy, which, due to the incentives provided by an electoral law that discourages candidates from campaigning locally and the long-term decline in party membership and organisational strength (Ignazi et al. 2010), have mostly been centred on mass-media techniques and, particularly, television (Grandi and Vaccari 2009). By contrast, Grillo proudly refused any opportunity to be interviewed by Italian newspapers or television programmes and forbade all M5S candidates to do so. Refraining from television was a conscious positioning tactic that allowed the M5S to ostensibly differentiate itself from other parties, which were constantly courting voters through it, as well as being a managerial decision that made it difficult for recognisable leaders other than Grillo to emerge within the movement. It was, however, also a risky strategy in a country where television is still a dominant channel of political communication. Of course, the fact that the M5S was not represented on talk shows and newscasts did not necessarily mean that it would not achieve any coverage, because Grillo attracted substantial media attention through some carefully crafted media stunts, such as swimming across the sea channel separating Calabria and Sicily to inaugurate the campaign for the Sicilian administrative elections in the autumn of 2012. However, during the 45-day official 2013 campaign period, the M5S was discussed for only 41 minutes in the main newscasts and political talk-shows of the principal television networks in the country, as opposed to 2 hours and 22 minutes for the Popolo della Libertà, 2 hours and 13 minutes for the Partito Democratico, and 1 hour and 30 minutes for the list promoted by Prime Minister Mario Monti (Grandi and Vaccari 2013). The success of the Movement's media strategy thus depended in large part on the intensity with which its prospective voters and supporters relied on communication channels other than television, chief among them being the Internet.

In order to assess the role of the Internet in the informational diets and political participation repertoires of M5S's voters, we relied on data from a post-election survey, conducted by the Itanes consortium, on a representative sample of the Italian voting-age population. We will assess the relationship between the respondents' vote for the Chamber of Deputies, differentiating between M5S voters and voters for other parties as well as non-voters, and respondents' Internet access and use of the main social media platforms, preferences for different channels of political information, and uses of the Internet to participate in various types of political activities.

We begin by looking at the extent to which M5S voters use the Internet and the main social networking platforms. As Table 6.3 shows, in the spring of 2013, 59 per cent of Italians had Internet access and, among them, 58 per cent used Facebook, and only 6 per cent used Twitter. Among those who voted for M5S, however, 74 per cent were online and, within this group, 73 per cent used Facebook, a substantially higher percentage than in the overall sample. By contrast, M5S voters were not particularly engaged in Twitter in spite of the fact that Grillo was by far the most followed Italian party leader during the campaign (Vaccari and Valeriani 2013). With respect to Internet usage, only supporters of two rather small left-wing parties – Rivoluzione Civile and Sinistra Ecologia e Libertà, which are aggregated as 'Left' in the table – outperformed those of the movement, and the other main parties in the election (the Partito Democratico, the Popolo della Libertà, and the Coalizione di Centro) lagged far behind. Moreover, M5S voters were the most likely to use Facebook in the whole sample.

Table 6.3 Use of the Internet, Facebook and Twitter by 2013 vote for the Chamber of Deputies

	Internet (%)	(N)	Facebook (%)	Twitter (%)	(N)
Left	87	(62)	65	9	(54)
Partito Democratico	58	(325)	46	4	(188)
Movimento 5 Stelle	74	(232)	73	5	(172)
Coalizione di Centro	62	(79)	43	2	(49)
Popolo della Libertà	48	(165)	57	9	(80)
Right	59	(39)	59	4	(22)
Other & non-voter	47	(306)	61	8	(143)
TOTAL	59	(1,208)	58	6	(706–9)

Note: 'Left' includes Rivoluzione Civile and Sinistra, Ecologia e Libertà; 'Right' includes Lega Nord, Fratelli d'Italia, La Destra, and Grande Sud. Percentages of Facebook and Twitter users are calculated based on Internet users only. Source: ITANES archive.

To the extent that, even in affluent countries, access to the Internet is unevenly distributed (Norris 2001) and that social media, however popular, are not used by all those who are online, the movement is well positioned to take advantage of digital media because its voters are more likely to be online and on the leading social networks. Simple access to and use of digital platforms, however, do not guarantee that voters will employ them to acquire political information or to engage with campaign activities. Indeed, research has shown that, although Internet use prompts politically interested citizens to increase their knowledge and involvement, it may encourage those who are detached from politics to avoid it altogether, and to employ the Web for entertainment instead (Prior 2007). Grillo's background as a comedian and his excessive, 'carnivalesque' language and style (Vaccari 2009) may have attracted citizens more eager to use the Internet to entertain than inform themselves.

To address these issues, we analysed the extent to which M5S voters relied on the Internet for political information during the 2013 campaign. Respondents were asked to identify their two most important sources of political news among television, radio, the Internet, newspapers, magazines, discussions with friends and family, and personal contacts with candidates. As shown in the bottom row of Table 6.4, an overwhelming majority of 90 per cent named television as one of their two favourite sources, confirming its long-established dominance in Italian political communication (Legnante 2007). M5S voters are no exception, being only slightly (84 per cent) less likely to name television as one of their two favourite sources. However, when it comes to the Internet, whilst less than one in five respondents (19 per cent) cited it among their top two sources, the percentage among M5S voters was almost double (33 per cent), and the highest among all parties' voters. Even though M5S voters are clearly more enthusiastic about the Web than the rest of the Italian population, however, digital media are still less popular than television and newspapers among them, just as they are in the whole sample.[11]

Table 6.4 The two main sources of political information by 2013 vote for the Chamber of Deputies (percentage values)

	Television	Newspapers	Family and friends	Internet	Radio	Magazines	Candidates	(N)
Left	78	56	17	32	5	3	3	(62)
Partito Democratico	91	44	19	15	8	3	1	(323)
Movimento 5 Stelle	84	37	21	33	6	2	2	(231)
Coalizione di Centro	93	43	25	12	9	2	2	(78)
Popolo della Libertà	98	35	16	14	4	3	3	(162)
Right	92	27	23	22	4	1	3	(38)
Other and non-voter	93	20	20	13	7	1	1	(287)
TOTAL	90	38	20	19	7	2	2	(1182)

Note: Aggregations are the same as in Table 6.3.
Source: ITANES archive.

The data also suggest that M5S voters are not entirely absorbed by digital media; they rely substantially on interpersonal communication as well. M5S supporters are just as likely as the rest of the population (21 per cent vs 20 per cent) to indicate personal conversations with family and friends as one of their two most important sources of political information. Indeed, in a separate question asking

11 The wording of the question and of the possible choices leaves open the possibility that respondents naming 'television' or 'newspapers' engaged with these sources at least in part through the Internet. For instance, they may have watched online videos from the website or the YouTube channel of a broadcast television programme, or they may have read news reports in the online edition of a newspaper.

respondents whether they had discussed politics during the campaign, M5S voters were substantially more likely than the overall sample to answer that they did so at least once a week (58 per cent vs 49 per cent), and a larger percentage of these voters also attended political meetings (25 per cent vs 20 per cent) and rallies (18 per cent vs 14 per cent). Altogether, these findings challenge the notion that the movement's reliance on the Internet for its communication and organisation implies that its supporters and activists are detached from offline activities. Indeed, among all the major parties that competed in the 2013 election, M5S was the only one to mount a significant campaign on the ground. It was centred on Grillo's 'Tsunami Tour' around many cities, and it culminated with the largest rally of the entire campaign on election eve in Rome. M5S supporters combine web-based and real-space repertoires of political action, and their online activities are not confined to a secluded 'cyberspace' aloof from political 'realities' on the ground (Vaccari 2013; Vaccari et al. 2013).

Further information on how M5S voters use the Internet for political engagement is yielded by some specific measures of the practice. Table 6.5 shows the frequencies with which the voters for various parties visited party or candidate websites and their social media profiles, watched online videos about the election, shared political content online, talked about politics over the Internet, and participated in events on the ground to which they had been invited on the Web. The results show that M5S voters were substantially more likely to use the Internet to engage with politics than were the rest of the sample. Similarly to our previous findings, the frequency with which M5S voters performed the activities considered was far higher than in the population as a whole, and the highest among all parties' voters. This pattern is exhibited by both information-oriented activities (visiting websites, connecting on social media, and watching online videos) and participation-oriented ones (sharing political content, discussing politics, and attending offline events after receiving an online invitation). The fact that 15 per cent of M5S voters (as opposed to 10 per cent in the whole sample) said that they had participated in an initiative that they had learned about via the Web further corroborates the argument that their use of the Internet has important implications for their offline involvement.

The fact that M5S voters are substantially more likely to share political messages and discuss political issues online can provide the movement with an important competitive advantage because its messages are more likely to travel across the Web through its supporters. Out of 100 respondents with Internet access who talked about politics online and shared political messages on the Web, 38 and 32, respectively, voted for the movement. This means that M5S's ideas and messages were overrepresented in online flows of political messages compared with the party's electoral appeal. The importance of these dynamics of interpersonal diffusion has been highlighted by Chadwick (2009), who discussed the potential of the 'information exuberance' that results from citizens' engagement in activities that require relatively little commitment, but where small contributions can be easily aggregated, and at times rapidly escalate into mass phenomena. This model

Table 6.5 Online political activities by 2013 vote for the Chamber of Deputies (percentage values among respondents with Internet access)

	Websites	Social media	Videos	Sharing	Discussion	Invitation	(N)
Left	37	30	35	30	15	11	(53–4)
Partito Democratico	30	22	28	21	14	9	(187–90)
Movimento 5 Stelle	43	36	44	28	22	15	(170–2)
Coalizione di Centro	20	20	18	10	4	8	(49–50)
Popolo della Libertà	15	16	19	20	10	11	(79–80)
Right	43	30	41	26	22	4	(22–3)
Other and non-voter	21	15	23	16	8	8	(140–4)
TOTAL	29	24	30	22	14	11	(706–9)

Note: Aggregations are the same as in Tables 6.3 and 6.4.
Source: ITANES archive.

is apparent in the M5S's approach to online communication. Key messages of the day usually come from Grillo's blog, the most read in the country, and they are then shared, often with a personal touch, by the movement's supporters through their own online devices, such as email or social media. Grillo often asks supporters to appropriate the content of his rallying cries by using a specific hashtag[12] to express their views. The leader's account then re-posts some of his supporters' messages, thus strengthening the idea of a distributed community engaged in propagation of the movement's ideas and acknowledging the contributions of the most active and creative supporters, which in turn constitutes an incentive for others to emulate them. Sara Bentivegna (2013) analysed the communication styles of party leaders on Twitter during the 2013 campaign and found that Grillo was by far the most likely to retweet other users' messages: 88 per cent of the M5S's leader's posts were retweets, substantially more than those of any other politician. By contrast, Grillo's account did not interact with users of the platform in any other way, a point that confirms the gap between M5S's rhetoric and praxis when it comes to engaging with citizens on the Web.

12 A hashtag is a keyword preceded by the symbol '#', which is used to characterise a conversational stream and distinguish it from other messages. Technically, when a user clicks on a hashtag, s/he can see all the messages that include it, irrespective of whether they were posted by accounts that s/he follows or not. Moreover, users can view which hashtags are more popular at any point in time, and can thus be drawn into discussions or collective acts of storytelling even if none of the accounts with which they are in contact are participating in them. Hashtags were first introduced by Twitter and later adopted by Facebook as well.

Conclusions

Our analysis has identified some evident contradictions between rhetorical claims by the M5S's leaders regarding the implications of the 'Internet revolution' for the future of politics and the structure of the movement itself, particularly the management of disagreement and organisational decision-making within the party. These findings show that what we have described as a 'mystique of the Web' becomes instrumental to the precise re-creation of reality through language (Edelman 1971, 1988) by M5S leaders in their speeches, writings and public performances.

Natale and Ballatore (2014, p. 117) have argued that the cyber-utopianism of the M5S leaders is an example of how the rhetoric of political change and the rhetoric of the digital revolution can be merged into a distinctive type of political discourse. As we have argued, this construction of reality may be interpreted as crucial for the movement, not just for presenting itself as an enlightened outsider in the Italian political arena, but also for the management of internal and external democracy, especially in protecting leaders against criticism and challenges from within.

As regards online primaries, we saw that participation was very limited, and that the rules on composing lists took only partial account of the (low) number of votes gained by candidates. Whilst the objective of preventing 'infiltration' by traditional parties or people external to the core of the most active members seems to have been fully achieved, the barriers to participation have discouraged the involvement and mobilisation of supporters and sympathetic citizens. The parlamentarie thus seem to have had the role of enabling 'recognition among the similar', rather than activating potential voters and mobilising supporters. As we have seen, the online voting procedure of the parlamentarie has been a somewhat exclusionary and opaque process favouring those with more experience and a leading role in the Meetup groups, and those most present and popular on social networking sites.

Finally, our survey data show that the Internet has maintained its importance for M5S voters as a channel of both political information and participation, as well as being a source of competitive advantage in electoral communication for the party. M5S supporters are more connected to the Internet and the main social media, more eager to obtain political information on the Web, and more likely to engage in online political endeavours of various kinds – including those that multiply the movement's message on the Web and span the boundaries between the online and offline realms – than the rest of the Italian population. However, although there is certainly much truth to the idea that the M5S has built part of its success on the ability to engage its voters through the Internet and make them effective conduits for online and offline person-to-person communication, the electoral success of the M5S is not rooted simply in an effective Internet strategy, but rather in the skilful use made of a diversified repertoire of integrated media.

The novelty of this model of communication can hardly be understated in a country where political communication has been dominated by a television-centric, mass-marketing approach over the last 20 years, and where digital media have played a smaller role compared to other Western democracies (Vaccari 2013). To the extent that the M5S will be able to refine its repertoire and adapt it to evolving political and electoral conditions, particularly the party's change in status from a fringe to a potentially governing party, it is likely to leave a lasting mark on Italian political communication.

References

Bentivegna, S. 2013. Stili di presenza dei leader politici su Twitter. In: I. Diamanti, L. Ceccarini, eds. *Sondaggi ed elezioni: Le regole del gioco e della comunicazione*. Firenze: Società Italiana di Studi Elettorali, pp. 246–66.

Bolgherini, S. and F. Gelli., eds. 2011. Elezioni primarie: controllo dei partiti o partecipazione popolare? *Partecipazione e Conflitto*, 1, Special Issue.

Bordignon, F. and Ceccarini, L. 2013a. Five Stars and a Cricket. Beppe Grillo Shakes Italian politics. *South European Society and Politics*, DOI: 10.1080/13608746.2013.775720.

———. 2013b. Tsunami' a 5 Stelle. In: I. Diamanti, ed. *Un salto nel voto. Ritratto politico dell'Italia di oggi*. Roma-Bari: Laterza, pp. 60–71.

Chadwick, A. 2009. Web 2.0: New Challenges for the Study of E-Democracy in an Era of Informational Exuberance. *I/S: A Journal of Law and Policy for the Information Society*, 5(1), pp. 9–41.

Chomsky, N. 2004. *Language and Politics*. Oakland, CA: AK Press.

Corbetta, P. 2013. Conclusioni. Un web-populismo dal destino incerto. In: P. Corbetta and E. Gualmini, eds. *Il partito di Grillo*. Bologna: Il Mulino, pp. 197–214.

Dal Lago, A. 2013. *Clic. Grillo, Casaleggio e la demagogia elettronica*. Napoli: Cronopio.

Edelman, M.J. 1971. *Politics as Symbolic Action: Mass Arousal and Quiescence*. New York: Academic Press.

———. 1988. *Constructing the Political Spectacle*. Chicago: University of Chicago Press.

Entman, R.M. 1993. Framing: Toward Clarification of a Fractured Paradigm. *Journal of communication*, 43(4), pp. 51–8.

Grandi, R. and Vaccari, C. 2009. Electoral Campaigning and the New Media. In: D. Albertazzi, C. Brook, C. Ross, and N. Rothenberg, eds. *Resisting the Tide: Cultures of Opposition under Berlusconi 2001–06*. New York and London: Continuum, pp. 46–56.

———. 2013. *Come si vincono le elezioni: Elementi di comunicazione politica*. Roma: Carocci.

Grillo, B. 2012a. I risultati delle Parlamentarie del M5S. *Beppegrillo.it* [blog] 6 December. Available at: http://www.beppegrillo.it/2012/12/i_risultati_delle_parlamentarie.html [Accessed 14 January 2014].

———. 2012b. Objective: Elections 2013. *Beppegrillo.it* [blog] 11 December. Available at: http://www.beppegrillo.it/en/2012/12/objective_elections_2013.html [Accessed 14 January 2014].

———. 2012c. Italian Primary Buffoonery. *Beppegrillo.it* [blog] 18 December. Available at: http://www.beppegrillo.it/en/2012/12/_italian_primary_buffoonery.html [Accessed 14 January 2014].

———. 2013a. Squirts of Digital Shit. *Beppegrillo.it* [blog] 24 March. Available at: http://www.beppegrillo.it/en/2013/03/squirts_of_digital_shit.html [Accessed 14 January 2014].

———. 2013b. Quando uno vale niente. *Beppegrillo.it* [blog] 11 June. Available at: http://www.beppegrillo.it/2013/06/quando_uno_vale.html [Accessed 14 January 2014].

———. 2013c. Gambaro a giudizio. *Beppegrillo.it* [blog] 13 June. Available at: http://www.beppegrillo.it/2013/06/gambaro_a_giudizio.html [Accessed 14 January 2014].

———. 2013d. Democracy Must be Revived – An Interview with Gianroberto Casaleggio *Beppegrillo.it* [blog] 24 June. Available at: http://www.beppegrillo.it/en/2013/06/democracy_must_be_revived_an_i_1.html [Accessed 14 January 2014].

———. 2013e. What is it? A platform? A portal? No, it's the M5S Operating System. *Beppegrillo.it* [blog] 3 October. Available at: http://www.beppegrillo.it/en/2013/10/what_is_it_a_platform_a_portal.html [Accessed 14 January 2014].

Ignazi, P., Bardi, L. and Massari, O. 2010. Party Organisational Change in Italy (1991–2006). *Modern Italy*, 15(2), pp. 197–216.

Lakoff, G. 2004. *Don't Think of an Elephant: Know Your Values and Frame the Debate*. White River Junction, VT: Chelsea Green Publishing.

Legnante, G. 2007. Cittadini, mezzi di comunicazione e politica. In: M. Maraffi, ed. *Gli italiani e la politica*. Bologna: Il Mulino, pp. 265–96.

Mosca, L. and Vaccari, C. 2013. Il Movimento e la rete. In: P. Corbetta and E. Gualmini, eds. *Il partito di Grillo*. Bologna: Il Mulino, pp. 169–96.

Movimento Cinque Stelle. 2013a. Regole per candidarsi e votare per le liste del MoVimento 5 Stelle alle politiche 2013. *Beppegrillo.it* [blog]. Available at: http://www.beppegrillo.it/movimento/regole_politiche_2013.php [Accessed 14 January 2014].

Movimento Cinque Stelle, 2013b. Codice di comportamento eletti MoVimento 5 Stelle in Parlamento. *Beppegrillo.it* [blog]. Available at: http://www.beppegrillo.it/movimento/codice_comportamento_parlamentare.php [Accessed 14 January 2014].

Mudde, C. 2004. The Populist Zeitgeist. *Government and Opposition*, 39(4), pp. 542–63.

Natale, S. and Ballatore, A. 2014. The Web Will Kill Them All: New Media, Digital Utopia, and Political Struggle in the Italian 5-Star Movement. *Media, Culture & Society*, 36(1), pp. 105–21.

Norris, P. 2000. *A Virtuous Circle: Political Communications in Postindustrial Societies*. Cambridge: Cambridge University Press.

———. 2001. *Digital Divide: Civic Engagement, Information Poverty, and the Internet Worldwide*. Cambridge: Cambridge University Press.

Pasquino, G. and Valbruzzi, M. 2013. Primarie per il premier: la selezione dei candidati tra innovazione e manipolazione. In: A. Di Virgilio and C.M. Radaelli, eds. *Politica in Italia. I fatti dell'anno e le interpretazioni*. Bologna: Il Mulino, pp. 119–40.

Pizzorno, A. 1987. Politics unbound. In: C.S. Maier, ed. 1987. *Changing Boundaries of the Political. Essays on the Evolving Balance between the State and Society, Public and Private in Europe*. New York: Cambridge University Press, pp. 27–62.

Prior, M. 2007. *Post-Broadcast Democracy: How Media Choice Increases Inequality in Political Involvement and Polarizes Elections*. New York: Cambridge University Press.

Sandri, G., Seddone, A. and Venturino, F. 2013. The Selection of Party Leaders in Italy. 1989–2012. In: J.B. Pilet and W. Cross, eds. *The Selection of Political Party Leaders in Contemporary Parliamentary Democracies. A Comparative Study*. New York: Routledge, pp. 93–107.

Vaccari, C. 2009. Web Challenges to Berlusconi: An Analysis of Oppositional Sites. In: D. Albertazzi, C. Brook, C. Ross, and N. Rothenberg, eds. 2009. *Resisting the Tide: Cultures of Opposition under Berlusconi 2001–06*. New York and London: Continuum, pp. 135–47.

———. 2013. *Digital Politics in Western Democracies: A Comparative Study*. Baltimore, MD: The Johns Hopkins University Press.

Vaccari, C., and Valeriani, A. 2013. Follow the Leader! Direct and Indirect Flows of Political Communication During the 2013 Italian General Election Campaign. *New Media & Society*, DOI: 10.1177/1461444813511038.

Vaccari, C., Valeriani, A., Barberá, P., Bonneau, R., Jost, J.T., Nagler, J. and Tucker, J. 2013. Social Media and Political Communication: A Survey of Twitter Users During the 2013 Italian General Election. *Rivista Italiana di Scienza Politica*, 43(3), pp. 325–55.

Valbruzzi, M. 2005. *Primarie. Partecipazione e leadership*. Bologna: Bononia University Press.

Chapter 7
The Movimento 5 Stelle and Social Conflicts: Between Symbiosis and Cooptation[1]

Lorenzo Mosca

Introduction

One of the reasons for the recent success of the Movimento 5 Stelle (M5S) has been deemed its capacity to engage with, and embed itself in, local conflicts on environmental issues, as well as the working conditions of employees in firms under restructuring.

Proximity with social movements is only one of the aspects that contribute to defining the identity of the M5S. While other chapters in this book focus on the innovative features of the party's organisation, its use of the internet, and its anti-establishment discourse, here the focus is on the linkage among the movement, social conflicts and local protests. There are three main dimensions that can shed light on this relationship: a) the proximity of the electoral programme and campaigns of Grillo and the M5S to social movement claims; b) the action repertoire and multiple belongings of the movement's elected representatives; c) electoral outcomes in areas with severe social conflicts.

In order to assess the movement's capacity to use local grievances and protests to define its political identity, the first part of this chapter illustrates the campaigns supported by Grillo over the past decade. It then discusses the official electoral manifestos of the M5S, singling out those parts explicitly concerned with conflicts and issues raised by social movements. Together with the programme presented in the 2013 general elections, other examples will be taken from the electoral programmes drawn up for subnational ballots.

The following section considers two important resources of the M5S: its repertoire of action, and the multiple belongings of its elected representatives at both the national and local level. While unconventional political action is a political resource used by powerless groups to enter the political arena by generating attention and support from the mass media, public opinion and powerful

1 I am particularly grateful to Giorgia Bulli, Piergiorgio Corbetta, Luca Pinto, Filippo Tronconi and Dario Tuorto for their helpful and constructive comments on an earlier version of this chapter.

actors (Lipsky 1968), multiple belongings and overlapping memberships can be considered the 'social capital of social movements', in that they are responsible for people's direct participation, network-building and mutual understanding (della Porta and Diani 2006). Analysis of the personal biographies of M5S MPs will show the incidence of manifold belongings and their use of unconventional forms of action. Biographies of some M5S representatives in local institutions are also considered because they provide anecdotal evidence of proximities and overlaps between social movements engaged in local social conflicts and M5S candidates.

The next section discusses the relationship between parties and movements in the electoral arena. It does so by examining the electoral performance of the M5S in areas where the movement gained a large amount of votes in the general elections of 2013. Consideration of those electoral results will show if the positive outcome was at least partially due to its capacity to occupy the political space of local protest movements generating electoral support.

The conclusion to the chapter discusses the relationship between the M5S and social movements in light of the current nature of this distinctive political actor.

Thematic Proximity to Social Movements

The thematic closeness of the M5S to Italian social movements can be assessed both by conducting a review of the main campaigns initiated or supported by Grillo since the beginning of the 2000s (well before the official birth of the M5S) and by analysing manifestos prepared for local and national elections. It is interesting to note that the majority of these campaigns have been promoted by local groups of citizens and associations against the ruling political parties. They have been given visibility by Grillo on his blog and have in some cases been successful.

In what follows, cases will be presented in which Grillo and members of his movement have demonstrated their tendency to join social conflicts, support demonstrators, and present themselves as spokespersons for many of the demands put forward by social movements (Biorcio and Natale 2013).

Grassroots Campaigns

At the beginning of 2000, Grillo was close to the 'Rete Lilliput' ecopacifist network (one of the main components of the global justice movement in Italy – see della Porta et al. 2006). He invited its activists (as well as those of other associations and groups) to promote their activities and campaigns during his shows staged in Italian squares and theatres (Mosca 2013). At that time, Grillo's engagement largely concerned environmental issues, often in connection with the negative impacts of neoliberal globalisation (see also Chapter 1). In 2003 he campaigned for an abrogative referendum promoted by the Italian federation of Greens against electrosmog (considered a cause of cancer). For a decade, he supported local mobilisations against large-scale infrastructures projected throughout the country.

He joined protests against new highways and high-speed trains, and he took part in the resistance mounted against major public works by, for example, the 'No Tav', 'No Dal Molin' and 'No Ponte' campaigns (della Porta and Piazza 2008; Caruso 2010).

In Val di Susa (Piedmont) he supported the campaign against high-speed trains ('No Tav') to such an extent that in May 2012 he was charged, as well as other activists, with the offence of trespass on a sequestered area of the valley (Tropeano 2012). He also supported a campaign against expansion of an American military base in Vicenza ('No Dal Molin') and also one to halt construction of a bridge across the Strait of Messina ('No Ponte').

Moreover, Grillo actively campaigned against plans to build local infrastructures – such as incinerators and similar facilities – alleged to pollute the environment and cause diseases. The most significant case of this opposition concerned the city of Parma, where a civic movement opposed to the construction of an incinerator has been active since 2006. Beside Parma, another important episode in the long fight against polluting facilities occurred in November 2012, when the M5S supported a successful referendum against an incinerator to be built in the northern region of Valle d'Aosta.

Other campaigns promoted or supported by Grillo concern issues that have been the object of mobilisations by social movements in the past decade. When the Italian comedian launched his blog at the beginning of 2005, he invited his supporters to write a letter to the president of the republic demanding the withdrawal of Italian soldiers from Iraq ('Via dall'Iraq'). In Italy at that time there was vociferous opposition against the war in Iraq, and it received strong support from public opinion, as shown by mass demonstrations and opinion polls (della Porta and Diani 2004; Verhulst and Walgrave 2010, p. 53).

Grillo has also promoted campaigns for consumer protection and against financial speculation. For instance, he has supported small shareholders in their actions to gain compensation for financial crashes: those of Argentine bonds, Parmalat (an Italian multinational dairy and food corporation), the Telecom Italia telecommunications company, and the Monte dei Paschi di Siena bank. Between 2006 and 2007 he embraced a successful campaign that persuaded the European institutions to abolish the cost of recharging mobile phones (Mosca and Santucci 2009).

The proximity between local conflicts and the M5S is evident in a region with a leftist tradition like Marche, where, after 2006 Meetup members joined local committees in their struggle against biomass plants planned by regional and local administrations (Gobbi 2012). In the same year, the 'No Pav' network (campaigning against the Piano area vasta – Wide Area Plan) – whose members were grassroots committees and citizens, environmental groups, political parties, rank-and-file unions, squats, and individuals – was created at a meeting held in Ancona. It opposed the construction of a building two million cubic metres in volume supposed to be erected in an 800,000 square metre industrial estate. Those opposing the Pav asked for a meeting with the regional council. Testifying to Grillo's role in the conflict was the decision of the protesters to declare him their spokesperson (Ansa 2006).

After promoting a petition to the President of the Republic, Grillo targeted other institutional representatives. He wrote two letters (in 2008 and in 2011) to the head of the Italian police to ask for accountability and democracy within the corps. This had been a demand typically associated with Italian social movements since the 1970s; and it returned to the top of their agenda after several cases of people being severely injured by the police during demonstrations: in particular, the Genoa anti-G8 protest, when a demonstrator was killed by a *carabiniere* (della Porta and Reiter 2004). As the comedian wrote in one of these letters:

> Recent days have seen the tenth anniversary of the G8 in Genoa and the 'macelleria messicana' (Mexican butchery) at the Diaz school ... I do not feel that it is right – and I believe that very many Italians feel the same – that someone found guilty (even though still not by the Court of Cassation) continues in service and has even been promoted ... Citizens should not have the slightest doubt about those delegated to protect them. They must have maximum trust and willingness to cooperate. I put two proposals to you, and I hope that you will support them. The first is to introduce a system for identification of every police officer like those of many other countries including the United States. The second is to hold a series of open meetings with the police in various cities during which every type of problem relative to safety and security is discussed. (Grillo 2011)

In 2011, Meetup groups were actively involved in supporting successful referenda on public water services, against nuclear energy, and legitimate impediment (*legittimo impedimento*).[2] As will be seen later, M5S activists were actively engaged in the organising committee of the referendum against the privatisation of water services.

On the occasion of a European general strike on 14 November 2012, students took to the streets in many Italian cities. The demonstrations resulted in clashes with the police, soon accused by the protesters of brutality and disproportionate reaction. Shortly thereafter, Grillo decisively sided with the student movement, inviting the policemen to 'take your helmet off and hug a protester' (Grillo 2012a).

In May 2013, the M5S campaigned for a local consultative referendum in Bologna on the public education system. The intention was to devote all resources for primary education to public schools and exclude private institutes from funding (a goal also included in the national programme). Although the M5S was the only party represented in the city council that supported the referendum from the outset, the consultation was supported by most of the citizens.

---

2 'The law on legitimate impediment (law 51/2010) precludes hearings for the prime minister [at that time, Berlusconi] and ministers in criminal cases in which they are involved as long as they can present a certificate stating that they have conflicting duties of government' (Dallara 2015). When still in government, this law has often been used by Berlusconi's lawyers to delay trials.

In November 2013, Grillo joined workers' demonstrations in Genoa against the privatisation of a local transport company. He declared:

> What I have seen is not just a strike, but a clash of two worlds. On the one hand, those who want to privatise; on the other, we who want to safeguard the common good of citizens earned by the sweat of the brows of our fathers and grandfathers ... We take the opposite view: that of the people who want to save the commons and public services. I went into the streets to participate in the event, to be with the workers, and to express publicly that all the citizens of M5S are on their side. (Grillo 2013a)

Again in December 2013, after a wildcat strike by the 'pitchforks movement',[3] Grillo published on his blog an open letter to the heads of the *carabinieri*, the police and the army. He made the following request: 'In the forthcoming demonstrations, order your men to take off their helmets and fraternise with the protesters. This would be a signal that is revolutionary, peaceful and extreme. And Italy will change' (Grillo 2013b).

Another interesting aspect emerging from the analysis of M5S campaigns concerns the conception of civic participation, which resembles that theorised by social movements. The M5S proposes a normative definition of the citizen as: a) someone controlling the work of elected representatives (Lanfrey 2011); b) someone interested in and informed about public issues and actively participating in politics. From this point of view, one of the most telling operations of the M5S has been its '*fiato sul collo*' (breathing down the neck) campaign, which consisted in the monitoring of several local assemblies accused of taking important decisions behind closed doors. The physical position of M5S MPs in the parliamentary assembly recalls this idea of control; they sit in the upper part of the chamber. Other initiatives include 'the map of power' promoted by Grillo via his blog and implemented at the local level by some Meetup groups. The latter have produced network maps revealing the connections between political and economic power in the management of public and private companies, and informing people on interpersonal relationships and exchanges among diverse actors (Lanfrey 2011, p. 163).

Electoral Manifestos

The analysis of electoral manifestos has been often employed to study political parties because it illuminates their official policy positions at a particular time, while also allowing comparison across time and space (Gabel and Hix, 2002).

3 During the winter of 2013, Italy was hit by a disruptive wave of protest that brought heterogeneous groups together in angry opposition to austerity policies. The protesters were extremely diverse (lorry drivers, farmers, small business owners, students, unemployed people, far-right supporters, and football hooligans). Their goals were not consistent although their common targets were the national government, the euro, and globalisation (Davies 2013).

Although focused on a single case, a qualitative investigation of the M5S's electoral programmes can be useful to grasp the salience given to social movement claims in its manifestos.

As its leader explicitly specified in a guide called 'Grillo for dummies': 'the M5S gives its backing to movements and campaign groups with shared objectives, as in the case of the 'no to nuclear', 'water stays public', 'No Tav' and 'No Gronda' campaigns' (Grillo 2012b).

Reference to the 'No Tav' is made in the M5S electoral manifesto drawn up for the general elections (doc. NP).[4] The intent to halt construction of a bridge across the Strait of Messina was expressed in the national electoral programme (ibid.). Like many other manifestos (including the national one), the M5S programme for regional elections in Emilia-Romagna in 2010 included the goal of 'zero waste' and stated that 'monsters which cannot survive without public funds such as nuclear power plants, incinerators and massive gas terminals will become unnecessary ... we plan a gradual phasing out of all the eight regional incinerators and landfills in the next fifteen years' (doc. RPER, p. 4). Opposition against locally unwanted land use in Parma became the core issue of the local programme (doc. MPP) and of the 2012 electoral campaign, when the M5S candidate – who pledged to halt construction of the local incinerator – was elected mayor.

Although the M5S declares itself to be beyond left and right, like many progressive movements it defends the welfare state against cuts, as well as the role of the state in providing services, and it proclaims its determination to protect vulnerable groups in society. More generally, reference to the concept of 'common goods' (public water, public education, public soil, etc.) protected against market dynamics, as propounded by Italian social movements, can be found in many of the M5S electoral manifestos. The programme presented for provincial elections in Trentino in 2013 devoted a section to this topic. It declared that 'each common good must have a 'citizens' parliament', composed of citizens, employees and administrators: all selected at random, without compensation or reimbursement, periodically renewed, and whose function is to supervise the actions of service providers and ensure their transparency' (doc. PPT, p. 3).

Other manifestos presented on the occasion of regional elections evidence the M5S's closeness to social movement claims in regard to the civil rights of LGBT and immigrants. The programme drawn up for regional elections held in Sicily in 2012 has a section devoted specifically to the former, including equal opportunities, laws against discrimination and homophobia (doc. RPS). The programme prepared for regional elections in Friuli-Venezia Giulia in 2013 advocated voting rights for immigrants in administrative elections, as well as a notion of citizenship based on *ius soli* (doc. RPFVG). This is an interesting difference with respect to the national level, where Grillo has always been ambiguous on the issue of immigration. He even censored an amendment to a parliamentary bill to abolish

4 Full details on the documents cited from now on can be found at the end of the chapter.

a law making illegal entry into the country a crime presented by two M5S MPs. He observed that 'a spokesperson cannot assume the right to make such an important decision in relation to an issue of such social concern without prior consultation with the public' (Grillo 2013c). Grillo deliberately avoids tackling divisive issues like immigration, since they could easily split his extremely diverse electorate (Bordignon and Ceccarini 2013). However, comparison between national and local manifestos shows that grassroots activists take a clearer and more progressive position on immigration.[5] To be noted is that these differences in policy positioning between local groups and the national leadership have to date been tolerated, contrary to other organisational aspects of the movement (see the concluding chapter of this book).

A proposal included in the programme for regional elections in Sicily recalls issues already raised in the past by social movements: the use of alternative indicators such as the Happy Planet Index, the green GDP, and the Gross National Happiness index measuring wealth, well-being and quality of life, beyond solely economic aspects (doc. RPS).

As Grillo's 'Tsunami tour' passed through many Italian squares during the electoral campaign preceding the general elections of 2013, he often repeated that 'no one will be left behind'. From this point of view, one of the most telling features of the electoral programme for the general elections was its reference to a guaranteed minimum income, another demand put forward by social movements (doc. NP).

As seen, although there is an evident thematic closeness to movements' campaigns and claims in the M5S's manifestos for local and general elections, references to specific issues are scarce. Such references are instead more frequent in manifestos prepared for local elections. For example, the programme for municipal elections held in Genoa in 2012 devoted a specific section to opposition against large-scale infrastructures: a new highway called the 'Gronda' and the '*terzo valico*' (third gateway; section of the high-speed/capacity Milan-Genoa railway line) (doc. MPG). In both the programmes for the Piedmont regional elections of 2010 and the Turin municipal elections of 2011, opposition to the high-speed train (Tav) was evident (doc. RPP and MPTU). Also the programme for the Lombardy regional elections of 2013 stressed opposition to new highways (doc. RPLO). Hostility to large infrastructures is also apparent in the programme prepared for the regional elections in Sicily (doc. RPS). One section specifically concerned the Mobile User Objective System (MUOS) – an ultra-high-frequency satellite network serving the US Navy – and argued for revision of the international treaties imposing military easements ('*servitù militari*') on the island,[6] as well as abrogation of the national law that created the company

5 Despite Grillo's opposition, the MPs' amendment was finally ratified by M5S members in an online consultation held on 13 January 2014 before the official vote in parliament.

6 Besides environmental impact, local residents fear cancer-inducing effects and other health hazards provoked by high power broadcast transmitters at mobile frequencies

in charge of erecting the bridge across the Strait of Messina. Opposition to the MUOS, as well as oil drilling in Sicily, formed part of the programme for Ragusa municipal elections of 2013 (doc. MPR), where the M5S had a mayor elected. A section of the programme for regional elections held in Basilicata in 2013 (doc. RPB) was devoted to opposition against oil extraction, which it accused of damaging the environment. The manifesto prepared for municipal elections in Taranto in 2012 referred to the controversy on the environmental pollution generated by the Ilva steelworks.[7] It stated: 'we believe that an agreement between politics and large industry is necessary to plan a clean future for Taranto. We believe that there should be a programme to protect jobs that envisages the conversion of production … We want to protect work and health' (doc. MPTA, p. 20).

The active participation of citizens is often envisaged by electoral manifestos. Planning, controlling and verifying the health system was explicitly mentioned in the programme for the regional elections held in Latium in 2013, and also foreseen was the role of citizens in monitoring CVs and their veto power in the selection of senior managers (doc. RPLA). The electoral programme for the city of Turin referred to citizens' involvement in urban planning, and to the regular consultation of young residents in order to identify their needs and priorities (doc. MPTU). Like many others, the manifesto prepared for Parma municipal elections stressed citizen participation via participatory budgeting and popular initiatives without a quorum, stressing that both instruments should not be consultative but instead binding on the local council (doc. MPP). Moreover, it also envisioned the experimental use of town meetings to collect citizens' proposals.

In sum, the analysis of electoral manifestos drawn up by the M5S for national and local elections clearly shows a sort of appropriation of social movement claims, ranging from environmental struggles to the defence of common goods, from expansion of civic rights to alternative ways to measure growth, from the protection of vulnerable social groups to direct participation by citizens in policy-making.

(Struggles in Italy 2013).

7 The Ilva plant in the southern Italian city of Taranto is the largest steelworks in Europe, employing 12,000 workers. The local economy almost entirely depends on it. In August 2012 the plant was closed by judicial order because of the damage that it had caused to the environment and the health of local residents. Eight of its senior managers were placed under house arrest. Ilva's management had already been condemned by a judicial inquiry in 2001 for neglecting work safety procedures and violating anti-pollution regulations. In September 2013 the European Commission stated that laboratory tests showed a heavy pollution of air, soil, surface and ground waters, both on the Ilva site and in nearby residential areas, and it urged Italy to fulfil its obligations under EU environmental directives.

Biographical Proximity to Social Movements

The analysis of individual biographies has played an important role in social movement studies. They have been used to trace trajectories of participation by social movement activists over time (Passy and Giugni 2000; Corrigall-Brown 2012). However, research on patterns of engagement by social movements in political parties (and vice versa) has been sporadic. In a seminal study on the protest cycle of the 1960s and 1970s in Italy, Tarrow stressed continuity between left parties and social movements, observing that 'rather than responding defensively to the new wave of movements, the Italian parties adapted quickly to their challenge by cooptation and preemption' (2012, p. 94). At that time, the protest was mounted by insurgents within 'old' organisations (parties and unions), and it was absorbed by the party system. Social movements did not politicise or create a new cleavage; rather, they acted according to the traditional right/left distinction. Accordingly, the Communist Party became the recipient of their struggles at the end of the protest cycle as it absorbed members of the movement into its structures. As Tarrow puts it:

> a look at several aspects of the relationship between the parties of the Left in Italy and the new movements that appeared in that period suggests that parties are more usefully seen as creative prompters in the origins, dynamics, and ultimate institutionalisation of new social movements than as old actors cast offstage by their movement detractors. (ibid., p. 96)

Bearing Tarrow's points in mind, we can observe that, differently from previous protest cycles, the M5S does not act according to the traditional left/right cleavage and that it did not emerge from within the existing party system; rather, it harshly criticised the old political actors. However, the purpose of our inquiry here is to illuminate the relationships between the M5S and social movements. As Diani and Fabbri (2014) have noted in a summary of Italian movements during the past decade: 'It is certainly the case, and it reflects in the biographies of the M5S MPs, that many M5S activists and groups have been involved in local initiatives, close to the global justice movement or to other campaigns such as the one on public water'.

This section focuses in particular on the individual proximity of M5S national elected representatives to social movements. Biographical closeness to movements has been assessed through analysis of CVs and videos prepared by the candidates for primary elections[8] (on the online consultation see Chapter 6 in this book) but

8 All candidates running in the online primary election were invited by the M5S's staff to furnish information on their personal biography (including professional and activist experiences) as well as a letter of intent regarding their future parliamentary activity, a presentation video, and links to their profiles on social networks (i.e. LinkedIn, Facebook, Twitter, YouTube, Meetup, etc.).

also via specific web searches on their personal blogs/web pages. Besides the analysis of M5S MPs profiles, brief reference is made to local candidates elected in areas particularly characterised by local conflicts.

As regards elected representatives, their biographies have been analysed by looking for explicit references to direct experience in social movements, local conflicts, mobilisations, demonstrations, and multiple memberships. The analysis has been performed by collecting information on the direct engagement of representatives in local conflicts, use of unconventional forms of participation, and organisational belonging besides the M5S. The expectation is that the more representatives' profiles are close to those of grassroots activists in terms of knowledge of conflicts, personal identification with local struggles, use of unconventional forms of action, and embeddedness in a dense network of civil society organisations, the more such expertise will form part of their action within institutions, and also influence their contribution to electoral programmes and parliamentary activity.

According to our records (Table 7.1), more than one-third of M5S MPs declared that they had either taken part in social movement demonstrations and campaigns or had overlapping memberships. This percentage was higher for senators (43 per cent) than for deputies (36 per cent). Considering the different forms of proximity to social movements, 11 per cent of deputies and 13 per cent of senators declared that they had used unconventional forms of action in the past (demonstrations, sit-ins, etc.) or that they had been involved in specific social movements (environmental, anti-mafia, no Tav, students etc.). The percentages of those declaring multiple memberships in civil society groups, associations, committees, etc. were 16 per cent for deputies and 17 per cent for senators. A minority of MPs (16 people) declared that they had experience of both forms of activism: 9 per cent of deputies and 13 per cent of senators.

Table 7.1 M5S MPs' proximity to social movements (percentages)

Dimensions of proximity to movements	**Deputies**	**Senators**	**All M5S MPs**
Unconventional forms of action	11.0	13	12.3
Multiple belongings	15.6	17	16.0
Both	9.2	13	9.1
None	64.2	57	62.6
Total	100.0	100	100.0
(N)	(109)	(54)	(163)

Reference to Local Conflicts and Social Movements

Focusing on the group of MPs most proximate to social movements can help shed light on the relationship between elected representatives and territorial conflicts. A large part of this 'vanguard' explicitly declared their opposition to high-speed trains. Some of these MPs had been elected in the northern region of Piedmont. where they had been directly involved in the mobilisation against the Tav. Emblematic of this closeness is a declaration by the leader of the protest who explicitly declared that he had voted for Grillo and stated with reference to the future MPs:

> through the M5S we present No Tav candidates who have an excellent chance of being elected ... we will bring a group of trusted people into the parliament that will break it up ... these candidates are people of our land, we know them well, they fought with us. They are No Tav through and through. (Baldolini 2013)

Some of the M5S representatives elected were activists with experience of the global justice movement of the early 2000s. As a deputy elected in Campania stated in his blog:

> I still believe that 'another world is possible' and I was in Genoa for the G8 summit in 2001, challenging the powerful who think that money is more important than the lives of people and the planet. Then I took part in the European social forum in Florence and marched from Perugia to Assisi against the war in Iraq.[9]

Sicily, too, is a region whose representatives are deeply embedded in local conflicts. Most of them have been personally involved in the anti-mafia movement,[10] as well as in the more recent protest against the MUOS. The importance of this issue for the M5S is evident if one considers that the movement's representatives in the Sicily regional assembly, who initially supported the centre-left governor, withdrew their confidence in the executive because, among other reasons, of its position on the MUOS. Part of the document announcing no confidence in the regional government is devoted to this topic. It states: 'during the electoral campaign, candidate Rosario Crocetta promised to rescind all permits ... but since he took office nothing has been done, not even after unanimous approval of a motion urging the government to adopt all useful means to revoke authorisations' (doc. MDCRS, p. 4–5). The regional M5S representatives also opposed plans to drill for oil in Valle del Belice and asked governor Crocetta to annul the permits already issued to Enel (Italy's largest electricity company) (doc. MTBRS).

While some MPs from Basilicata have engaged in the fight by the 'No Triv' movement against oil drilling, some representatives from Apulia have been involved

9 http://galloluigi.wordpress.com/sono [Accessed 17 February 2014]

10 Their membership of the anti-mafia movement was mentioned to explain why, instead of abstaining (as decided by their group), some of them contributed to the election of the candidate of the centre-left coalition to the Senate presidency, Piero Grasso, in order to prevent the election of Renato Schifani, proposed by the centre-right coalition and opposed because of his alleged relationship with the mafia (Pini 2013).

in the controversy surrounding the Ilva steelworks, a highly sensitive issue because demands to reduce pollution and protect the environment may have negative consequences in terms of employment. Among the elected representatives were also two MPs, one in Tuscany and the other in Sicily, who used their professional expertise to organise class actions or appeals to administrative tribunals to block the construction of high-speed train infrastructures and incinerators.

The salience of certain issues for candidates of the M5S from the social movement milieu helps explain why explicit references to conflicts and movement claims are made in the electoral manifestos.

Reference to Organisational Experience

Shifting the attention from direct participation in social conflicts and movements to the organisational experience of elected M5S representatives is useful for exploration of the potential contribution of overlapping affiliations. As scholars have noted when analysing the dynamics of contention, multiple belongings ease the amalgamation of different sectors of a movement because they facilitate personal contacts and the growth of informal networks (della Porta and Diani 2006, pp. 127–9). This in turn favours individual participation, the spread of information, the development of links, mutual understanding, trust and collaboration among different groups, and resource mobilisation (ibid.). Bearing these virtues of overlapping memberships in mind, we now focus on the role that they play in the M5S.

As seen, multiple belongings concern 16 per cent of M5S MPs. The organisational affiliations declared by parliamentarians are rather heterogeneous: they range among unions (Confederazione Generale Italiana del Lavoro and rank-and-file unions), fair trade and ethical purchasing groups (Gruppi d'acquisto solidale), the happy degrowth movement, non-profit associations (i.e. Mani Tese, Associazione Italiana per la Donazione di Organi e tessuti and Associazione Donatori Midollo Osseo), anti-mafia committees (i.e. Libera, Addio Pizzo and Agende Rosse), environmental groups (i.e. Zero Waste, Critical Mass, Legambiente and Greenpeace), voluntary associations (i.e. Associazione Nazionale Privi della Vista ed Ipovedenti and Associazioni Volontari Italiani Sangue), student groups (Collettivi), NGOs (i.e. Emergency, Amnesty International, and African Medical and Research Foundation), cultural and sport associations, and a plethora of local single-issue groups. Past experiences in political parties concern very few cases, being limited to Verdi, post-communist parties, La Rete, and Lega Nord.

Other significant experiences by MPs in grassroots campaigns concern the referendum on public water privatisation. Numerous members of the M5S joined water committees, and played key roles within many water organisations (Cernison 2013). One deputy elected in Latium was a member of the campaign's main coordinating committee, and many local groups were active in collecting signatures for the referendum, mobilising citizens, and campaigning on the issue.

Multiple memberships also seem to be a significant characteristic of some successful candidates elected by the M5S at the local level. The mayoral candidate for the Genoa city council in 2012 was also the spokesperson of the 'No Gronda' coordination group. Elected to the local assembly with other activists, he led a long campaign against a project to widen the highways around Genoa. In Parma, some members of the local government have been leading members of the committee for fair waste management (comitato 'Gestione Corretta Rifiuti') opposed to the planned construction of an incinerator. In Jesi, since 2006 the birth of an environmental committee (Comitato per la tutela della salute e dell'ambiente della Vallesina) was promoted against the project to build a biomass plant. A MP elected in the same region is the vice-president of that committee. The president of the committee was the mayoral candidate in the municipal elections of 2012 and he won almost 18 per cent per cent of votes.

Multiple belongings can favour osmosis between the social movement milieu and political parties. They operate as a facilitating mechanism that enables the appropriation of resources from one field to the other, capturing issues and forms of action, and even coopting activists from the social movement arena. Indeed, the M5S attracts local movements' activists because they tend to see it as a means to give visibility to their claims in the political agenda and to open windows of opportunity for issues neglected by institutions.

Unconventional Forms of Action Inside and Outside Institutions

After the foregoing short overview of overlapping memberships, consideration of the M5S's action repertoire is useful to complete the picture. As seen, around 12 per cent of M5S MPs declared familiarity with unconventional forms of action. The tactical emulation and imitation in terms of repertoire of action typical of resource-poor actors is functional for the M5S to gain media attention and public visibility (Lipsky 1968).

Rallies and marches had been organised by Grillo before the official birth of the M5S. The M5S's repertoire of action comprises forms of unconventional action that have not been discarded since the movement's entry into the national parliament: occupations, public protests, sit-ins, and demonstrations have often been used by M5S MPs. The importance of unconventional action was confirmed by Grillo in December 2013, when he organised the third V-Day in Genoa to go 'beyond' simple opposition. This was a follow-up to the V-Days of 2007 (Bologna) and 2008 (Turin), mass demonstrations which anticipated some of the most important claims put forward by the M5S (see Chapter 1).

To ratify their closeness to the campaign against high-speed trains, one month after the general elections of 2013 a large group of M5S MPs joined a demonstration organised by the No Tav movement in Val di Susa to oppose a project enjoying bipartisan consensus in the national and regional parliaments. On that occasion, the spokesperson of M5S senators stated:

> The high-speed train between Turin and Lyon is one of our main battles. Definitely one of the next things to do is establish a commission of inquiry on the

> Tav [to shed light on] the abuses that have been committed, the breaches of the regulations, and the use of force against the protesters. (Huffington Post 2013)

He also added 'we consider the Tav useless, we hope to be able to prove this and stop its construction' (*Il Fatto Quotidiano* 2013a). During the same day, on the other side of the peninsula (Calabria, in the far south), three MPs took part in a demonstration against water privatisation in Vibo Valentia. As one of them noted, referring to the demonstration in Val di Susa: 'different regions but the same battle for common goods' (*Il Dispaccio* 2013).

Some months later, elected M5S representatives organised a sit-in outside the Rai national public television centre to protest against its editorial policy (*La Repubblica* 2013a).

In October, some M5S MPs demonstrated outside the Tirreno Power electricity company in Vado Ligure to protest against the use of coke and the project to expand the local thermal power plant (*La Stampa* 2013a).

In December, the movement's MPs took part in a nocturnal sit-in organised outside the headquarters of the ministry of the economy to press for the creation of a fund generated by the restitution of part of M5S MPs' monthly salary and reserved for small and medium-sized enterprises (*La Repubblica* 2013b).

These are only some examples of protests organised or joined by the movement's MPs. However, as will be shown below, the real novelty consists in the unconventional forms of action undertaken by M5S elected representatives, not just outside institutions but also internally to them. The interesting aspect is that forms of confrontation disrupting normal parliamentary routine have been brought from the streets into the representative institutions by members of those same institutions. The protest actions staged by M5S MPs within the institution par excellence (the parliament) often consist of filibustering and symbolic acts with high spectacular content intended to attract media coverage because their 'fundamental communicative elements are public visibility and the "dramatizing" of tones' (Bordignon and Ceccarini 2014). There are only a few and sporadic antecedents of such practice in the Italian parliament's history, and they can be mostly associated with the Partito Radicale and the Lega Nord (Biorcio 2003; Tarchi 2003; Novelli 2006). This phenomenon relates to a process of mediatisation and popularisation (Mazzoleni and Schulz 1999; Mazzoleni and Sfardini 2009) that has deeply affected politics and institutions in recent decades. Representative institutions, in fact, have shifted from being places for discussion among MPs to loci of public exposition under the media gaze (Novelli 2006). Actions staged by the M5S's MPs within the parliament are often symbolic in nature 'clearly addressed to the television cameras rather than to the colleagues who are present … even though those events are not new in some respects, the 5 Star MPs push the exceptionality further, transforming it into a true 'style' of parliamentary action' (Bordignon and Ceccarini 2014). Some examples of unconventional action in the chambers of parliament follow.

In April 2013, M5S MPs occupied the parliament to protest against the institutional delay in forming a government following the general elections of

February 2013, and to demand that a central role be restored to the representative assembly (*La Stampa* 2013b).

In September 2013, a group of M5S MPs occupied the roof of the lower chamber to oppose a reform of the constitution that they considered illegitimate from the procedural point of view. This act resembled the student and worker protests of previous years (Caruso et al. 2010). As the MPs put it:

> We act like the blue-collar workers who climb onto the roofs of factories to protest. This is the only way to wake up a sleeping country. We have done everything possible by tabling amendments and asking for discussion in plenary session, but we have been ignored. We have nothing else left to do. (*Il Fatto Quotidiano* 2013b)

In December, a noisy protest took place in the lower chamber. It resulted in mutual accusations among party representatives, clashes, and sanctions on the M5S MPs who occupied the government benches to oppose ratification of an agreement among Albania, Greece and Italy on construction of a 'Trans Adriatic Pipeline' (TAP) believed likely to damage the environment of the Apulian coast (Spagnolo 2013).

However, unconventional action within institutions escalated in January 2014 – 'two days of guerrilla warfare' according to *Il Fatto Quotidiano* (2014) – when a bill reforming the electoral system seemed about to be passed by the parliament without the M5S's support. During a parliamentary debate on revaluation of the shares of private shareholders in the national bank (Bankitalia), M5S MPs occupied the government bench as well as the commission for constitutional affairs. They shouted, hurled insults, and physically confronted other MPs. They verbally attacked the president of the lower chamber for blocking their filibustering with a 'guillotine',[11] and they also opened a formal procedure for impeachment of the president of the republic.

This effort to 'de-institutionalise the institutions' by the M5S MPs (Bordignon and Ceccarini 2014) was obviously intended to direct public attention to certain issues via means particularly suited to attracting media coverage.

Geographical Proximity to Social Movements

Despite Tarrow's call for closer attention to be played to electoral contention – defined as 'a set of recurring links between elections and movements that powerfully

11 This is a procedure included in the regulations of the senate (but not explicitly foreseen by the regulations of the lower chamber) that can be employed by the president of the assembly in cases of filibustering to grant the right of the parliamentary majority to convert a decree into law without examination of all the amendments after a certain period of time (*La Repubblica* 2014).

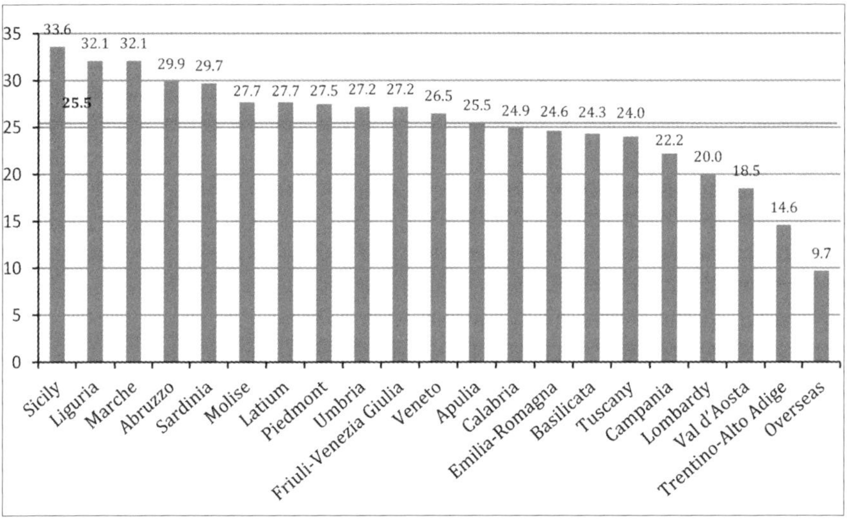

Figure 7.1 The M5S's electoral penetration by region (percentages)
Source: Elaboration on Ministry of the Interior data (http://elezioni.interno.it).

shape movement dynamics and electoral outcomes' (2012, p.94) – and regardless of a growing body of empirical evidence on relations between movements and elections, 'these remain largely separate areas of inquiry in both sociology and political science' (ibid.). The Italian case may offer a significant opportunity to start filling this gap in the literature.

Another way to investigate the M5S's closeness to social movements, in fact, is to analyse its electoral results so as to determine whether there is an association between the presence of strong local conflicts and votes gained in a particular geographical area. An investigation of this kind certainly risks giving social conflicts greater weight than they effectively have in influencing electoral behaviour. However, the purpose of this exploratory analysis is not to establish a direct and causal relationship between social conflicts and electoral outcomes. With this caveat in mind, mapping the main areas of social conflict and trying to match them with electoral results can still be considered a fruitful exercise.

The attention will focus on areas where Grillo gained more votes in the lower chamber in the general elections of 2013, bearing in mind that the national average percentage for his party was 25.5 per cent. After a first inspection of the results, one notes that out of 20 regions, 3 had the highest shares of votes for Grillo (over 30 per cent): Liguria, Marche and Sicily (Figure 7.1). As already said, all these are regions characterised by significant territorial conflicts.

As Table 7.2 shows, in 15 provinces (out of a total of 110) the M5S gained over 30 per cent of the votes: 6 were located in Sicily, 4 in Marche, 3 in Liguria, 1 in the eastern part of Emilia-Romagna (Rimini), and 1 in the northern part of Latium (Viterbo). The previous sections have already discussed the importance of resistance against the MUOS in Sicily (Caltanissetta) where there is also fierce opposition to the US military base in Sigonella (Catania) and the pollution generated by the biggest oil refinery in Europe (Siracusa), as well as popular resistance against oil drilling (Trapani).[12] In Liguria, there are various conflicts centered on new highways (Genoa), high-speed trains, thermal power plants (Savona), and garbage dumps (Imperia). In regard to Marche, during the past decade a dense network of committees has mobilised on environmental issues, and the results of this activation were already evident in the 2012 municipal elections (Gobbi 2012). Concerning Latium, a coordination of self-styled 'No coke' groups has been active for years in the Viterbo province (Binotto 2012a) and may have partly contributed to the M5S's electoral success in that area. As for Emilia-Romagna, mobilisations against a project for rapid bus transit along the coast between Riccione and Rimini started in 2011. They were soon supported by the M5S, whose three representatives elected to the local assembly called for a referendum to oppose its construction. They denounced the poor management of the local bank and the local airport, whose governing bodies consisted of representatives of the dominant local party (Partito Democratico).

Table 7.2 Provinces with greatest M5S electoral penetration (percentages)

Provinces	%	s.d.
Ragusa (Sicily)	38.26	3.9
Trapani (Sicily)	38.13	5.3
Siracusa (Sicily)	36.91	5.7
Imperia (Liguria)	34.02	5.1
Caltanissetta (Sicily)	33.55	6.1
Agrigento (Sicily)	33.42	7.3
Rimini (Emilia-Romagna)	33.42	3.7
Savona (Liguria)	32.76	5.0
Catania (Sicily)	32.72	5.1
Pesaro and Urbino (Marche)	32.18	6.2
Fermo (Marche)	32.04	3.2
Genoa (Liguria)	31.93	6.5
Ancona (Marche)	31.83	3.8
Ascoli Piceno (Marche)	30.91	4.7
Viterbo (Latium)	30.27	4.7

Source: Elaboration on Ministry of the Interior data (http://elezioni.interno.it).

12 Interestingly, in July 2013 M5S MPs, regional representatives, and local activists organised a 'No oil tour' of Sicilian industrial areas to show their environmental risks and heighten awareness of the 'dark side of black gold' (Movimento 5 Stelle Sicilia 2013).

In order to relate local conflicts to votes, individual municipalities were also considered. According to the data, in 106 municipalities (out of a total of over 8,000) the M5S gained more than 40 per cent of votes, and in 431 more than 35 per cent. In the first seven municipalities – all located in Piedmont (six in the province of Turin and one in the province of Cuneo) – the M5S electoral consensus was over 50 per cent. These are small municipalities for the most part located in Val di Susa, and they can be easily related to the No Tav campaign. Significantly, the municipality of Venaus – one of the symbols of the No Tav movement – is where the M5S gained the highest share of its votes (58.1 per cent).

Among the 30 municipalities in which the movement gained over 45 per cent of the votes, at least 19 were affected by significant territorial conflicts. If we consider the 105 municipalities where the movement gained more than 40 per cent, at least 54 were affected by major local conflicts: among them, those concerning the Tav, the MUOS, the Gronda, thermal power plants, oil drilling and the Ilva factory in Taranto.

Other local conflicts not mentioned above can help explain, at least partially, electoral results in other areas. Among them, of substantial importance appears the opposition against a pipeline in the Gulf of Trieste, the campaign against an incinerator plant in Parma, protests against garbage dumps in Albano and Bracciano (Rome), workers' mobilisation against closure of the Alcoa aluminum factory of Portovesme and miners' opposition to cessation of Carbosulcis in Gonnesa (Sardinia), popular opposition against oil drilling in Pisticci and Policoro (Basilicata) as well as a national nuclear waste storage plant in Scanzano Ionico (Binotto, 2012b), and mobilisations against pipelines in Galatina and Brindisi in Apulia.

Concluding, to be noted is that: a) most territorial conflicts associated with good electoral performances by the M5S concern environmental issues, and only rarely other themes such as factory closures or restructuring; b) Abruzzo seems an 'outlier' in the relation between protest and electoral outcomes: it is a region with significant electoral penetration by the M5S in some provinces but less active in term of social conflict (mostly focused on oil extraction).

Colonising and Appropriating Social Movement Forms and Struggles

Before concluding, it should be stressed once again that the distinctive nature of the M5S and its proximity to social movements pertains to a peculiar political creature and should not be overstated. Indeed – as demonstrated in other chapters in this book – the M5S differs from the other Italian parties also in terms of its organisational structure, communication strategies, democratic conceptions and practices, etc.

This chapter has considered three main dimensions in order to investigate the M5S's proximity to social movements: a) programmatic proximity (by analysing its campaigns and electoral manifestos at the local and national level);

b) biographical proximity (by examining the profiles of M5S MPs and other elected representatives at the local level in order to find references to unconventional forms of action and multiple belongings); c) geographical proximity (by investigating its electoral outcomes in areas characterised by strong social conflicts).

As the analysis has shown, albeit in a fuzzy, contradictory and inconsistent way, the M5S has captured activists, grievances, claims and action forms from social movements of the past decade.

In terms of issues, M5S claims range from open hostility to war to defence of 'common goods', from opposition against large-scale infrastructures and incinerators to demands for civil rights, from support for consumer protection campaigns to condemnation of acts of violence by the police. Contentious themes have been colonised and appropriated over time by local groups and activists, and by Grillo through his blog.

In regard to activists, a significant proportion of elected M5S representatives in parliament and local assemblies originate from the social movement milieu, and also from leading positions in local mobilisations. In fact, they conceive the M5S as a chance to make their claims more visible and resonant in the policy arena: elected representatives tend to act as spokespersons of territorial grievances, facilitating access to data and institutional opportunities that can be publicly disclosed and shared (Lanfrey 2011, p. 163). As one M5S MP claimed: 'The choice of being a candidate is due to the desire to give voice to all these people, bringing into the parliament and translating into law all the experiments that grassroots movements have done, within associations and local committees'.[13]

Unconventional forms of action have been imported into the institutional arena by elected representatives actively involved in local conflicts and with multiple belongings.

This appropriation of issues and repertoires is clearly apparent in the biographies of M5S MPs and in the movement's electoral manifestos. This proximity can be considered as one factor (among others) explaining the electoral successes of the M5S. Although a direct and casual relationship between conflict appropriation and electoral success cannot be proved empirically, the data show that, in many cases, the provinces and municipalities in which the M5S has obtained most of its votes are characterised by strong territorial conflicts captured by Grillo's political creature.

Once protests enter the public arena, Grillo and the M5S rapidly appropriate them, sharing activists, frames and forms of action with newborn movements and campaigns. More in general, Grillo seems to embrace a strategy of attunement with different sectors of public opinion. When a conflict arises, he immediately sides with the protesters through personal participation and public declarations on his blog. However, as Caruso has observed, the relation that Grillo establishes with other social movements with which he shares specific campaigns is a peculiar one:

13 https://sistemaoperativom5s.beppegrillo.it/candidati/luigi_gallo.html [Accessed 17 February 2014].

> 'Now I represent you' is the message. 'In my comprehensive message there is also room for you, you do not need to express your own point of view' … Rarely is this relation a joint effort, a shared purpose. More often the M5S works independently and in 'parallel' on the same issues as pursued by social movements, trying to represent them electorally and presenting those struggles as its own. (Caruso 2013)

As a former spokesperson of the M5S in the lower chamber declared to the leader of the Partito Democratico during a meeting held to explore the M5S's willingness to support a centre-left government and which was streamed online: 'We don't meet the social bodies [trade union and enterprise representatives] because we are the social bodies' (Bordignon 2013, p. 218).

To conclude: although the M5S has been considered a positive development by some social movement activists, who have personally engaged with it, the movement has some peculiar features that impede the consolidation of an ongoing alliance with social movements. Diani and Fabbri (2014) see three main factors that hinder continuing cooperation: a) a limited coalitional capacity due to the rejection of strategic collaborations with groups somehow linked to existing political parties; b) substantial dependency on a hierarchical and unelected leadership; c) absolute denial of the left/right cleavage that still retains salience for social movement activists.

References

Ansa. 2006. Quadrilatero: rete no pav marche, presidio contro progetto, regione esca ambiguità, chiesto un consiglio con Beppe Grillo. *Ansa* [online] 30 March. Available at: http://89.97.204.228/fparticolipdf/106371.pdf [Accessed 17 February 2014].

Baldolini, S. 2013. No Tav, Val di Susa. Intervista a Alberto Perino: 'Con Grillo veri compagni di viaggio, il M5s prenderà percentuali bulgare in Val di Susa'. *L'Huffington Post* [online] 14 February. Available at: http://www.huffingtonpost.it/2013/02/14/con-grillo-veri-compagni-di-viaggio-il-m5s-prendera-percentuali-bulgare-in-val-di-susa_n_2685795.html [Accessed 17 February 2014].

Binotto, M. 2012b. La lezione di Scansano. In: A. Caramis and R. Rega, eds. 2012. *Conflitti insostenibili. Media, società civile e politiche nelle controversie ambientali*. Roma: Edizioni Nuova Cultura. pp. 129–91.

———. 2012a. Giocarsi la centrale. Un esperimento di analisi dei conflitti politico-territoriali come 'modelli di gioco'. In: A. Caramis and R. Rega, eds. *Conflitti insostenibili. Media, società civile e politiche nelle controversie ambientali*. Roma: Edizioni Nuova Cultura. pp. 219–55.

Biorcio, R. 2003. The Lega Nord and the Italian Media System. In: G. Mazzoleni, J. Stewart and B. Horsfield, eds. *The Media and Neo-populism: A Contemporary Comparative Analysis*. Westport and London: Praeger Publishers, pp. 71–94.

Biorcio, R. and Natale, P. 2013. *Politica a 5 stelle. Idee, storia e strategie del movimento di Grillo*. Milano: Feltrinelli.

Bordignon, F. 2013. *Il partito del capo. Da Berlusconi a Renzi*. Rimini: Maggioli.

Bordignon, F. and Ceccarini, L. 2013. Five Stars and a Cricket. Beppe Grillo Shakes Italian Politics. *South European Society and Politics*, 18(4), pp. 427–49.

———. 2014. The 5 Star People and the Unconventional Parliament. *Studia Politica. Romanian Political Science Review*, 1.

Caruso, L. 2010. *Il territorio della politica. La nuova partecipazione di massa nei movimenti No Tav e Dal Molin*. Milano: FrancoAngeli.

———. 2013. Un movimento bifronte. *Il Manifesto* [online] 9 March. Available at: http://www.albasoggettopoliticonuovo.it/2013/03/un-movimento-bifronte-di-loris-caruso-il-manifesto-9-marzo-2013 [Accessed 17 February 2014].

Caruso, L., Giorgi, A., Mattoni, A. and Piazza, G., eds. 2010. *Alla ricerca dell'Onda. I nuovi conflitti nell'istruzione superiore*. Milano: FrancoAngeli.

Cernison, M. 2013. *Online Communication Spheres in Social Movements Campaigns: The Italian Referendum on Water*. PhD thesis. Fiesole: European University Institute.

Corrigall-Brown, C. 2012. *Patterns of Protest: Trajectories of Participation in Social Movements*. Stanford: Stanford University Press.

Dallara, C. 2015. Berlusconi's impact and legacy on the Italian judicial system. *Modern Italy*, 20(1), forthcoming.

Davies, L. 2013. Italy Hit by Wave of Pitchfork Protests as Austerity Unites Disparate Groups. *The Guardian* [online] 13 December. Available at: http://www.theguardian.com/world/2013/dec/13/italy-pitchfork-protests-austerity-unites-groups [Accessed 17 February 2014].

della Porta, D., Andretta, M., Mosca, L. and Reiter, H. 2006. *Globalization from Below. Transnational Activists and Protest Networks*. Minneapolis and London: Minnesota Press.

della Porta, D., and Diani, M. 2004. 'No to the War with No Ifs or Buts': Protests against the War in Iraq. In: V. Della Sala and S. Fabbrini, eds. *Italy between Europeanization and Domestic Politics*. New York and Oxford: Berghahn books, pp. 200–218.

———. 2006. *Social Movements: An Introduction*. Second edition. London: Wiley-Blackwell.

della Porta, D. and Piazza, G. 2008. *Voices of the Valley, Voices of the Straits: How Protest Creates Communities*. New York: Berghahn Books.

della Porta D. and Reiter, H. 2004. *Polizia e protesta. L'ordine pubblico dalla Liberazione ai 'no global'*. Bologna: Il Mulino.

Diani M. and Fabbri, M. 2014. Social Movements Italian-Style: When Non-Party Organizations Matter. In: A. Mammone, G.A. Veltri and E.G. Parini,

eds. *Handbook of Contemporary Italy: History, Politics, and Society*. London: Routledge.
Gabel M. and Hix, S. 2002. Defining the EU political space. An Empirical Study of the European Elections Manifestos, 1979–1999. *Comparative Political Studies*, 35(8), pp. 934–64.
Gobbi, O. 2012. Le centinaia di comitati delle Marche. in difesa del paesaggio. In: A. Pizzo and P. Sullo, eds. *No Tav d'Italia. Facce e ragioni dei cittadini che difendono il territorio*. Napoli: Intra Moenia. pp. 199–212.
Grillo, B. 2011. Open letter to Antonio Manganelli. *Beppegrillo.it* [blog] 20 July. Available at: http://www.beppegrillo.it/en/2011/07/20/open_letter_to_antonio_mangane.html [Accessed 17 February 2014].
———. 2012a. Soldier Blue. *Beppegrillo.it* [blog] 15 November. Available at: www.beppegrillo.it/en/2012/11/soldier_blue.html [Accessed 17 February 2014].
———. 2012b. Grillo for Dummies. *Beppegrillo.it* [blog] 6 November. Available at: www.beppegrillo.it/2012/11/grillo_for_dummies.html Accessed 17 February 2014].
———. 2013a. Grillo con i lavoratori a Genova. *Beppegrillo.it* [blog] 22 November. Available at: www.beppegrillo.it/2013/11/beppe_grillo_con_i_lavoratori_a_genova.html [Accessed 17 February 2014].
———. 2013b. Open Letter to the Leaders of the Security Forces. *Beppegrillo.it* [blog] 11 December. Available at: www.beppegrillo.it/en/2013/12/open_letter_to_the_leaders_of.html [Accessed 17 February 2014].
———. 2013c. The Crime of Clandestinity. *Beppegrillo.it* [blog] 10 October. Available at: www.beppegrillo.it/en/2013/10/the_crime_of_clandestinity.html [Accessed 17 February 2014].
Huffington Post. 2013. No Tav: il giorno della marcia Susa-Bussoleno, parlamentari M5s e Sel in cantiere, Crimi: 'Chiederemo commissione d'inchiesta'. *L'Huffington Post* [online] 23 March. Available at: http://www.huffingtonpost.it/2013/03/23/no-tav-il-giorno-della-ma_n_2938415.html [Accessed 17 February 2014].
Il Dispaccio. 2013. Vibo, parlamentari del Movimento 5 Stelle alla manifestazione 'No Alaco': 'Ricorreremo a tutti gli strumenti che il Parlamento ci metterà a disposizione'. *Il Dispaccio*, [online] 23 March. Available at: http://ildispaccio.it/vibo-valentia/18994-vibo-parlamentari-del-movimento-5-stelle-alla-manifestazione-no-alaco-ricorreremo-a-tutti-gli-strumenti-che-il-parlamento-ci-mettera-a-disposizione [Accessed 17 February 2014].
Il Fatto Quotidiano. 2013a. Val Susa, in migliaia al corteo No Tav. Cinque Stelle: 'Commissione d'inchiesta'. *Il Fatto Quotidiano* [online] 23 March. Available at: http://www.ilfattoquotidiano.it/2013/03/23/val-susa-parlamentari-5-stelle-ai-cantieri-tav-militarizzazione-assurda/539765 [Accessed 17 February 2014].
———. 2013b. Riforma della Costituzione, i 5 Stelle occupano il tetto della Camera per protesta. *Il Fatto Quotidiano* [online] 6 September. Available at: http://www.ilfattoquotidiano.it/2013/09/06/riforma-della-costituzione-5-stelle-occupano-tetto-della-camera-per-protesta/703283 [Accessed 17 February 2014].

———. 2014. Camera, due giorni di guerriglia. Boldrini a M5S: 'Minacce e violenze, ora sanzioni'. *Il Fatto Quotidiano* [online] 30 January. Available at: http://www.ilfattoquotidiano.it/2014/01/30/camera-due-giorni-di-guerriglia-m5s-ricorso-contro-ok-a-italicum-in-commissione/862619 [Accessed 17 February 2014].

La Repubblica. 2013a. Grillo, lite con Letta sul Porcellum. E i Cinque stelle 'occupano' la Rai. *La Repubblica* [online] 30 September. Available at: http://www.repubblica.it/politica/2013/09/30/news/grillo_rai-67574973 [Accessed 17 February 2014].

———. 2013b. Stipendi tagliati, sit-in del M5S per poterli restituire. *La Repubblica* [online] 17 December. Available at: http://www.repubblica.it/politica/2013/12/17/news/restitution_day_m5s-73832478 [Accessed 17 February 2014].

———. 2014. Parlamento, ecco cos'è la ghigliottina. *La Repubblica* [online] 29 January. Available at: http://www.repubblica.it/politica/2014/01/29/news/parlamento_ecco_cos_la_ghigliottina-77239250 [Accessed 17 February 2014].

La Stampa. 2013a. 'Assedio' dei Cinque Stelle alla Tirreno Power di Vado. *La Stampa Savona* [online] 26 October. Available at: http://www.lastampa.it/2013/10/26/edizioni/savona/assedio-dei-cinque-stelle-alla-tirreno-power-di-vado-naHdzsfsw9JKAfYT7xdFjL/pagina.html [Accessed 17 February 2014].

———. 2013b. La sfida dei Cinque Stelle: occuperemo il Parlamento. *La Stampa* [online] 8 April. Available at: http://www.lastampa.it/2013/04/08/italia/politica/i-stelle-confermanoa-l-occupazione-delle-camere-ora-basta-scherzare-xOWSYGeAJuOIwdBPKwHeVO/pagina.html [Accessed 17 February 2014].

Lanfrey, D. 2011. Il MoVimento dei grillini tra meetup, meta-organizzazione e democrazia del monitoraggio. In: L. Mosca and C. Vaccari, eds. 2012. *Nuovi media, nuova politica? Partecipazione e mobilitazione online da MoveOn al MoVimento 5 stelle*. Milan: Franco Angeli, pp.143–66.

Lipsky, M. 1968. Protest as a Political Resource. *The American Political Science Review*, 62(4), pp. 1,144–58.

Mazzoleni, G. and Schulz, W. 1999. 'Mediatization' of Politics: A Challenge for Democracy. *Political Communication*, 16(3), pp. 247–61.

Mazzoleni, G., and Sfardini, A. 2009. *Politica pop. Da 'Porta a Porta' a 'L'isola dei famosi'*. Bologna: Il Mulino.

Mosca, L. 2013. A Year of Social Movements in Italy: From the No-Tavs to the Five-Star Movement. In: A. di Virgilio and C. Radaelli, eds. *Italian Politics: Technocrats in Office*. New York: Berghahn, pp. 267–85.

Mosca, L., and Santucci, D. 2009. Petitioning Online. The Role of E-Petitions in Web Campaigning. In: S. Baringhorst, J. Niesyto and V. Kneip, eds. *Political Campaigning on the Web*. Bielefeld: Transcript. pp. 121–46.

Movimento 5 Stelle Sicilia. 2013. Riflettori sui rischi delle zone industriali siciliane. Parte il 'No oil tour' con parlamentari e attivisti M5S. *sicilia5stelle.it* [online] 10 July. Available at: http://www.sicilia5stelle.it/2013/07/riflettori-sui-rischi-delle-zone-industriali-siciliane-parte-il-no-oil-tour-con-parlamentari-e-attivisti-m5s [Accessed 17 February 2014].

Novelli, E. 2006. *La turbopolitica. Sessant'anni di comunicazione politica e scena pubblica in Italia*. Milano: Bur Rizzoli.

Passy, F. and Giugni, M. 2000. Life-Spheres, Networks, and Sustained Participation in Social Movements: A Phenomenological Approach to Political Commitment. *Sociological Forum*, 15(1), pp. 117–44.

Pini, V. 2013. Sul web lo sconcerto dei militanti M5S. 'Grasso non può essere paragonato a Schifani'. *La Repubblica* [online] 16 March. Available at: http://www.repubblica.it/politica/2013/03/16/news/sul_web_m5s_boccia_schifani-54696196 [Accessed 17 February 2014].

Spagnolo, C. 2013. Gasdotto Tap, è bagarre alla Camera. Il governo spalle al muro sui tempi. *La Repubblica Bari* [online] 4 December. Available at: http://bari.repubblica.it/cronaca/2013/12/04/news/gasdotto_tap-72701125 [Accessed 17 February 2014].

Tarchi, M., 2003. *L'Italia populista. Dal qualunquismo ai girotondi*. Bologna: Il Mulino.

Tarrow, S. 2012. *Strangers at the gates. Movements and states in contentious politics*. Cambridge: Cambridge University Press.

Tropeano, M. 2012. Baita abusiva a Chiomonte. Grillo e 21 No Tav a processo. *La Stampa*, [online] 3 May. Available at: http://www.lastampa.it/2012/05/03/cronaca/baita-abusiva-a-chiomontegrillo-e-no-tav-a-processo-ZOHD4IcJ3purdmKnY7RLXO/pagina.html [Accessed 17 February 2014].

Verhulst, J. and Walgrave, S. 2010. The Issues and Context behind the Demonstrations. In: S. Walgrave and D. Rucht, eds. *The World Says No to War. Demonstrations against the War on Iraq*. Minneapolis and London: University of Minnesota Press, pp. 42–60.

Documents

doc. NP: national program
doc. RPB: regional program Basilicata
doc. RPER: regional program Emilia-Romagna
doc. RPFVG: regional program Friuli-Venezia Giulia
doc. RPLA: regional program Latium
doc. RPLO: regional program Lombardy
doc. RPP: regional program Piedmont
doc. RPS: regional program Sicily
doc. PPT provincial program Trentino
doc. MPG: municipal program Genoa
doc. MPP: municipal program Parma
doc. MPR: municipal program Ragusa
doc. MPTA: municipal program Taranto
doc. MPTU: municipal program Turin

doc. MDCRS: motion for denial of confidence to the regional governor of Sicily (*allegato all'ordine del giorno della seduta del 29 ottobre 2013*)
doc. MTBRS: initiative aimed at revoking oil drilling in Valle del Belice (*iniziative finalizzate alla revoca delle trivellazioni nella Valle del Belice*)

Chapter 8

A Vote(r) Like Any Other? Exploring the Protest Component in the Vote for the Movimento 5 Stelle

Gianluca Passarelli and Dario Tuorto

Introduction

The electoral success of the Movimento 5 Stelle (M5S) has often been interpreted as the result of its ability to occupy the space of radical protest against the forces of the "old politics", identified first and foremost with the existing parties and their leaders. *Tutti a casa*! (Everybody home!) is the rallying cry that best states the movement's ambition to promote a radical renovation of the Italian political elite. The combined effect of this anti-party stance, a (quasi) charismatic leadership and an aggressive electoral campaign, is that the M5S has been, perhaps too simply, labelled as a populist party. Indeed, some specifically populist traits are present in the movement's rhetoric and political action. In particular, the dualism of 'we' (the people) against 'them' (the politicians), which basically represents the core of populist thinking (Hermet 2001) – has been widely stressed as a message and as a tool for the party's propaganda. Thanks to its intrinsic capacity to include movements of all sorts, in the case of M5S the term populism has been used especially by commentators and politicians. After all, the populist tradition has a long history in Italy (Tarchi 2003), but only the recent decline of all the other parties (Lega Nord, Popolo della Libertà) (Passarelli and Tuorto 2012, 2013), which, in recent years, exploited this 'political capital', has produced the conditions for a new political and electoral scenario.

That said, the reference to populism in this case might be considered, to some extent, misleading. Indeed, the label appears, at the same time, too vague and too general. The axiom 'this is a populist party, *so* its voters are populist as well' is of no help if the aim is to understand what underlies electoral choices. Populism is often treated as a *catch-all* category in which parties and voters are contained, where the attention is focused mainly on the parties' characteristics and strategies rather than on voters' motivations. On the contrary, the concept of *protest voting*, which has also been widely used to identify Beppe Grillo's supporters, appears more theoretically grounded and useful when attempting to explain voting behaviour. By shifting the attention from populism to protest, the focus falls on concepts such as political distrust, discontent, resentment, all those attitudes and opinions which citizens develop and address to the democratic system, the 'establishment', the elite, and the (incumbent) governments or, in general, to the 'old' parties.

The partially unexpected result in the 2013 elections (Bordignon and Ceccarini 2013), when M5S obtained 25 per cent of the votes, radically changed the Italian political scenario, but it also gives rise to a significant research question: to what extent and for how many voters did the anti-political sentiments really lead to the decision to choose M5S? (Passarelli et al. 2012). Was it mainly a protest vote or a 'normal' vote driven by values or opinions on policies?[1] In order to measure the effectiveness of the 'protest' component in M5S voters it is appropriate, as a first step, to carefully clarify and define what political protest is, against which objects or actors it is addressed and which voters make use of these arguments and resources to orient themselves in the electoral arena. Once the analytical dimensions have been laid out, it becomes more fruitful to attempt to test the hypothesis of the vote for M5S as a protest vote.

The Concept of Protest Vote

From a Downsian perspective protest voting is basically irrational. If voters do not cast their votes for the party that is closest to their policy preferences, then they should not vote at all. On the other hand, if voters no longer prefer party A, but instead rank party B higher, then protest voting disappears in favour of a simple switch of alignments (Kang, 2004). Political protest in disaffected voters may produce both deliberate abstention and voting for an 'extremist' party, or a new or outcast party. Politically dissatisfied voters may temporarily withdraw their support from their preferred candidate/party even if that party has a good chance of winning, in the hope that this signal of disaffection will lead to downstream improvements in that candidate's/party's performance (Kselman and Niou 2011). This motive makes protest voting an expression of voice rather than an exit, a strategic behaviour known under the term 'voting with the boot' (Van der Eijk and Franklin 1996). Moreover, protest voting could reflect not only and simply an expression of disaffection. Indeed, it should also include an element of attraction for 'different' parties. But which type of parties? Some of the parties that may be included in this list are, of course, the anti-system parties. For Sartori (1976, p. 133), a party qualifies as anti-system if it 'would not change – if it could – the government, but the very system of government'. As a further specification, Sartori adds that 'not all the anti-system parties are such in the same sense: the negation covers, or may cover, a wide span of different attitudes ranging from "alienation" and total refusal to "protest"' (Ibidem, p. 132). This definition applies above all to extreme leftist and rightist parties, but also secessionist and religious fundamentalist parties can be included in the category and, more generally, parties

1 For an analysis of issue- or value-based voting decisions for the M5S, see Colloca and Corbetta's chapter in this volume.

that undermine the legitimacy of the regime in which they operate, like populist or new radical right parties.

A conceptual clarification is necessary when the protest vote is considered in relation to, and sometimes as a synonym of, apathy. Protest voting is *not* in itself an apathetic behaviour: it assumes the configuration of a complete electoral act lived as a disaffection against the established parties and/or those usually voted for. While political apathy refers to (political) indifference and a sense of estrangement from (or rejection of) the prevailing political system, political protest seems to be more strictly linked to a condition of political alienation and implies a certain (minimal) connection with the political system, even when it is configured as alienation against *all*.

The debate on the protest vote is flourishing and, although there is no unique shared definition of such a phenomenon (and corresponding parties that should attract protest), it is probably more fruitful to concentrate on those common features and methodological tools that may be used to measure it. In literature, the 'protest vote' is generally considered a vote primarily cast to scare the elite, but also a vote in which political attitudes are expected to be of minor importance (Van der Brug et al. 2000). The idea of protest voting necessitates something against which these voters are protesting, some kind of disapproval, the result of political distrust (Bergh, 2004). A vote for non-established parties incorporates in its anti-elitist position a certain amount of dissatisfaction, and is expected to frighten or shock the élites from mainstream parties (Van der Brug and Fennema 2007).

These definitions allow us to narrow down the field of interest to a vote: a) against the establishment; b) not driven by policy preferences. With regard to the first aspect – a vote 'against' – a protest in a ballot box is given when citizens make a choice expressing a certain amount of radicalism, criticism, dissatisfaction against the established parties in the national parliament, even without any sentiment of true and genuine sympathy for a party that they could vote for (Bowler and Lanoue 1992; Van der Brug et al. 2000; Van der Eijk and Franklin 2009). Protest voting may be defined as the level of dissatisfaction with how the established parties and system, as well as the government and the parliament, have performed. On the basis of these different objects of protest, Bergh (2004) has differentiated the political protest into two distinct but interrelated dimensions corresponding to 'system discontent' and 'elite discontent'. The former is directed at the political system and the elements of the established democratic politics such as party politicians in general, institutions or the functioning of democracy. The latter selects, as its target, the incumbent government and its performance in terms of its day-to-day policy outputs, but also other parties including those in opposition (Hosch-Dayican 2011).

To what extent was the M5S's electoral success due to a general resentment against the established parties, the so-called *casta* (the clique)? Did it mainly refer to more specific and reasoned evaluations about political actors, their responsiveness and ability to handle crucial issues? Or, did the voters cast their vote for M5S because they were active, genuine supporters of the party? This question partially recalls the distinction between 'instrumental' and 'expressive' voting (Brennan and Hamlin, 1998). An instrumental voter is mainly led by the motivation of having an influence; the voter elaborates a rational, deliberate calculation of cost-benefits and, for this, needs some knowledge about party programmes and policy positions. An expressive voter, on the other hand, would not necessarily be interested in the outcome of the election or driven by specific parties' policy positions, because benefits and costs derive from expressing support or opposition to the candidates/system as an end in itself (Brennan 2001, p. 225). In terms of the protest vote, this latter position implies that the focus has to be placed on political alienation rather than on policy preferences or attitudes, because voters are mobilised mainly by the need to express their grievances and are less interested in the programme or policy positions of the party (Van der Brug et al. 2000; Van der Brug and Fennema 2007). As a means of expressing lack of support for the government, the protest vote should concern all those parties perceived as being far from government influence, regardless of their ideological position (Bergh 2004). In contrast, if a protest vote is read as instrumental, it stands for more than a generic punishment for established parties. New parties would gain 'protest votes' also by emphasising some issues that are important to a growing and relevant share of voters (Van der Eijk and Franklin, 2009). In this view, voters may combine political dissatisfaction with ideological and issue considerations such as left-right position (Van der Brug, 1998) and attitudes toward immigration, as in the case of extreme right or populist right parties (Ignazi 2003; Mudde 2007; Rooduijn 2012). Or, in other terms, there may be a spurious effect, when the policy preferences are the real cause of an apparent protest effect and protest voters distrust the politicians only because they see the issue differently (Bergh 2004).

An important corollary of this debate concerns the assumptions about the socio-political profiles of protest voters. A piece of literature on radical right parties focused on the so-called 'angry white men' or 'losers of modernity' (Betz 1998), those categories of manual workers with lower education who might lose their jobs as a result of the rapid changes occurring in post-industrial societies and who feel insecure. However, this model provides only a partial explanation for the vote for populist parties, especially the most important and successful ones, which are generally representative of all social strata (Van der Brug and Fennema 2009). Given the peculiar socio-demographic characteristics of the M5S electorate (very young, with a high level of education, frequent internet users, as all the empirical analysis conducted in Italy in the last years have pointed out (Corbetta and Gualmini 2012; Itanes 2013), much more promising suggestions in this field might be found in the classic model of 'critical citizen'. The long-lasting process of value change that affected political culture, as described by Inglehart (1990), would have moulded new citizens who are more educated, competent and politically informed – the *sophisticated non-partisans* (Dalton 1996) – less prone to sustain passively the big mass parties and willing to participate directly in public life, especially in non-traditional forms of political engagement. In particular, several studies conducted on young people of different countries (Henn et al.

2002; Muxel and Cacouault 2001; Bontempi and Pocaterra 2007) have observed a high level of civic sense and satisfaction with democracy, a non-refusal of the vote as a participative resource, together with a strong hostility and scepticism towards the traditional political process, with a preference for protest as a way to express their opinions.

Data, Methods, and Hypotheses

This chapter investigates the diffusion of protest attitudes among M5S voters and the impact that different dimensions of protest have had on voters' choices in the 2013 elections. In order to develop the theoretical questions highlighted in the previous pages, we concentrate on the measure of political protest in all its multifaceted dimensions, trying to disentangle the most important meanings and examining, at the same time, which categories of voters – less or more connected to politics – make use of these tools to decide. The theoretical debate discussed above supports the notion that the protest dimension is expected to be particularly relevant in the explanation of the vote for new parties with characteristics similar to those of M5S. In order to correctly assess this influence, we adopt Bergh's classification of political protest into the two distinct dimensions of 'system discontent' and 'elite discontent'. Using bivariate and multivariate analysis (logistic regression models), our study aims to understand: a) whether voters of different parties have exhibited, with different intensity, negative feelings towards politics; b) to what extent political protest (and which kind of political protest) can explain the vote for M5S; c) in which ways the use of political protest depends on (and changes according to) the capabilities of voters' personal political resources.

We assume that the vote for the M5S in the 2013 general elections can largely be explained, more than for other parties, by the effects of political protest in both its two components of (more radical) system distrust and (less radical) élites distrust. Indeed, the M5S has strongly emphasised voters' protest against the old parties, particularly the two largest ones (Partito Democratico (PD) and Popolo della Libertà (PDL)), which in 2011–2013 were governing as a coalition. In this way, the M5S had the opportunity to stress its willingness to present itself as a party overcoming the left-right cleavage. Such new parties often obtain votes by opposing existing establishment and politicians, and criticising their negative performances. Moreover, we hypothesise that the impact of political protest is reinforced (not weakened) by the presence of a high level of political engagement. Those more prone to support M5S were mostly those voters who are sensitive to political domains and discontent. This should be particularly true when the measure of elite discontent is taken into account, because a more focalised indicator of protest is expected to combine better with higher political awareness.

The data come from a post-electoral survey carried out by Itanes. The research was conducted in March 2013 – a month after the Parliamentary elections – as piece of a more general programme of investigation into the electoral effects of the economic and political crisis in contemporary Italy.[2] The post-electoral survey was based on about 1,500 face-to-face interviews.

The Protest Vote and its Components

A vote for a new (self-defined as anti-system) party such as M5S incorporates, in all likelihood, a certain amount of protest as expression of disaffection with politics and/or, more specifically, with political actors and institutions. Following a recent classification of political discontent (Bergh 2004; Hosch-Dayican 2011), we distinguish between a protest against the political system and a protest against the political élites. The system protest is operationalised through a combination of variables related to certain feelings which assume political relevance: a) political trust/distrust; b) efficacy/alienation; c) belief in a functioning party democracy. All these dimensions allow us to understand and evaluate how the democratic system is organised and works. On the other hand, the elite protest concerns: a) perception of the state of the (personal/national) economy; b) judgments on government performance and attribution of responsibility for the crisis; c) opinion of leaders. In general, it assumes, as specific and focalised object of criticism, the incumbent party or parties, perceived as unable to solve collective problems.[3]

Tables 8.1 and 8.2 display, in detail, a large array of indicators related to political discontent and allow us to see how it is spread among the whole electorate. Following our hypothesis, we expect a particular concentration of these negative attitudes and opinions among M5S voters. As a first result, the tables indicate, for the electorate as a whole, the general prevalence of a critical position along almost all the indicators, both those referring to the political institutions and those concerning how political actors worked. At the same time, the data show that political discontent is significantly higher among M5S voters than among supporters of any other party. This wider diffusion of negative feelings concerns, for instance, the dimension of 'trust': more than 40 per cent of M5S voters display a minimal (or zero) confidence in Parliament, and 60 per cent of them have no trust in political parties, while the corresponding percentages for other voters are respectively around 20 per cent and 30 per cent. Moreover,

2 Formally established in 2007, the Itanes association (Italian National Election Studies) promotes a research programme on electoral behaviour in Italy mainly through electoral mass surveys. See www.itanes.org/en.

3 Given the peculiar contingency of the 2013 Italian elections, identifying the incumbent parties is somewhat problematic. The incumbent government was led by professor Mario Monti and entirely composed of technocrats. The government was formed in November 2011, after the resignation of the former Prime minister Silvio Berlusconi, and was supported in parliament by a large coalition which also included the two main parties: the Popolo della Libertà and the Partito Democratico. In this sense, all parties can be included in the category of incumbent, with the exception of the Lega Nord.

Table 8.1 Indicators of system discontent among M5S voters and other selected groups of voters

	M5S voters	Centre-left (PD) voters	Centre-right (PDL) voters	Non voters	Cramers' V (M5S vs others)
Efficacy (% that strongly agree)					
People like me have no say in what the government does	56.6	45.5	51.8	61.8	0.078
Sometimes politics seems so complicated that a person like me cannot really understand what is going on	58.8	45.4	54.9	59.9	0.099
Those we elect lose touch with the people	72.6	57.2	62.5	64.0	0.123
Parties are only interested in people's votes, not in their opinions	65.5	49.8	58.5	70.0	0.106
Trust in political institutions (% none)					
Parliament	40.9	17.0	23.2	37.3	0.190
Parties	59.2	31.4	35.0	55.3	0.231
President of the Republic	18.5	2.8	6.7	12.4	0.256
European Union	20.5	4.9	11.5	20.7	0.218
Belief in functioning party democracy (% that totally disagree)					
Parties are necessary to protect the interests of different groups and social classes	24.2	10.0	14.6	15.5	0.195
Parties allow citizens to participate in political life	34.1	15.3	19.7	24.1	0.202
Without parties democracy would not exist	24.8	5.1	8.9	16.0	0.258
N	232	325	165	269	

M5S voters typically show little belief in the rule of parties as an instrument for participation or advocacy in democracy. In addition to this systemic discontent, Beppe Grillo's supporters are also characterised by a very intense expression of discontent towards the political élites. In a scenario of generalised negative views of the government's performances, M5S voters express, therefore, the most critical evaluations about the economy (in particular in terms of its future prospects) and about how the two governments of the XVI legislative term (Berlusconi and Monti) have faced up to the effects of the crisis. But the most important peculiarity that this preliminary analysis reveals is probably that those attributions of negative responsibility among M5S voters turn out to be generalised to all the political class, included the opposition leader Bersani, whose rating is unexpectedly worse than the corresponding ratings attributed to the incumbent leaders. Furthermore,

Table 8.2 Indicators of elite discontent among M5S voters and other voters

	M5S voters	Centre-left (PD) voters	Centre-right (PDL) Voters	Non voters	Cramers' V (M5S vs others)
Economic evaluations					
State of the national economy. retrospective: very much worsened	68.5	57.8	64.5	61.2	0.109
State of the national economy, prospective: very much worsening	43.1	23.0	30.7	35.6	0.199
Relative deprivation: fear of losing job: very strong	14.7	6.6	4.9	7.0	0.158
Evaluation of government performance: % very negative					
Berlusconi government on the economy	48.0	52.8	3.6	24.5	0.202
Monti government on the economy	28.9	12.0	36.4	28.2	0.184
Responsibility for economic crisis % very responsible					
Berlusconi government	24.2	23.6	0.0	10.8	0.169
Monti government	8.3	2.5	10.5	9.3	0.153
Leaders' ratings: score 0–10. means					
Berlusconi (PDL)	1.5	1.1	7.4	3.3	0.243
Monti (incumbent prime minister)	2.5	4.0	2.5	2.7	0.234
Bersani (PD)	3.2	5.7	2.4	3.6	0.264
N	232	325	165	269	

political discontent among M5S supporters is not only higher when compared with other voters, but also when the group of non-voters is taken into account. This is a very important finding, because abstainers normally express the most distrustful, alienated and critical positions.

After showing how protest is spread across the whole Italian electorate and particularly concentrated among the M5S voters, we examine the impact of political protest through a logistic regression (Table 8.3), whose models test the (differential) effects, on the probability of voting for M5S, of the two additive indexes of 'system discontent' and 'elite discontent'.

Model 1 (baseline) reports the coefficients for the main socio-demographic variables and the left-right self-placement dimension. At this first step, the only relevant finding is the considerable effect of age, with the younger more likely oriented towards a vote for M5S. As expected, left-right division does not discriminate, confirming the (self) representation of the party as a post-ideological actor able to drain votes from both the ideological sides. The impact of the two components of political protest is tested in Model 2. Confirming the results of

Table 8.3 Effect of 'protest' on the probability of vote for M5S. Logistic regressions

	Model 1: Baseline	Model 2: System discontent	Model 3: Elite discontent	Model 4: Interaction
Sex (female)	+0.153	+0.091	+0.137	+0.080
Age (<35)	+0.936***	+0.767***	+0.940***	+0.784***
Zone (South)	+0.236	+0.237	+0.557**	+0.242
Education (low)	+0.029	+0.149	+0.062	−0.114
Occupational status (employed)	−0.084	−0.117	−0.161	−0.123
Left-Right position (scale, 0–1)		−0.038	+0.001	+0.004
System discontent (min–max, scale 0–1)		+4.100***		−5.024***
Elite discontent (min–max, 0–1)			+3.845***	−5.231**
System discontent *elite discontent				+13.267***
Constant	−1.782***	−3.854***	−4.225***	−0.382
Pseudo R-square	0.049	0.143	0.144	0.278
N	738	738	738	738

Note: **: p<0.01; ***: p<0.001.
The dependent variable is coded 0 (vote for other parties) and 1 (vote for M5S). The two components of political protest – *system discontent* and *elite discontent* – are additive indexes consisting of all the variables in Table 8.1 (system discontent) and Table 8.2 (elite discontent). Both the indexes are normalised.

bivariate analysis, regressions clearly show that these dimensions are both relevant and significant, even after controlling the socio-demographic and ideological variables. The positive effect of system discontent appears to be a little stronger than elite discontent (beta coefficient of +4.100 against +3.845). But, as reported in Model 4, the maximum effect is reached when discontent is high on both dimensions. All these findings indicate that political protest is not only relevant in general as an explanation of the vote for M5S, but it also assumes a more concrete pattern. In fact, it appears particularly efficacious when it focuses on specific political objects and when this resentment is combined with that addressed against the political system as a whole.

The importance of the protest dimension as explanation of voters' choices in the 2013 elections is clearly visible in Figure 8.1, which reports the predicted percentages of vote for the main parties under the effect of lower/higher political discontent (an additive index of system discontent and elite discontent). While the predicted values for PD and PDL significantly decline according to the growth of political discontent, the trend for M5S is inverse. The probability of attracting voters not critical or only moderately critical toward politics is not higher than those expressed by other parties. In the absence of criticism, voters chose mainly

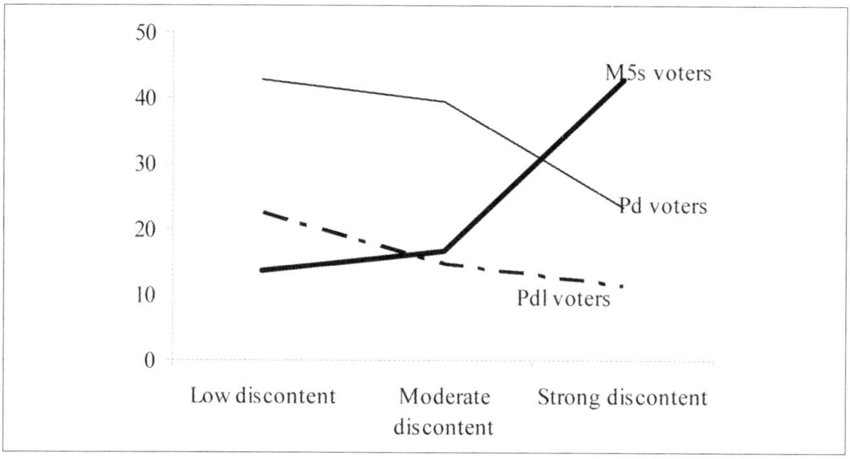

Figure 8.1 Predicted percentage of voting for M5S, PD and PDL by intensity of political discontent

Note: Estimates are calculated using Margins with Stata. We run one separate regression model for each dependent variable (voted/not voted for M5S, PD, PDL). *Political discontent* index a (normalised) sum of the two indexes of *system discontent* and *elite discontent*, and assume three values (low, moderate and strong discontent). Covariates introduced as a check are also included in Table 8.3. Values on Y-axis are predicted percentages of vote for M5S and derive from a multiplication per 100 of predicted probabilities 0–1. Predicted percentages are not comparable with simple percentages of bivariate analysis because they are controlled for the effects of socio-demographic covariates.

PD, to some extent PDL and only minimally M5S. But when the level of criticism among the electorate grows, the predicted percentages of votes for M5S becomes very high (43 per cent against 23 per cent for PD, 11 per cent for PDL) and the M5S becomes the most widely preferred party.

Protest as a Tool for Engaged, Detached or Both Types of Voters?

As we outlined in the first pages of this chapter, protest may assume different meanings if expressed by highly engaged citizens or by citizens who feel politics. In this section, we investigate the interaction between political discontent and political engagement. Did the relationship assume a positive direction (more engagement, more protest) and foster a vote in favour of M5S? Or, alternatively, was the protest (and the vote for a protest party such as the M5S) massively spread among those voters disengaged and detached from politics?

The typology reproduced in Table 8.4 summarises the different combinations of these two dimensions. With regard to the dimension of protest we use the same general index of Figure 8.1, using the whole range of variables reported in Tables 8.1 and 8.2. Political engagement derives from a combination of attitudinal (level of 'interest in politics') and behavioural variables (scale of 'political activism'). The first group of voters selected through this procedure fits the well-known category of 'critical citizens' (Norris 1999), but they report a higher score on both the dimensions of discontent and engagement. For this group a high degree of criticism is reinforced by a condition of political attentiveness. Moving to the other group of discontented – those more critical and, at the same time, disengaged – they are classified as 'anti-politics voters'. The remaining cells contain two groups of voters who are largely indifferent, with non-negative attitudes towards politics: the 'integrated citizens' (those highly engaged), and the 'apathetic citizens' (those with a low level of engagement: Milbrath 1965; De Luca 1995).

The results reported in Table 8.4 show that M5S's electorate is largely composed of a significant component of 'critical citizens', with a percentage (45 per cent) that is double that registered for centre-left PD voters (connoted as 'integrated citizens'), and triple in the case of centre-right PDL voters (Passarelli and Tuorto 2013). Together, the two groups of politically discontented voters ('critical citizens' and 'anti-politics citizens') cover 70 per cent of M5S voters. In contrast, the corresponding percentages for centre-left (PD) and centre-right (PDL) parties only reach a third of the electorate; and also non-voters display a minor relevance of discontent (56 per cent). The effect of this over-representation is that the categories of 'integrated citizens' and 'apathetic citizens' count less or are absolutely marginal (20 per cent against the average level of 32 per cent in the first case, only 9 per cent against 21 per cent for the latter) (Table 8.4).

Table 8.4 Typology of political discontent and political engagement among M5S voters, PD voters, PDL voters and non-voters

	M5S voters	PD voters	PDL voters	Non-voters	Total
Political discontent: against the system and the elite					
Critical citizens (engaged+ high discontent)	44.9	22.6	15.0	21.1	25.8
Integrated citizens (engaged + low discontent)	19.9	48.8	27.9	12.6	31.8
Anti-politics citizens (disengaged + high discontent)	26.0	11.8	18.6	35.3	20.9
Apathetic/passive citizens (disengaged + low discontent)	9.2	16.8	38.6	31.1	21.4
Total	100.0	100.0	100.0	100.0	100.0
N	232	325	165	269	1197

Note: the total does not include 'other voters' (206 cases).

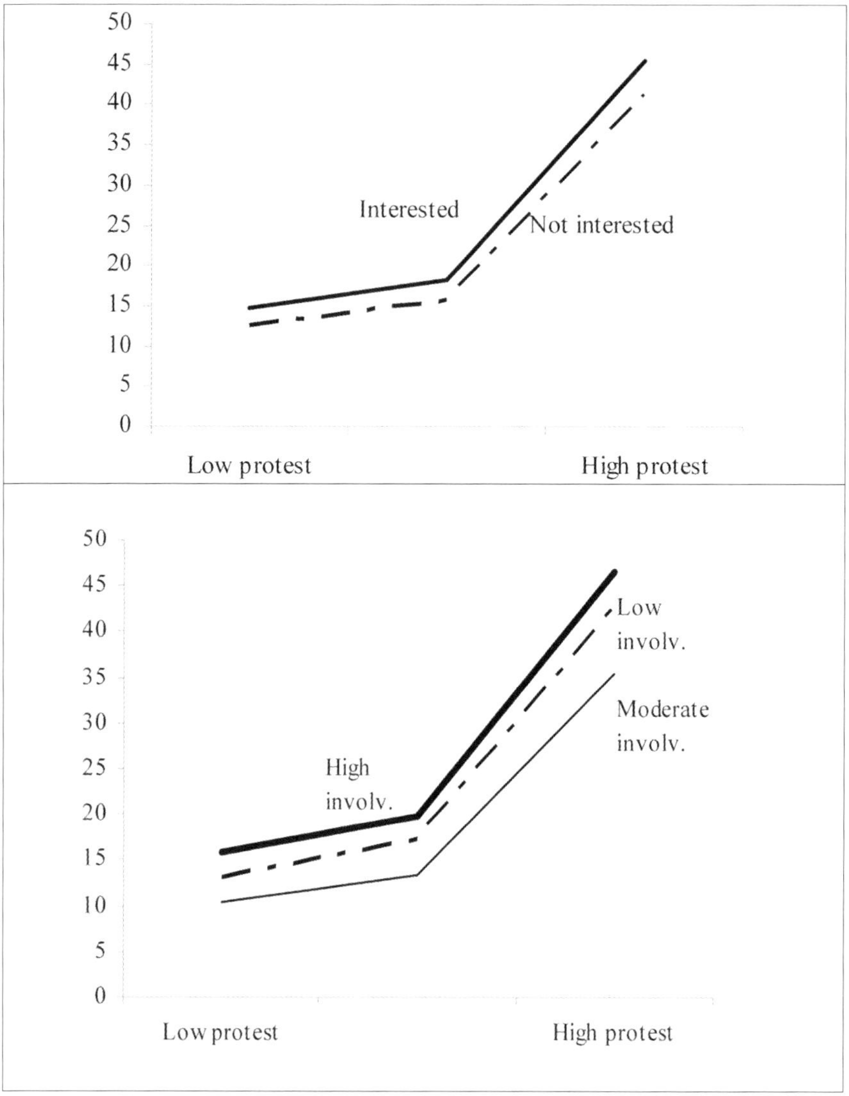

Figure 8.2 Probability of vote for M5S by level of political protest, for different groups interested/ not interested, involved / not involved in politics

Note: Estimates are calculated using Margins with Stata. All the groups of voters derive from a dichotomisation of the variable 'interest in politics' (*much+enough v. a little+none*) and the articulation of the variable 'political involvement' into three categories (no political action = low involvement; one political action = medium involvement; more than one political action = high involvement). *Interested* (N = 554); *Not interested* (N = 952); *Low involvement* (N = 894); *Medium involvement* (N=305); *High involvement* (N = 309). Values on Y-axis are predicted percentages (see Figure 8.1).

This typology helps clarify the characteristics of M5S voters' profiles, but it does not give any information about the relationship between political discontent, political engagement and vote choice. For which group of voters did political discontent increase the probability of voting for M5S? Is political protest a typical resource available for and used by the peripheral and detached voters or, alternatively, does it concern firstly those most connected and aware of the political process? Figure 8.2 describes how the probability of voting for M5S changes according to the intensity of political discontent among voters with different levels of political engagement. In general, negative opinions on the political system and political elites positively affect the level of support for M5S, with an exponential increase in correspondence with high discontent. Nevertheless, in the absence of a political activation the effect of protest seems to be weaker not stronger, coherently with what the hypothesis (H2) maintains. Although differences are not remarkable (politically engaged exceed the other group by around 3–5 percentage points) this relationship is confirmed for both measures of political engagement. This means that system discontent and elite discontent have functioned as interchangeable dimensions, both boosting the probability of voting for M5S among the most engaged voters. Figure 8.2 also suggests a further finding. When the profile of engaged and non-engaged in politics are compared, voters who are in touch with politics always display a higher (predicted) percentage of votes for M5S, regardless of how political discontent is expressed. Indeed, the two lines in each figure remain parallel, showing a similar effect of political protest for both groups. We can conclude that not only voters detached and distant from politics have used discontent as a substitutive resource to select the preferred party. Political protest acted as a further instrument of expression also for active and motivated citizens who represent, as described in Table 8.4, a significant component of M5S's electorate.

Conclusion

In this chapter we have evaluated the causes of voting for M5S, looking at the crucial dimension of political protest. As a general result, the empirical analysis confirms that political protest, in all its components, has acted as a crucial predictor of M5S votes. Compared with other electorates, voters who cast ballots for M5S in the 2013 elections were actually more politically dissatisfied and they have systematically expressed feelings of distrust or alienation with more intensity. At the same time, they exhibited worse perceptions of the economy, government, parties and political leaders. Another conclusion of our study concerns the characteristics of political protest associated with the vote for M5S. Such a political choice is not simply driven by resentment against the system in its corrupted and inefficacious components, which the populist rhetoric usually foments, but it also shows more reasoned evaluations on how politics and politicians have actually worked. In fact, the highest impact of political protest on the vote for M5S is reached when the two dimensions (system discontent and elite discontent) combine their effects, and the generic criticism is reinforced by focalised judgements on specific topics. Lastly, an in-depth analysis on specific sub-groups of voters with different levels of engagement and interest in politics reveals that political protest has functioned as a stronger determinant of voting patterns for all voters more connected with politics, suggesting a model of 'critical citizens' instead of 'apathetic citizens'.

We would argue that the M5S is basically a party which is able to gather together a strong protest component. However, protest does not sound as a generic expression, but it seems to be consciously oriented. M5S voters are protesting more actively than the rest of the electorate and, at the same time, the vote is protest-driven, especially among those who are politically engaged. Therefore, we are faced with an angry vote that is also aware and informed. On this point, our findings are in line with other research on populist parties, which emphasises the relationship, or better the interaction, between generic and specific claims, expressive and instrumental voting.

References

Bergh, J. 2004. Protest voting in Austria, Denmark and Norway. *Scandinavian Political Studies*, 27(4), pp. 367–89.

Bontempi, M. and Pocaterra, R., eds. 2007. *I figli del disincanto: giovani e partecipazione politica in Europa*. Milano: Mondadori.

Bordignon, F. and Ceccarini, L. 2013. Five Stars and a Cricket. Beppe Grillo. Shakes Italian Politics. *South European Society and Politics*, 18(4), pp. 427–49.

Bowler, S. and Lanoue, D.J. 1992. Strategic and Protest Voting for Third Parties: The Case of The Canadian NDP. *Political Research Quarterly*, 45(2), pp. 485–99.

Brennan, G. 2001. Five Rational Actor Accounts of the Welfare State. *Kyklos*, 54(2–3), pp. 213–34.

Brennan, G. and Hamlin, A. 1998. Expressive Voting and Electoral Equilibrium. *Public Choice*, 95(1–2), pp. 149–75.

Corbetta, P. and Gualmini, E. eds. 2012. *Il partito di Grillo*. Bologna: Il Mulino.

Dalton, R.J. 1996. *Citizen Politics: Public Opinion and Political Parties in Advanced Industrial Democracies*. New York: Chatham House.

De Luca, T. 1995. *The two faces of political apathy*. Philadelphia: Temple University Press.

Henn, M., Weinstein, M. and Wring, D. 2002. A Generation Apart? Youth and political participation in Britain. *British Journal of Politics and International Relation*, 4(2), pp. 167–92.

Hermet, G. 2001. *Le populismes dans le monde. Une histoire sociologique. XIXe-XXe siècle*. Paris: Fayard.

Hosch-Dayican, B. 2011. Populist Party Choice in Germany and the Netherlands. The Protest Vote Hypothesis Revisited. 10th Dutch-Belgian Political Science Conference, Amsterdam, 9–10 June 2011.

Ignazi, P. 2003. *Extreme Right Parties in Western Europe*. Oxford: Oxford University Press.

Inglehart, R. 1990. *Culture Shift in Advanced Industrial Society*. Princeton: Princeton University Press.

Itanes. 2013. *Voto amaro: disincanto e crisi economica nelle elezioni del 2013*. Bologna: Il Mulino.

Kang, T.W. 2004. Protest Voting and Abstention under Plurality Rule Elections. An Alternative Public Choice Approach. *Journal of Theoretical Politics*, 16(1), pp. 79–102.

Kselman, D. and Niou, E. 2011. Protest voting in plurality elections: a theory of voter signalling. *Public Choice*, 148(3–4), pp. 395–418.

Milbrath, L.W. 1965. *Political Participation: How and Why Do People Get Involved in Politics?* Chicago: Rand McNally.

Mudde, C. 2007. *Populist Radical Right Parties in Europe*. Cambridge: Cambridge University Press.

Muxel, A. and Cacouault, M. eds. 2001. *Les jeunes d'Europe du Sud et la politique: une enquête comparative, France, Italie, Espagne*. Paris: L'Harmattan.

Norris, P., ed. 1999. *Critical Citizens: Global Support for Democratic Governance*. Oxford: Oxford University Press.

Passarelli, G. and Tuorto, D. 2012. *Lega & Padania. Storie e luoghi delle camicie Verdi*. Bologna: Il Mulino.

———. 2013. *Berlusconi tra elettori fedeli e defezioni*. In: Itanes, ed. 2013. *Voto amaro. Disincanto e crisi economica nelle elezioni del 2013*. Bologna: Il Mulino. pp. 71–82.

Passarelli, G., Tronconi. F., and Tuorto, D. 2013. *Dentro il movimento. Organizzazione, attivisti e programmi*. In: P. Corbetta and E. Gualmini, eds. *Il partito di Grillo*. Bologna: Il Mulino, pp. 123–67.

Rooduijn, M., de Lange S.L., and van der Brug W. 2012. A populist Zeitgeist? Programmatic contagion by populist parties in Western Europe. *Party Politics* [online] 20 April. Available at: http://ppq.sagepub.com/content/early/2012/04/19/1354068811436065.abstract [Accessed 4 June 2014].

Sartori, G. 1976. *Parties and Party Systems*. Cambridge: Cambridge University Press.

Tarchi, M. 2003. *L'Italia populista. Dal qualunquismo ai girotondi*. Bologna: Il Mulino.

Van der Brug, W. 1998. The Informed Electorate: Political Perceptions and Party Behaviour. *Acta Politica*, 33(1), pp. 20 55.

Van der Brug, W. and Fennema, M. 2007. What Causes People to Vote for a Radical-Right Party? A Review of Recent Work. *International Journal of Public Opinion Research*, 19(4), pp. 474–87.

Van der Brug, W., Fennema M. and Tillie, J. 2000. Anti-Immigrant Parties in Europe: Ideological or Protest Vote? *European Journal of Political Research*, 37(1), pp. 77–102.

Van der Eijk, C. And Franklin, M., eds. 1996. *Choosing Europe? The European Electorate and National Politics in the Face of Union*. Ann Arbor: University of Michigan Press.

———. 2009. *Elections and Voters*. Basingstoke: Palgrave Macmillan.

Chapter 9

Beyond Protest: Issues and Ideological Inconsistencies in the Voters of the Movimento 5 Stelle

Pasquale Colloca and Piergiorgio Corbetta

Introduction

The main goal of this chapter is to understand whether the voters of the Movimento 5 Stelle (M5S) are a chaotic assortment of individuals united only by their protest against the political establishment (or, at most, by a confused desire for change), or whether they share common values, a vision of democracy and fundamental political attitudes. The question is therefore whether we are faced with the complete ideological heterogeneity that typifies populist movements, or whether we can identify in the M5S electorate a significant level of political and ideological homogeneity. In the former case, we can expect a rapid decline of the movement, despite its incredible success in the 2013 general elections; in the latter case, we will try to trace the borders and discover the content of a new social and political entity that is potentially able to deeply influence Italian politics in the coming years.

In our search for an ideological thread that may connect the political orientations of M5S voters, we must necessarily make reference to the left-right dimension. Indeed, in the wake of the general elections held in February 2013, the question asked by everyone – observers, analysts and ordinary citizens – was: 'Is this a 'right-wing' or a 'left-wing' political movement?'

If we wish to place the M5S in a 'political family', we have no doubt that it falls within the vast area of populism. Nevertheless, saying that the M5S is a populist movement is to say little about its ideological nature. Indeed, both historians and political analysts agree that populism is not an ideology. Paul Taggart (2000) says that 'populism serves many masters and mistresses' (ibid., p. 10) and points out that 'populism has been a tool of progressives, of reactionaries, of democrats, of autocrats, of the left and of the right. The reason for this adaptability lies in the 'empty hearth' of populism: populism lacks to key values. While other ideologies contain, either implicitly or explicitly, a focus on one or more values such equality, liberty and social justice, populism has not such core to it' (ibid., pp. 3–4).

Thus, according to Taggart – and a similar view has been expressed by other scholars of populism, such as Mény and Surel (2000) and Taguieff (2002) –

populism is not a true ideology; rather, it is a 'chamaleontic' political style (Taggart 2002, p. 70) that can be applied to various ideological models: a kind of dress for all seasons. Nevertheless, we should add that, historically, this dress has almost always been worn by the right, at least in Europe (Mudde and Kaltwasser 2011; Mudde 2013). In Italy, too, right-wing parties have always been more able than those on the left to interpret the insecurity and dissatisfaction of the electorate in a populist manner (Ruzza and Fella 2009).

In this regard, the M5S constitutes an anomaly. Indeed, in Italy the common perception is that, if the movement does have a political colour, it can be identified more with the left than with the right. This impression chiefly stems from the origin of the movement, which arose at the beginning of the century in the wake of the environmentalist movements and of critical consumerism and opposition to the multinationals and high finance.

Beppe Grillo has always rejected the labels of both right and left. Indeed, his statements on the issue have been both numerous and insistent. We will quote a few: 'The days of ideology are over. The 5 Stars Movement is not fascist; it is neither right nor left. It is above and beyond' (Grillo 2013a). 'The 5 Stars Movement is neither on the left nor on the right. It is a movement of Italians' (Grillo 2013b). And so on.

In the analysis that follows, we will focus not on the official positions of the movement, but rather on the opinions of its followers, particularly those of M5S voters. This is what interests us, and it is an issue on which few cognitive elements are available. Our starting point will be the survey conducted in the wake of the February 2013 elections by the Itanes (Italian National Election Studies) group on a sample of 1508 voters. The survey consisted of face-to-face interviews, which have enabled us to explore a range of political issues that can be traced back to left-right ideology.

Before analysing the data, however, it is worth asking a question: 'Does the left-right dichotomy still make sense today?' As is well known, this debate was triggered almost half a century ago by Daniel Bell's provocative statement on 'the end of ideology': 'The ideologies … which emerged from the nineteenth century … today are exhausted' (Bell 1965, p. 402). The truth of this claim, however, has always aroused serious doubt among political scientists, and the attempts to validate this prediction empirically have not been very successful (see, among others, Inglehart and Klingemann 1976; Jost 2006; Mair 2007). For what concerns Italy, in a previous study we found empirical evidence to support the thesis that 'the left-right dimension continues to be very meaningful for citizens and to perform decisive functions of political orientation', and that 'the social representations of left and right mainly perform two functions previously fulfilled by ideologies: social and individual orientation' (Corbetta, Cavazza and Roccato 2009, p. 638).

Position and Distribution of M5S Voters on the Left-Right Scale

The first question dealt with here is whether M5S voters are grouped around a sufficiently well-defined centre of gravity in the left-right spectrum, or whether they constitute a hodgepodge containing a bit of everything – from the radicalism of the alternative left, as exemplified by the no-global or Occupy Wall Street movements, to right-wing neo-populism in the style of Le Pen or Haider. And if they do have an ideological focus, where is this located on an ideal scale from 0 to 10, where 0 is taken to indicate extreme left and 10 extreme right? In statistical terms, we want to define the mean and standard deviation of the left-right variable among M5S voters.

To answer this question, we must first define the instrument used to determine where the individual stands in the left-right continuum. Traditionally, the position of the interviewee on this scale is ascertained from the following question: 'Many people use the terms 'left' and 'right' when they talk about politics. This diagram shows a line of boxes going from left to right. Thinking about your political opinions, in which box would you place yourself?'

This is the simplest way of operationalising the variable, in that the answer to a single question settles the entire issue. Nevertheless, some problems arise. Interviewees may give a predetermined ideological answer ('I've always been on the left'), or they may determine their own position according to that of their favourite party ('I vote for the PDL, so I'm on the right'): in both cases, we have statements that are detached from any concrete content (for instance, someone who claims to be 'on the left' may then adopt a right-wing stance on law and order). Then again, we may encounter an ideological refusal to answer the question ('I'm neither on the right nor on the left'), even when the individual holds clearly defined positions on classical ideological themes such as social inequality or the issue of public vs private. Such refusal is frequently encountered among M5S voters, both because the left-right divide may appear to belong to the 'old' political system, and because Beppe Grillo has repeatedly labelled this ideological reference as misleading.

For these reasons, we need to look more closely at the contents of the left-right dimension. In doing so, we are aided by the Itanes survey data, in which the opinions of the respondents are explored in several directions in terms of political and value contents linked to left-right ideology. From the survey conducted 15 questions of this type were available. To evaluate their true connection with the left-right dimension, we correlated each question with the respondents' self-placement on the left-right scale and selected those with a statistically significant ($p < 0.001$) correlation coefficient (Pearson's r). Ten questions were utilized.[1]

---

1 The 10 questions are reported in simplified form in Fig 1. The replies to the first four questions were placed on a 1–7 scale; the subsequent six questions on a 1–4 scale. For the purpose of comparison, the measurements were then normalized to a 0–10 scale.

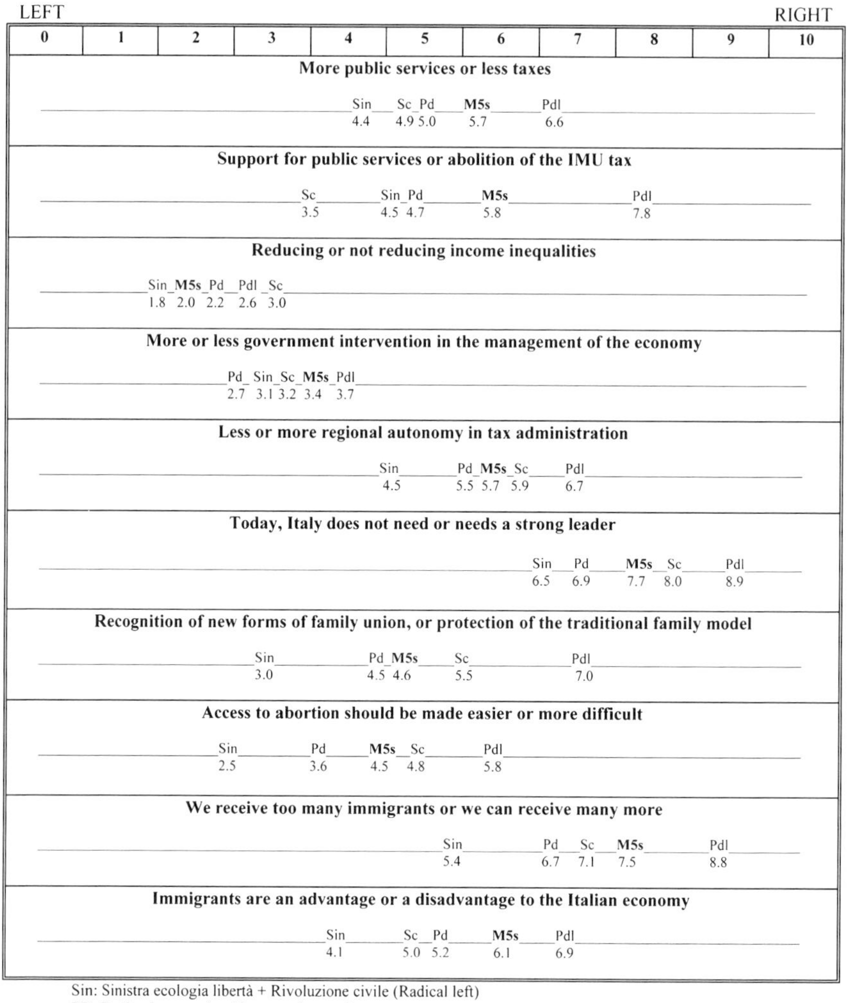

Sin: Sinistra ecologia libertà + Rivoluzione civile (Radical left)
PD: Partito democratico (Democratic party)
M5S: Movimento 5 stelle (Five Stars Movement)
SC: Scelta civica (Civic choice)
PDL: Popolo delle libertà (People of freedom)

Figure 9.1 Mean self-positioning of voters for principal parties on left-right issues

First of all, Figure 9.1 shows the mean self-positioning of voters for the main parties[2] on each issue on a scale from 0 (left) to 10 (right). We focused on five

2 Voters for the various parties were classified according to how they reported having voted for the Chamber of Deputies.

political groupings: the radical left;[3] the Partito Democratico (Democratic Party, PD) (Bersani); the M5S; the Scelta Civica (Civic Choice, a centrist movement led, at the time of the election, by Prime Minister Mario Monti); the Popolo della libertà (People of Freedom, PDL) (Berlusconi).[4] It can easily be seen that – with only one exception – M5S voters place themselves between the PD and the PDL, in a substantially central position among the parties. This finding in itself suggests that these voters do not display a clear left or right ideological connotation.

However, what interests us is the overall position of the respondents on the left-right axis, rather than on specific issues. We therefore calculated an additive index on the 10 items (Chronbach's $\alpha = 0.68$), thus obtaining a score from 0 to 10 for each individual (0 = extreme left; 10 = extreme right). Table 9.1 reports the means of these scores among the voters for the political groupings considered. This confirms the central position of M5S voters, whose mean score of 5.2 falls between those of the PD (4.1) and the PDL (7.4).

As mentioned earlier, however, what interests us more than the mean value of this variable is its spread. Indeed, a mean score of 5 on a scale from 0 to 10 may result either from the concentration of all scores around the value 5 or from the widespread scattering of scores over the whole range. We analyzed this spread both through the application of the statistical index 'standard deviation' and through its graphic representation. Table 9.1 indicates that M5S voters display the greatest standard deviation of all the parties. Even more revealing is Figure 2, which shows that, while the radical left, PD and PDL voters are fairly closely clustered (around the values of 1, 1–2 and 8–10, respectively), the M5S electorate exhibits marked variation, being distributed over practically the whole range of values from 1 to 10 (somewhat flat curve). In terms of the left-right dimension, therefore, M5S voters are distinctly more heterogeneous than those of the other parties.

Table 9.1 Index of left-right issues: mean and standard deviation

	Mean	Standard deviation*	N
Radical left	3.28	3.16	62
Partito Democratico	4.14	3.07	325
Movimento 5 Stelle	5.22	3.25	232
Scelta Civica	4.63	3.07	57
Popolo della Libertà	7.39	2.90	165

Note: *Mean standard deviations of the items.

3 Combining voters for the two parties in this area – Sinistra ecologia e libertà (Left for Ecology and Freedom) and Rivoluzione civile (Civil Revolution)

4 It would have been interesting to include the Lega Nord, but the sample contained too few cases.

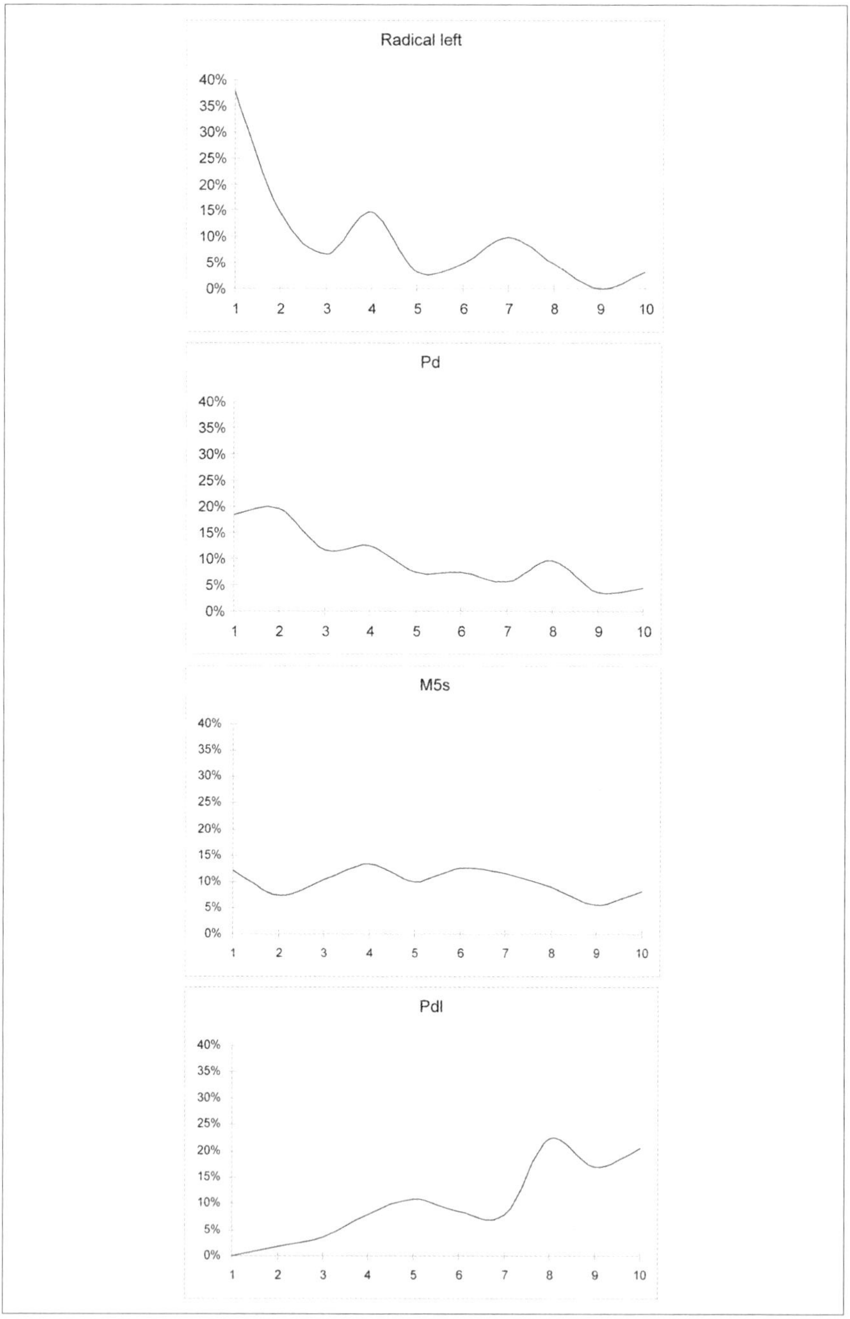

Figure 9.2 Distribution of left-right issue index among voters for the principal parties (1 left, 10 right)

In short, this first analysis yielded two findings: a) the M5S electorate does not – on average – display a clear ideological connotation in the left-right dimension, falling halfway between the PD and PDL; b) M5S voters are less compact than those of the other parties, displaying greater ideological diversification.

Inconsistency on the Left-Right Scale

As we have seen, M5S voters exhibit diversity in terms of their left-right placement. However, another form of diversification can be discerned – not among individuals, but within each individual. Indeed, each individual's score on the left-right axis results from the mean of responses to 10 questions. In this case, too, however, the same mean value may emerge from different distributions of values. Thus, the phenomenon already seen at the aggregate level is also at play at the individual level. At the aggregate level, the question is one of homogeneity/heterogeneity among individuals; at the individual level, it is one of the internal consistency/inconsistency of the individual.

The hypothesis that we wish to investigate here is that M5S voters display greater ideological inconsistency than voters for the other parties. Is it possible to demonstrate that the left-right dimension has less meaning for them than for other voters? That they are less ideological?

To answer these questions, we calculated an 'intra-individual inconsistency index' in the same way as we had previously calculated the index of inter-individual diversity; to do so, we applied to each individual the standard deviation among the 10 variables measuring ideology presented in Figure 1. Table 9.2 shows the mean values of this inconsistency index among the voters for the five parties considered. It can be seen that M5S voters have the highest value of intra-individual inconsistency.[5]

Table 9.2 Left-right intra-individual inconsistency index: mean by party voted

	Mean	N
Radical left	2.96	60
Partito Democratico	3.11	324
Movimento 5 Stelle	3.43	229
Scelta Civica	3.21	58
Popolo della Libertà	3.39	161

5 It can also be seen that the greatest ideological consistency is shown by voters for the radical left; this finding is also plausible.

What does the fact that M5S voters on *average* display greater ideological inconsistency than those of the other parties actually mean? Once again, the mean value may hide the presence of various subgroups. It is a fairly common opinion among commentators and political analysts that, within the large body of the M5S electorate, two 'spirits' coexist: one 'on the left' and one 'populist'. The left-wing spirit is claimed to have originated in the initial founding phase of the movement, which emerged in the wake of environmentalist and no-global agitation, and to have been subsequently strengthened by an influx of ex-PD voters in the run-up to the February 2013 general election. By contrast, the populist spirit (bereft of ideology) is thought to have blown in after the success of the movement – at the polls and, especially, in the media – in the 2012 administrative elections. This second wave is deemed to have been made up of scantly ideological voters who were substantially disappointed by the other populist movements in Italy: the Lega Nord (Bossi), the Italia dei Valori (Di Pietro) and the Popolo della Libertà (Berlusconi) itself.

In other words, behind the high mean ideological inconsistency of M5S voters an ideologically consistent and compact core of leftist voters may be hiding. In order to test this hypothesis, we subdivided the electorate according to the typology presented in Table 9.3, in which we operationalised the individual left-right position with the mean of the 10 left-right issues for each respondent, and the individual ideological inconsistency with the standard deviation of the 10 left-right issue scores within each respondent. The two variables were dichotomized at the median cut-points and crossed. On the basis of this operation, we isolated three types of voter (see Table 9.3): voters who were inconsistent , 'consistent leftist' voters, and 'consistent rightist' voters. In this way, we placed all the inconsistent voters (non-ideological, and hence neither leftist nor rightist, whom we could call typically 'populist') in a single category, while we can consider 'leftist' and 'rightist' only those voters who adhere fairly systematically to one of the two ideological areas. If the above-mentioned hypothesis were true, we should find a large number of 'consistent leftist' voters in the M5S.

Table 9.3 Typology A: Individual ideological inconsistency and left-right position

	Left	Right
Inconsistency	**Inconsistent**	
Consistency	**Leftist consistent**	**Rightist consistent**

The result of this analysis is reported in Table 9.4, which first of all reveals a high proportion of inconsistent voters in the M5S – the highest of all the parties, as was to be expected in the light of the previous table on the mean of this variable. However, this high proportion is not counterbalanced by a marked presence of 'consistent leftist' voters, the mean value of these latter being similar to that seen in the electorate as a whole (and, naturally, well below those of the radical left or the Partito Democratico).

Table 9.4 Typology A by party voted

	Radical left	Partito Democratico	Movimento 5 Stelle	Scelta Civica	Popolo della Libertà	Total
Inconsistent	40.0	41.4	58.9	56.2	56.9	50.7
Leftist consistent	48.3	45.5	29.7	28.1	9.4	28.1
Rightist consistent	11.7	13.0	11.4	15.8	33.8	21.2
Total	100.0	100.0	100.0	100.0	100.0	100.0
N	60	323	229	57	160	1454

Note: the column "Total" refers to the whole sample, including people not answering on voted party.

We may also add, however, that the opposite is not true either; indeed, we do not find an appreciable proportion of 'consistent right' voters in the ranks of the M5S (about the same modest level as in the radical left or Partito Democratico). This contradicts Grillo's post-election assertion, 'Thank heaven that we are here; otherwise, you'd have Golden Dawn (the Greek ultra-right movement) in Italy' (quoted in Merlo, 2013a).

Here, we may also explore a second hypothesis, which is fairly similar to the first. It has been claimed that two circles of voters can be discerned within the M5S electorate: a tight inner circle made up of highly committed people who are identifiable with leftist ideology – we could call them 'militants' – and a slacker outer circle comprising more mobile, fluctuating, even occasional voters, who are ideologically ambivalent and contradictory. According to this hypothesis, it is the inner circle which gives the party its political identity, and it is this circle which must be observed in order to understand the true political nature of the movement. This hypothesis differs from the previous one in that it focuses on the presence of 'leftist' voters in the M5S not so much in terms of their numbers as in terms of the 'quality' of their presence, i.e. their proximity to the 'centre' of the party; being more committed, they are more influential.

To test this hypothesis, we operationalised identification with the Movement in three different ways on the basis of three questions: respondents' self-assessed closeness to the party, their approval of Grillo as a leader, and their probability of voting for the M5S again in the future.[6] The results of this analysis are shown

6 The three questions were: 1) Perceived closeness: 'How close do you feel to this party? (low: a mere sympathizer; high: quite/very close); the percentages regard only those

in Table 9.5. On operationalising closeness to the Movement in the three ways mentioned above, our data clearly indicate that the 'consistent leftist' voters are present in the same measure both in those who are 'closest to the party' and in the ordinary sympathizers: in the low and high category of perceived closeness to the Movement, the leftist consistent are 29.6 per cent vs 27.3 per cent; in the low and high approval for Grillo they are 30.4 per cent vs 28.1 per cent; in the low and high probability of voting M5S again they are 29.4 per cent vs 29.6 per cent.

Table 9.5 Typology A by closeness to the party (only M5S voters)

	Perceived Closeness		**Judgement on Mr Grillo**		**Probability of voting M5S again**	
	Low	High	Low (0–6)	High (7–10)	Low (0–6)	High (7–10)
Inconsistent	64.8	59.1	58.9	59.6	57.8	59.4
Leftist consistent	29.6	27.3	30.4	28.1	29.4	29.6
Rightist consistent	5.6	13.6	10.7	12.3	12.8	11.3
Total	100	100	100	100	100	100
N	71	88	112	114	109	115

Thus, the data refute both hypotheses that the M5S electorate includes a considerable body of ideologically left-wing voters. Indeed, the group of voters that we have called 'leftist consistent' does not have a *quantitative* relevance, in that it cannot counterbalance, even in part, the weight of the 'inconsistent' voters. Nor does it have a *qualitative* relevance, in that it is not particularly well represented in the hard core of those who identify most closely with the Movement.

Non-ideology and post-ideology

It therefore emerges from the analyses conducted so far that M5S voters are more 'inconsistent', in terms of their left-right profile, than the voters of other parties. For them, the left-right dimension has less meaning than it does for the rest of the electorate; they find it harder to recognize their place in it and

who, in answer to previous two questions, said that they felt closer to the M5S than to any of the other parties; 2) Judgment on Mr Grillo as leader: 'I will read you the names of some politicians. If you have heard of them, tell me how you rate them on a scale from 0 to10, where 0 means a completely negative judgment and 10 a completely positive judgment'; 3) Probability of voting M5S again: 'Regardless of how you voted in the recent election, how likely would you be to vote for the following parties or alliances in the future: M5S (scale 0–10)'.

exhibit greater contradictions. But what does this mean? How should we interpret these contradictions?

Let us now return to the fact that the term 'inconsistency' – as we have used it so far – does not hide a judgmental connotation; it should not therefore be interpreted in either a negative or a positive sense. Indeed, the fact that an individual manifests contradictions on the left-right axis (e.g. by favouring higher taxes and increased spending on social services, while at the same time opposing state intervention in the economy) can be interpreted in two ways. Expressing contradictory positions may stem either from the inadequate political culture of the respondent – who does not recognize himself in the definitions, who misunderstands them, or who replies at random in order to hide his own ignorance – or from a far more general state of dissolution of the ideologies and political culture of the twentieth century. How can these two positions be distinguished?

In accordance with a line of research that we have already developed (Corbetta and Roccato 2006), we believe that an indicator that can distinguish between these two positions is the respondent's level of political information. In a politically well-informed person, contradictory responses concerning the various dimensions that have traditionally been ascribed to the left-right split may be interpreted as symptomatic of a cultural decline of the ideological schemes that have ideally delineated the principal ideological axis of politics for almost two centuries. By contrast, in an individual who is poorly informed and politically alienated, contradictoriness may be a sign of uncertainty, poor knowledge of the political lexicon and ideological confusion. Thus, we would have a simple form of contradictoriness that stems from deficient political culture, and a more complex form of contradictoriness that can be traced back to the crisis of traditional references, and which chiefly involves those who are politically and culturally more sophisticated.

We therefore analysed our data in accordance with this interpretative paradigm and constructed a typology in which 'inconsistent' voters were subdivided, on the basis of a variable of political information (measured by means of three questions on political knowledge),[7] into incompetent and competent; we will call incompetent inconsistent voters 'confused', and competent inconsistent voters 'post-ideological' (Table 9.6). The results are fairly clear (Table 9.7): the high level of inconsistency seen in M5S voters is due to the above-average presence of those voters whom we have called 'post-ideological', that is, politically well-informed individuals who nevertheless display contradictoriness with regard to the left-right ideological axis:

It is not easy to define the features of this 'post-ideology'. In politics, whenever new situations prove difficult to define, it is common practice to attach the prefix 'post' to old terms; in the Italian context, we need only cite: 'post-Christian

7 The three questions were: 1) Do you know who elects the President of the Republic? 2) Do you know, more or less, how many deputies there are in the Chamber of Deputies? 3) How many years can a person serve as President of the Republic?

Table 9.6 Typology B: individual ideological inconsistency and political knowledge

	Low political knowledge	High political knowledge
Inconsistent	**Confused**	**Post-ideological**
Consistent	**Consistent**	

Table 9.7 Typology B by party

	Radical left	Partito Democratico	Movimento 5 Stelle	Scelta Civica	Popolo della Libertà	Total
Consistent	60.0	58.5	41.1	43.9	43.2	49.3
Confused	20.0	20.7	33.6	31.6	35.6	31.4
Post-ideological	20.0	20.7	25.3	24.6	21.3	19.3
Total	100	100	100	100	100	100
N	60	323	229	57	160	1454

Note: the column "Total" refers to the whole sample, including people not answering on party voted.

Democrats', 'post-communists', 'post-fascists'. Nor is this practice limited to politics; indeed, in broader conceptual settings, we find such terms as post-industrial or post-modern . In such cases, the prefix 'post' gives the idea of a historical parabola, of a decline and a new beginning, of a link between present and past. It does not, however, confirm new conceptual identity; it merely serves to identify the starting point of the new political movement-thought-group and does not help to define its characteristics. Naturally, this is not only a matter of terminological difficulty; behind it lies a conceptual difficulty. Beneath the inadequacy of names lies the uncertainty of contents.

In this context, we can only present a few data on the socio-demographic profile of typology B among the M5S voters. As can be seen in Table 9.8, post-ideological M5S voters are mostly men, slightly younger than the average and better educated; they are more cultured than the other groups (they read more newspapers, watch less TV and display a medium-higher level of cultural consumption). In short, those whom we have called post-ideological voters belong to a segment of the population that is of a medium-high cultural level.

Conclusions

The extraordinary success of the Five Star Movement in the February 2013 general elections aroused two different sentiments in the Italian public, or at least

Table 9.8 Typology profile (mean values on M5s voters, N = 229)

	Sex (% male)	Age	Education (years of study)	Newspaper reading[a]	TV watching[b]	Cultural consumption index[c]
Leftist consistent	57.4	43.0	12.7	4.0	3.6	4.2
Rightist consistent	50.0	41.6	10.2	2.5	4.0	2.6
Inconsistent post-ideological	58.6	40.4	13.0	4.6	3.4	3.5
Inconsistent confused	27.3	42.4	10.6	2.7	4.3	2.8

Notes: a) Range 1 (never) – 9 (every day); b) Range 1 (never) – 9 (more than 6 hours a day); c) Based on 6 cultural activities, range 0–6.

in the sector most attentive to the country's political destiny: surprise and concern. Surprise on account of the unexpected size of that success, in that no party, either in Italy or elsewhere in Europe, had ever won 25 per cent of the valid votes cast in a national election on its début. Concern because the political colour of the movement was (and still is) decidedly ambiguous, and because Beppe Grillo's scathing anti-system propaganda seemed deliberately designed to strike fear into the supporters of democratic orthodoxy. At the time, the question asked by everyone – from the most sophisticated analyst to the man in the street – was a simple one: are these people on the left or the right?

But precisely because the question was simple, the answer was difficult and complicated. It was difficult because the true question centred on the political opinions and attitudes of those citizens who had decided to vote for the M5S, and not on the ideology and official policy proposals of the movement. Indeed, the answers that have been hazarded so far as to whether the movement stands on the left or the right have been based on the origin of the movement itself, on the personal biography of Beppe Grillo and on the speeches and statements of its leader.

When it first appeared on the Italian political scene, the M5S was deemed to belong to the area of the radical left, or rather to the green wave that swelled up in Western Europe in the 1980s – what would then also be called the 'libertarian left' (Kitschelt 1988), as opposed to the 'traditional left' of a social-democratic-labour nature. What pointed to this interpretation was the central position of environmental issues, critical consumerism, demands for the direct participation of citizen-voters, and opposition to the multinationals and to high finance. As Vignati recounts in the first chapter of this book, Beppe Grillo himself 'was born on the left … and his shows have always gained the attention and appreciation of the left-leaning public …'.

Over time, however, starting from the movement's entry into the electoral arena towards the end of the first decade of the twenty-first century, some of the previously blurred outlines came into better focus. For instance, we may think of the immigration issue (and Grillo's anti-immigration stance), the question of taxes (and his support for some forms of tax revolt), and the growing hostility towards Europe and the Euro. We may also think of the tenacious anti-institutional attitude of the more intransigent M5S deputies (who symbolically occupied the Chamber of Deputies, who physically prevented the normal functioning of parliamentary sessions, and who engaged in filibustering);[8] not to mention the perennially violent tone of Grillo's speeches, the language of which verges on insult and increasingly resembles the truculent style of the Lega Nord and populist groups on the extreme right. All of this also seems to point to a transformation in the movement's electoral base, which has increasingly diverged from the original nucleus. Above all, as the 2014 European elections draw near, parallels have been evoked between the M5S and the populist movements of the extreme right operating in various European countries, from France to Austria and the Netherlands.

In this regard, the position of Eugenio Scalfari – the founder and still now chief editorialist of *La Repubblica*, the Italian daily newspaper most widely read on the left – is emblematic. In his vehement denunciation, Scalfari welds the accusation of 'anti-political' to that of right-wing extremism. He has written: 'This is a campaign of the right, a xenophobic, anti-immigration right, disdainful of all ideology, against political parties (all parties, without exception) and against the institutions, from the President of the Republic to the Prime Minister and the ministers (all ministers) of the government, and against the judiciary and the Constitutional Court … [Grillo] wants to demolish all of the existing architecture, but his objective is reactionary, in that he yearns for dictatorship: his own. It is the same strategy adopted by Le Pen's French National Front and by the anti-Europe movement in Germany, Greece, Denmark and Holland' (Scalfari, 2013).

But this is an extreme view. Indeed, in the same newspaper, another authoritative commentator, Barbara Spinelli (2013), has expressed disagreement 'with the harsh judgment on the anti-European protest movements that have sprung up … Those who listen to Grillo … will not encounter nationalism nor true anti-European sentiment … This does not mean that the M5S can be likened to Marine Le Pen or to the neo-Nazis in Greece and Hungary'. Nevertheless, the fear of an ideological bond between the M5S and the extreme right populist movements in Europe has arisen in more than a few observers of Italian politics, especially foreign observers.

Our conviction is that both interpretations of the M5S – as 'leftist' or 'rightist' – are based on prejudicial and value-laden representations rather than on a solid sociological description of those who vote for this party. Our research revealed a variegated picture, which can be summarized by the following points:

1. Those who voted for the M5S in the February 2013 general election are not, for the most part, on the left nor on the right. *On average* (and this is an important specification), they stand somewhere around the centre of

8 On this point, see Chapter 7 in this volume.

the left-right political spectrum (only slightly left of centre), between the Partito Democratico and the Popolo della libertà ('People of Freedom').

2. The mean central position on the ideological scale might be the result of two ideologically opposed groups. Specifically, it has been claimed that the M5S electorate embraces a leftist area of protest-oriented/environmentalist origin or disillusioned former Partito Democratico voters, and a non-ideological populist area. This hypothesis, however, is not confirmed by our data, which do not indicate a significant presence of those whom we have called 'consistent leftist' voters. Nor did we identify any considerable presence of 'consistent rightist' voters.
3. The M5S electorate does not have a leftist nucleus, not even one that is quantitatively modest but qualitatively significant. According to a current hypothesis, those voters who most closely identify themselves with the movement – we might call them militants – are 'leftist'. However, our data indicate that, among those who are 'closest to the party', 'consistent leftist' voters are no more numerous than ordinary sympathizers.
4. By contrast, the M5S has more 'non-ideological' or 'inconsistent' voters than the other parties. These voters are people who give contradictory answers to questions concerning the left-right axis, in that some of their answers are 'leftist' while others are 'rightist'. However, our data show that this greater presence of 'inconsistent' voters is not due to a lack of information or to scant interest in political issues; rather, it stems from what we might call a knowing rejection of the left-right ideology.

In conclusion, those who voted for the M5S in February 2013 cannot be defined as being either on the left or on the right. It should be noted that being neither left nor right is an advantage at the time of consensus-gathering, especially if this hinges on protest. However, it becomes an insurmountable handicap when the time comes to make proposals and to frame a policy, whether in government or in opposition; indeed, if the party were to adopt a rightist stance, it would upset its leftist supporters, and vice versa.

Thus, we can say that the 5 Stars Movement lacks a unifying *ideological* principle. And this is added to its lack of unifying *sociological* principles, in that it is a *catch-all* party in the sense that it does not have a privileged social class (see Chapter 4 in this volume), as did Berlusconi's populism, which appealed to the self-employed, the professional classes, and the private as opposed to the public sector. Nor does it have a geographical connotation, like that of the Lega Nord, a populist movement but with territorial roots.

This lack of unifying principles was probably at the root of the movement's sudden electoral success. However, it also exposes the movement to the risk of electoral collapse, or at least considerable shrinkage, though the uncertainty of Italian politics renders such forecasts extremely chancy.

We can conclude by saying that the ideological uncertainty of the M5S is the clearest example of the fact that populism can be dressed in any political colour.

The current ideological uncertainty of the M5S may also be due to the fact that its electorate – precisely because this party has emerged so recently – probably contains a considerable number of swing voters, i.e. people who voted M5S only out of a confused desire for change and novelty, and who may well abandon the movement on the next electoral occasion. Only when the M5S has freed itself from this uncertain vote and has developed a stable 'hard core' of voters who are faithful in the long term will we be better able to explore the characteristics of its political culture and, especially, to understand more fully whether, and to what degree, the movement is the fount of a 'new' political culture, which we have called 'post-ideological' and which currently appears to have muddled features and blurred outlines.

References

Bell, D. 1965. *The end of ideology: On the Exhaustion of Political Ideas*. Glencoe, IL: Free Press.

Corbetta, P., Cavazza, N. and Roccato, M., 2009. Between Ideology and Social Representations: Four Theses Plus (a New) One on the Relevance and the Meaning of the Political Left and Right. *European Journal of Political Research*, 48(5), pp. 622–41.

Corbetta, P. and Gualmini, E. 2013. *Il partito di Grillo*. Bologna: Il Mulino.

Corbetta, P. and Roccato, M. 2006. Autodefinizioni. Il lessico della politica. In: P. Catellani and P. Corbetta, eds. *Sinistra e destra. Le radici psicologiche della differenza politica*. Bologna: Il Mulino, pp. 45–71.

Grillo, B. 2013a. Il M5S non è né di destra né di sinistra *Beppegrillo.it* [blog] 11 January. Available at: http://www.beppegrillo.it/2013/01/il_m5s_non_e_di_destra_ne_di_sinistra.html [Accessed 4 June 2014].

———. 2013b. Il M5S non è di sinistra (e neppure di destra) *Beppegrillo.it*, [blog] 19 May. Available at http://www.beppegrillo.it/2013/05/il_m5s_non_e_di.html [Accessed 4 June 2014].

Inglehart, R. and Klingemann, H.D. 1976. Party Identification, Ideological Preference and the Left-Right Dimension among Western Publics. In: I. Budge, I. Crewe and D. Farlie, eds. *Party Identification and Beyond*. London: Wiley, pp. 243–73.

Jost, J. 2006. The End of the End of Ideology. *American Psychologist*, 61(7), pp. 651–70.

Kitschelt, H. 1988. Left-Libertarian Parties: Explaining Innovation in Competitive Systems. *World Politics*, 40(2), pp. 194–234.

Mair, P. 2007. Left-Right Orientations. In: R.J. Dalton and H.D. Klingemann, eds. *The Oxford Handbook of Political Behaviour*. Oxford: Oxford University Press, pp. 206–22.

Mény, Y. and Surel, Y. 2000. *Par le peuple, pour le people*. Paris: Fayard.

Merlo, F. 2013. Elezioni 2013, Grillo è l'Alba dorata italiana. *la Repubblica* [online] 25 February. Available at: http://video.repubblica.it/dossier/movimento-5-stelle-beppe-grillo/elezioni-2013-merlo-grillo-e-l-alba-dorata-italiana/120625/119108 [Accessed 4 June 2014].

Mudde, C. 2013. Three decades of populist radical right parties in Western Europe: So what? *European Journal of Political Research*, 52(1), pp. 1–19.

Mudde, C. and Kaltwasser, C.R. 2011. *Voices of the Peoples: Populism in Europe and Latin America Compared.* Kellogg Institute Working Paper 378. Notre Dame, IN: Kellogg Institute for International Studies.

Ruzza, C., and Fella, S. 2009. *Re-inventing the Italian Right. Territorial Politics, Populism and 'Post-Fascism'*. London: Routledge.

Scalfari, E. 2013. Se vince Grillo il paese va a rotoli. *la Repubblica*, 11 March, p. 1.

Spinelli, B. 2013. Europa, l'ufficio lettere smarrite. *la Repubblica*, 6 November, p. 1.

Taggart, P. 2000. *Populism*. Buckingham: Open University Press.

———. 2002. Populism and the Pathology of Representative Politics. In: Y. Mény and Y. Surel, eds. *Democracies and the Populist Challenge*. Basingstoke: Palgrave, pp. 62–80.

Chapter 10

Conclusion: The Organisational and Ideological Roots of the Electoral Success

Filippo Tronconi

Introduction

The electoral result of the M5S in the 2013 general elections has been astonishing. In its first electoral participation at national level, only three years after its official birth, this party obtained slightly less than nine million votes for the Chamber of Deputies (25.6 per cent) and 7.4 million for the Senate (23.6 per cent), gaining 109 and 54 seats respectively. In the competition for the Lower Chamber it was the most voted party, with some 40,000 votes more than the Partito Democratico.[1] This is by far the most successful party entry in the history of post-war Western European democracies. As a point of reference, Berlusconi's Forza Italia, in its first electoral appearance in 1994, a few months after its official birth, 'only' achieved 21 per cent of the votes.

If one looks at other successful 'newcomers' around Europe, the comparison is even more surprising. Until the 1970s, due to the 'freezing' of cleavage structures (Lipset and Rokkan 1967; Bartolini and Mair 1990), the successful entry of new parties into the electoral arena has been extremely rare, and mainly due to the re-activation of old cleavages. This is for instance the case of the Volksunie in Belgium, formed in 1954 by Flemish nationalist activists (De Winter 1998). In the same year's general elections this party won 2.2 per cent of the votes and one seat, while the first significant result arrived only 11 years later (6.7 per cent of the votes, 12 seats).

More recently, scholars have widely described two waves of new political parties, the left libertarian and the new radical right.[2] The German Grünen are among the first and probably the most well-known example of the first kind. This party was founded in 1980 and achieved representation in the national parliament

1 If one considers only the votes expressed in Italy. According to the Italian legislation, a few seats are reserved for Italians living abroad, among whom the M5S did not score equally well. Considering the overall number of votes, the Partito Democratico is the most voted party (8,932,615 votes, with the M5S getting 8,797,902 votes).

2 See, among many others, Kitschelt (1988), Müller-Rommel (1989) on the emergence of left libertarian parties; Ignazi (1992), Kitschelt (1995), Norris (2005) on the new radical right.

three years later (27 seats, 5.6 per cent of the votes), reaching its highest result to date in 2009 (10.7 per cent of the votes and 68 seats in the Bundestag). The French Front National, one of the most successful radical right parties, was founded in 1972, but its first electoral breakthrough was in 1986 (9.6 per cent of the votes, 35 seats), while its best result in elections for the National Assembly was in 1997 (14.9 per cent, but only one seat, due to the majoritarian French electoral system). The Danish Fremskridtspartiet (Progress Party) had a different electoral history. Born in 1972 as an anti-tax party, it immediately achieved a remarkable result in the 1973 parliamentary elections, becoming the second most voted party behind the Social Democrats, with 15.9 per cent of the votes and 28 seats. However, it was not able to repeat that result in the following elections, and slipped below 10 per cent in the eighties, to finally disappear from the Danish Folketing in 2001. Its successor, the Dansk Folkeparti (Danish People's Party) was launched in 1995 and received between 7.4 and 13.8 per cent of the votes in the electoral competitions of the last two decades.

The Lijst Pim Fortuyn in the Netherlands, obtained 17 per cent of the votes and 26 seats in its first electoral competition in 2002, becoming the second most voted party; however the party disappeared a few years later, after its founder and leader was murdered.[3] From this quick and partial survey of some of the most successful 'new' parties of Western Europe, it appears evident that the electoral success of the M5S in 2013 represents a truly outstanding case which requires explanation.

In political science three kinds of factors have been identified as plausible explanations for the rise and success of new political actors in consolidated democracies. First, success might be favoured by institutional conditions that make it easier for challengers of existing parties to access the competition. This is sometimes referred to as electoral contestability (Bartolini 2002, pp. 90–92). Secondly, a party might profit from an innovative organisational structure that makes it easier to mobilise its electoral base, or to have access to the necessary resources (e.g. funding). In general, the organisational advantage consists of being able to better exploit some relevant change in the environment. This was the case, for instance, of the innovative organisation of mass parties in Europe in times of enfranchisement. Third, the success of a challenger can originate from its ability to intercept the expectations and needs of a segment of the electorate that existing parties are not (or are no longer) able to represent. This refers, in other words, to occupying the 'right spot' in the political space, one that is either genuinely new, i.e. defined by a new dimension of competition, or has been left unguarded by existing parties. An example of the first kind can be the rise of a Eurosceptic party in a country that has recently joined the European Union; an example of the second kind can be an independentist party losing its credibility after signing an agreement that is perceived as betraying the aspirations for self-rule of the peripheral region, thus allowing the rise of a new hard-liner competitor. The first

3 Pim Fortuyn was killed by an environmental and animal-rights activist a few days before the 2002 elections.

of these factors is a system-level explanation, affecting the chances of success of all potential challengers of the existing party system, while the other two are party-level explanations, affecting the probabilities of emergence of individual political actors.

In the next pages I will assess the relative significance of each of these three arguments in the case of the M5S, building on the evidence gathered so far in the previous chapters of this volume. In the last section I will then move to some conclusive speculations on the uncertain prospects for the sustainability of the success of this party in the long run.

Explaining the Success: Electoral Contestability

Contestability refers to the openness of the electoral competition to the entry of new political parties. Openness is in turn shaped by the presence and permeability of institutional barriers, such as incentives and constraints determined by electoral rules, but also the existence of elected assemblies below the state level, or access to state resources. A low electoral threshold and easy access to public resources (funding and channels of communication) are expected to reduce the costs of party entry. Moreover, new parties can find it easier to gain initial visibility (and representation) at other levels, and later exploit this resource to boost their chances at general elections. Thus, countries characterised by significant representative arenas at sub-state or supra-state level, provide better opportunities for new parties to emerge. Beyond that, elections for the European Parliament and for regional assemblies are often characterised by distinctive electoral behaviours: given the second-order nature of these elections (Reif and Schmidt 1980; Schakel and Jeffery 2013), small and emerging parties often perform better than they do in general elections.

Although apparently obvious, the fact that higher institutional barriers make it more difficult for new political subjects to gain representation has not been empirically confirmed. The most comprehensive comparative studies (Harmel and Robertson 1985; Hug 2000; Tavits 2006) fail to reach a conclusive proof of the relevance of these explanations for the electoral breakthrough of new parties.

The case of the M5S appears to be in line with the contradictory evidence of these studies. The current Italian electoral system was introduced in 2005 by the centre-right coalition led by Silvio Berlusconi. It is based on proportional representation plus a majority bonus to be awarded to the party or coalition receiving the highest number of votes nationwide. Also, and more relevant to the present argument, a rather complex system of multiple thresholds is present. Lists competing individually must overcome a 4 per cent nationwide threshold in order to gain seats in the Chamber of Deputies and an 8 per cent threshold on a regional basis in order to gain seats in the Senate. Coalitions, to be formally declared in advance, must reach 10 per cent of the votes for the Chamber and 20 per cent of the votes, on a regional basis, for the Senate. Lists included in a coalition overcoming the threshold must receive 2 per cent of the votes for the Chamber and 3 per cent of the votes for the Senate.[4] These are rather demanding thresholds for newcomers, especially if they choose not to join one of the main coalitions. Before the M5S, in the three elections in which the electoral system was adopted (2006, 2008 and 2013), only one party overcame the threshold without being included in one of the two main coalitions – the Unione di Centro in 2008 (with 5.6 per cent of the votes).

The access to state resources (public funding and communication on state networks) is relatively easy, but only for parties already represented. Thus, the M5S was not entitled to any public funding before obtaining its first regional representatives in 2010 (in the two regions where it was able to gain representation, Emilia-Romagna and Piedmont). Furthermore, it must be noted that one of the flagship battles of the movement is precisely for the abolition of any public funding to parties, and that the M5S takes pride in giving back all the money received from the State (Grillo 2012a, 2013a). Also access to the main media was limited during the 2013 electoral campaign. Legnante et al. (2013, p. 38) report that Beppe Grillo was present only in 7 per cent of front-page news and in 5 per cent of the time dedicated to information TV programmes during the 90 days preceding the vote. As a term of reference, the leader of the PD, Pierluigi Bersani, had 18 per cent and 13 per cent of the space in newspapers and on TV respectively; Silvio Berlusconi 35 per cent and 19 per cent.

The third hypothesis concerns the existence of 'alternative electoral arenas'. The M5S was initially conceived as a 'brand' connecting lists competing exclusively on a local basis. This was in fact the case in 2008 and 2009, when a number of 'Amici di Beppe Grillo' (Friends of Beppe Grillo) lists took part in municipal elections. Participation in the 2010 regional elections probably marked a turning point in this strategy, proving that the movement was able to run also on a non-strictly local competition. Particularly important, in this respect, were the regional elections in Sicily in October 2012. Beppe Grillo invested heavily in the electoral campaign in this region,[5] and the excellent result (14.9 per cent) gave the movement a clear boost to the campaign for the national elections to be held only a few months later.

To sum up on this point, political science literature does not provide conclusive evidence on the effects of contextual institutional factors on the probability of new parties to get representation at national level. Be it as it may, in our case, two of these factors, namely the electoral system and access to state resources, should be considered as limiting the probability of success of the M5S. On the contrary, the existence of relevant electoral arenas at sub-state level might have favoured the emergence of this party as a credible competitor also at national level.

4 See Massetti (2006) for details.

5 The opening of the electoral campaign of the M5S was marked by Grillo's swim across the Strait of Messina, which received enormous media attention, and started off his tour around the Sicilian cities.

Explaining the Success: Organisation

Several studies have emphasised the importance of the organisational aspects on the initial stages of party development (Panebianco 1982; Harmel 1985; Harmel and Såsand 1993). Harmel and Såsand (1993), in particular, offer an overview of challenges parties have to address to establish themselves as consolidated actors in the political arena. Three phases of party development are pinpointed: 1) *Identification*, when the party needs to develop a recognisable message and communicate it; at this stage the leader is normally the only relevant figure within the party; 2) *Organisation*, when from a one-person operation the party evolves into an organisation: here the need for members' coordination and leadership control over the party's emerging apparatus becomes visible. In particular, the party now has to face risks of factionalism, between members who prefer a pragmatic approach and do not exclude a path towards 'normalisation' and members who aim to keep the pure, original message of the party; 3) *Stabilisation*, when the focus is moved from internal organisation to the building of a solid and credible image within the political system, in order to build alliances with other political forces and eventually become an acceptable coalition member. Harmel and Såsand's main idea is that different leadership styles are needed in order to effectively tackle the different challenges of each phase of development. In the first phase the ideal leader is a 'creator and preacher', with an authoritative or charismatic personality and communication skills. In the second phase the leader must be an 'organiser', able to delegate part of his or her tasks and willing to institutionalise the internal rules of the party. In the third phase, finally, the leader must be a 'moderator and stabiliser, someone with good personal credentials for credibility and dependability'. The troubles for the emerging party begin when the founding leader does not possess the skills needed to advance to the second and third organisational stages and is not willing to give way to a more suitable heir; in alternative, or in addition, a potential source of problems is given by the overlap of two phases, typically the first two. In other words, too much and too fast success can be harmful to the party, as it makes it necessary to accomplish the identification and the organisation tasks simultaneously.

How does this apply to the case of the M5S? The analyses presented in previous chapters of this volume[6] suggest that several organisational features could represent important elements for understanding the emergence and initial success of this party.

In short, the defining aspects of the M5S from the organisational point of view can be reduced to 1) a charismatic leadership; 2) the total absence of meso-structures connecting the 'party in central office' to the 'party on the ground'; 3) an effective use of the internet – and specifically of the social network meetup.com – as a tool for the recruitment of members.

6 See in particular Chapters 2 and 3 on party organisation and activists.

The relevance of a charismatic leadership for the emergence and initial success of a party hardly needs any explanation. Charisma is an exceptional resource outwards where the leader's skills as a 'preacher' are needed to mobilise supporters around the party's message. It is also a resource inwards, as a way to keep the party cohesive, where cohesion is given by the fact that only those who benefit from the leader's support and faith have authorised access to the party's 'inner circle' (Panebianco 1982, p. 131). Furthermore, as the party is totally identified with the charismatic leader, he or she is the only one in a position to dictate the official party line, thus avoiding (or immediately resolving) any possible internal conflict. This point is directly connected with the second aspect we referred to above, namely the absence of intermediate organisational structures between the party in central office and the party on the ground. Indeed, the party in central office can be reduced to Grillo himself, or to the Grillo-Casaleggio duo.[7] By definition, a charismatic leadership is antithetical to the idea of bureaucratisation that is associated with the creation of the formal apparatus that is typical of traditional mass parties. This would in fact limit the leader's control over the party and constrain his freedom of action. These notions are not new. Charismatic leadership is known to lead towards a paradoxical situation: the party is strongly centralised, but its institutionalisation is unlikely. Centralisation is in fact the result of members' loyalty to the leader, not to the party as such, to the point that the hypothetical retirement of the leader from his political role would be likely to lead to the disappearance of the party itself. While the lack of any organisational structures above the local level might be seen as an obstacle to the development of the party in the long run, I argue that it was instead an asset in the early stages of the M5S lifespan, and contributed to explain its success in the 2009–2013 electoral cycle. The absence of an intermediate organisational structure was often mentioned in order to underline the difference between the M5S and rival parties also on this point[8] and to build a rhetoric of politics handed back to ordinary citizens, as opposed to politics managed by party bureaucrats.

This leads us to our third point – the use of the internet. Though often alluded to in the political debate, however, this aspect needs to be addressed in detail, as myths and realities are mixed when referring to the relationship between the internet and the M5S. The rhetoric of an internet-based party is to a large extent exaggerated, if one considers that during the 2013 electoral campaign 84 per cent of M5S voters declared that they used television as a source of political information, while the internet is cited by 33 per cent, which is even less than newspapers (37 per cent) (see Chapter 6 in this volume). Also the claim that the M5S is realising

7 Throughout this chapter I will refer to Beppe Grillo as the leader of the party, as he is most of the time the public voice of the M5S. Nonetheless, the role of Gianroberto Casaleggio is certainly significant in shaping the strategy of the party, as described in the first chapter of this book.

8 The 'non-statute' of the movement states that 'the M5S is not a political party, nor is it foreseen to become a political party in the future'.

a new model of direct democracy working through constant online consultation and deliberation does not correspond to observable facts. The online selection of candidates for the parliamentary elections of 2013, held on 3–6 December 2012 – the so-called 'parlamentarie' – suffered from restrictive rules for participation,[9] leading to a low turnout. About 20,000 voters, two thirds of those entitled to vote, took part in these primaries, according to the figures released by Grillo. This figure should be compared to the 3.1 million participating in the analogous initiative of the Partito Democratico a few weeks before. Low participation led in turn to the selection of candidates receiving an extremely low number of preferences. On average, deputies had received only 133 votes in the primaries (with a minimum of 22 votes) while 131 primary votes were necessary to be elected as senators (with a minimum of 28). After the 2013 elections, online votes were adopted also for selecting the candidate of the M5S for the office of President of the Republic and for taking other decisions, among which the expulsion of several deputies and Senators from the movement. In all these cases the turnout rate was lower than observed in the 'parlamentarie'. Moreover, the decision of what issues to submit to the procedure of electronic voting and when, is always unilaterally taken by Beppe Grillo, and external checks on the security and transparency of vote operations have never been possible, as the digital infrastructure on which such votes are expressed is strictly proprietary.

If the promises of a digital revolution in the internal democratic procedures have not been kept, the internet has nonetheless been a crucial instrument for the birth and development of the M5S. As shown in Chapters 2 and 3, the truly original aspect of the organisation of this party lies in the interconnection between virtual and physical arenas of recruitment and activism. The meetup.com platform was crucial for establishing a network of Grillo's followers and put them in contact with each other in local communities. Meetup.com turned out to be an ideal tool to transform the atomised audience of Grillo's blog into an organisation with roots in many local communities and an 'army' of activists ready to mobilise and to bring the ideas and rallying cries of the leader from the blogosphere into squares. At the same time it was functional to the goal of keeping the complexity of internal organisational structures to a minimum, reaffirming its original nature of movement party.

To sum up on this aspect, the emergence of the M5S has taken advantage of a charismatic leadership, but also of its ability to stress its difference from the bureaucratic organisational model of traditional parties. This was achieved through a party in central office kept to a minimum (Grillo himself, the web entrepreneur Gianroberto Casaleggio and a not well defined staff that manages the blog), an extensive use of the meetup.com platform as a tool for organising the local units of activists, and a total absence of intermediate bodies between these two levels. Going back to the Harmel and Svåsand concepts introduced above, this organisational

9 Only those who had registered in the movement and sent a digital copy of their ID by 30 September 2012 were entitled to vote. Also candidacies were restricted to non-elected candidates at previous local and regional elections.

model has proven perfectly suitable for the *identification* phase, and has borne the shock wave of a sudden electoral success of unexpected dimensions. The first months after the 2013 elections, however, have shown the limits of this model as the party faces its *organisation* phase. The tightening of Grillo's control over the party, made manifest by the expulsion of numerous MPs and other local activists and elected representatives, can be seen as a symptom of growing underground tensions within the party. I will go back to these difficulties in the concluding section, after examining the ideological explanation of the party's success.

Explaining the Success: Ideological Positioning

If one takes a look at the 2013 electoral manifesto of the M5S, there can be little doubt about its positioning in the ideological space of Italian politics. Indeed, according to the right-left index of the Manifesto Project Database (Volkens et al. 2013), the M5S is located on the extreme left, well beyond the mainstream left represented by the Partito Democratico and even the radical left represented by Sinistra Ecologia Libertà and the umbrella list of Rivoluzione Civile (Figure 10.1). This is in sharp contrast with the figures shown in the previous chapters of this volume. Pedrazzani and Pinto argue that about half of M5S voters in 2013 elections voted for right of centre parties in 2008, while radical left voters were only 11.7 per cent (see Figure 4.5). Also Colloca and Corbetta underline the fact that M5S voters are evenly distributed along the whole ideological spectrum. Furthermore, if one looks at a number of individual issues – ranging from state intervention in the economy to abortion rights – M5S voters almost invariably locate themselves in a median position between mainstream left and mainstream right parties (see Figures 9.1 and 9.2). How do we make sense of these contradictory facts? How was a party presenting itself with radical left ideological positions able to get votes from both leftist and rightist voters? In order to give an answer to this puzzle, I will shortly recall the steps leading to the making of the M5S manifesto. This will allow us to place the M5S more realistically into the space of Italian politics.

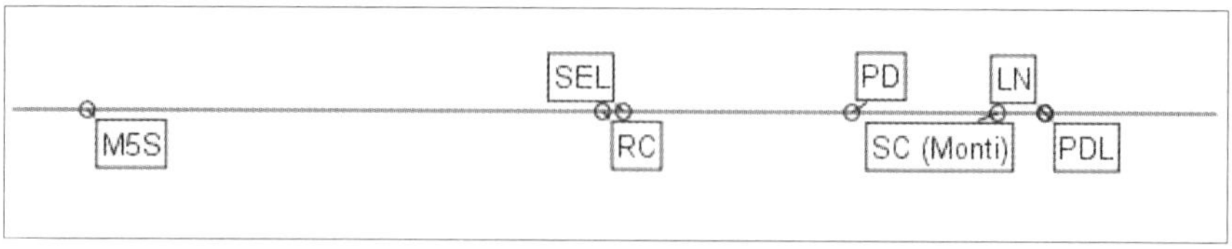

Figure 10.1 The location of the main Italian parties in 2013, according to the left-right index of the Manifesto Project Database

Note: The M5S positioning is based on the 2009 manifesto.
Source: https://manifesto-project.wzb.eu/.

The first manifesto was proposed by Grillo at a national meeting of meetups held in Florence in March 2009, which means several months before the official birth of the party. The *Carta di Firenze*, a guideline for the 'Amici di Beppe Grillo' civic lists contesting local elections in the same year, consists of 12 points dealing with public water management, the environment (mainly referring to a correct waste management), public transport, energy efficiency and renewable energy, and internet connectivity.

A more detailed manifesto was presented on the occasion of the official launching of the M5S in Milan in October 2009. The 120 items in this 15-page document are divided into seven sections (State and citizens, Energy, Information, Economy, Transport, Health, Education), and presented by Grillo himself (2009) as 'all utopian, thus all feasible'. This has remained the official manifesto of the movement up to the present day, and never updated since its first release, in spite of Grillo's statement that 'there will be time to discuss it together online, to improve it, to amend it in the next months' (Grillo 2009). Grillo (2012) claims that it 'has been drafted online, thanks to thousands of contributions and the help of experts on specific issues', but to the best of my knowledge, no traces have remained on the internet about this discussion.

If one considers the content of this manifesto (Movimento 5 Stelle 2009), it immediately appears obvious why it can be classified as a radical leftist party. Overall, the manifesto describes a party with liberal views on the libertarian-authoritarian dimension, and a strong pro-state orientation on the state-market dimension, beyond the 'obvious' focus on anti-establishment and anti-party stances. The sections on 'State and citizens' and on 'information' go to the core of this anti-establishment message of the M5S, both towards elected officials and communication company owners. In the first section a number of proposals are directed towards the moralisation of politics ('ineligibility for election for convicted citizens'), in favour of tools of direct democracy ('referenda to abrogate and propose laws without a quorum', 'bills to be published online at least three months before their approval in order to get comments from citizens'), against what are perceived to be 'privileges' of politicians ('MPs' salaries in line with the national average'). The section on information, finally, beyond stressing again the issue of internet connectivity, calls for enhanced pluralism limiting the share of ownership of editorial companies (no more than 10 per cent of capital share) and abolishing public contributions to newspapers.

The other sections are generally fragmentary and in many cases poorly written, but point to a rather clear *Weltanschauung*, close to many left-libertarian movements around Europe, based on post-materialist values, environmental safeguards, ethical consumerism and a critique of current developments of globalised capitalism. A few examples of these positions can be provided. In the energy section, for instance, a rather detailed overview of existing Italian and European regulations on energy efficiency is provided with proposals that mainly refer to a strict implementation of existing rules and to fiscal advantages for promoting the production of energy from renewable sources. The transport section is mainly focused on the 'immediate stop' to the public works related to the high-speed train in Val di Susa[10] and the promotion of environmentally-friendly urban mobility, although in much more generic terms: 'deterrent to the use of motor-driven private means in urban areas', 'bus lanes in urban areas', 'efficient connections among various forms of public transport'. The health section is generally concerned with the preservation of a public, universal-access health system, ('free access to public health services', 'separation of careers of private and public sector doctors', 'funding of independent [health] research, with funds destined for military research') and information towards prevention, a healthy lifestyle and ethical consumerism ('an independent, public and permanent program of health education, on aiming to achieve a correct use of drugs, their risks and benefits'). The same attention towards the preservation and improvement of the public sector is present in the education section. The economy section insists on transparency in the banking system, empowerment of consumers and private savers vis-à-vis the big companies, the development of a system of local production, distribution and consumption of goods (particularly in the food industry). On the issue of public expenditure, a general remark is made on the need to 'reduce the public debt with strong intervention on the costs of the State, cutting waste and introducing new technologies in order for citizens to access information and services without turning to intermediaries'.

The third crucial stage of this 'manifesto in the making' is represented by Grillo's letter to Italians of February 6, 2013, in the midst of the electoral campaign. The letter (Grillo 2013b) is a perfect summary of Grillo's typical arguments and tones:

> Italy must become a community. No one must be left behind. It's intolerable, inhuman, to see the queues of people who have been turfed out of their jobs a few years before retirement age, people turfed out of their homes, and people who are unemployed waiting at the Caritas soup kitchens while the people who have plunged the country into poverty are going around with bodyguards, in official blue cars and with no financial problems. The parties are the main ones responsible for this situation. They have occupied the State. They have sold it off. They have taken out its flesh from the inside. Now, thanks to the newspapers and the TV channels that they control, they present themselves as the saviours of the fatherland, they, the very people who have fleeced it and used it for their own interests. … I'm not asking for your vote. I'm not interested in your vote without your participation in public affairs, without your direct involvement. If your vote for the M5S is simply a way of delegating someone to decide for you, then don't vote for us. If we are to change this country, then we have to do it all together. There's no other way. We will come out of the darkness and once more we will see the stars'.

10 As we have seen in Lorenzo Mosca's chapter, this has been one of the main battles of the M5S since its birth, and even before, in Beppe Grillo's theatre shows.

The letter is followed by '20 points to come out of darkness' which are presented as a synthesis of the 2009 manifesto, but actually update and amend it in significant ways, in order to include several topics recurrent in Grillo's 2013 campaign. Some points recall the previous document slightly amending it,[11] others are totally new. In particular, five points cover totally new issues: 'immediate measures to reinvigorate small and medium sized enterprises', 'calling a referendum on Italy's stay in the Euro', 'abolition of IMU (tax on house property) on primary residence', 'primary residence not subject to distraint', 'abolition of Equitalia (public agency for collection of taxes)'. What is most striking is that all these new pledges are clearly oriented to appeal to conservative voters, or voters from social groups that have consistently supported right-wing parties in the last decades. The Lega Nord and Berlusconi's Popolo della Libertà have always been largely majoritarian among small entrepreneurs, especially in the north-east of the country; opposition to the European common currency has increasingly been adopted by the Lega Nord as a campaign slogan; the suppression of taxes on real estate have been at the centre of Berlusconi's electoral campaign both in 2006 and in 2013.

One further issue, crucial in Grillo's campaign tour, although not mentioned in the '20 points' is opposition to amend legislation on citizenship in the direction of the so-called *ius soli*. This was among the proposals of the Partito Democratico and rejected by the Lega Nord and the other parties on the right.

All this clearly defines a political strategy aimed at expanding the area of potential voters of the M5S, blurring its position on the left-right dimension of competition, and keeping a strong hold on the anti-establishment issues. In fact while the economic crisis made a populist political discourse more attractive to a wide range of the electorate, the parties that built their fortunes exploiting these issues – the Lega Nord on the right and the Italia dei Valori on the left[12] – were facing their worst difficulties, being in turn hit by accusations of mismanagement of public money.

This strategy was amply rewarded in the 2013 election. As the chapter of Passarelli and Tuorto demonstrates, the electoral appeal of the M5S was successful in intercepting protest voters, a growing segment of the Italian electorate, not only among citizens alienated and distant from politics, but also among people traditionally engaged with politics but disappointed (or even disgusted) by the main political parties. At the same time, as we have seen in Colloca and Corbetta's

11 For instance, the first of the 20 points refers to a universal basic income, whereas the 2009 manifesto referred to a 'guaranteed unemployment income', which is substantially different. The fifth point is about 'abolishing public funding to parties' whereas the previous manifesto referred to 'abolishing electoral reimbursement'.

12 Italia dei Valori (Italy of Values) is the party founded by the former anti-corruption judge Antonio Di Pietro, protagonist of the Tangentopoli investigations at the beginning of the nineties. The Italia dei Valori was allied with the Partito Democratico in the 2008 elections, getting 4.4 per cent of the votes and reaching a record of 8 per cent in the 2009 European elections.

chapter, the vague and contradictory ideological positioning of the M5S was specifically designed to gather votes from the most diverse set of voters, ranging from the extreme left to the extreme right. While we might be tempted to observe that the M5S was electorally successful *in spite of* its contradictory positioning, a recent stream of political science literature (Meguid 2008; Rovny 2013) suggests instead that the M5S could be successful precisely *because of* this position blurring. In a multidimensional competition setting, the argument goes, one should not only consider the position of parties along the main dimensions of competition, but also issue salience and issue ownership. Typically, new parties emerge because they are able to impose a new issue as relevant, or to pick up an issue that is felt as relevant by wide sectors of the population but still not politicized by established parties, or to pick up an issue on which existing parties are not or no longer considered as credible. If a party is successful in introducing a new issue, the overall structure of competition changes. In this new setting, the challenger party has a clear incentive to reinforce its ownership over the new issue, while blurring its position on the pre-existing one(s). Position blurring, in turn, can result from not taking any position on an issue or – if this is not possible because of its saliency – from projecting vague, contradictory or ambiguous positions on it. The aim of this strategy is to minimise the risk of alienating voters that would otherwise perceive their distance from the party on that specific issue (see Rovny 2013, pp. 5–6).

In the Italian scenario the M5S was able, on the one hand, to present itself as the most credible owner of the anti-establishment issue, which was particularly salient in 2013 due to a number of scandals involving politicians from all traditional parties, including the former champions of the moralisation of politics. On the other hand, its strategy involved blurring its position on the main left-right axis of competition. This was achieved by appealing to leftist voters with the emphasis on the environment, the pledge for a universal basic income, support for the public health and education systems, all issues that have been present in the M5S's political discourse since its very origins. At the same time, rightist voters could consider voting for a party that was in favour of lowering taxes on house property, critical towards the Euro, sympathetic towards the expectations of small entrepreneurs and cautious towards any opening on immigration policy, all issues added to the original manifesto and particularly emphasised during the 2013 campaign.

Here to Stay? Concluding Remarks on the Uncertain Future of the M5S

We started this concluding chapter wondering where we could trace the origin of the unprecedented, astonishing electoral success of the M5S in the general elections of February 2013. We looked for hints for an answer in three areas: a favourable institutional setting, organisational innovations and the ideological profile of the party. We can now safely discard the first answer – indeed, the M5S had to overcome rather high institutional barriers, both in terms of electoral threshold and access to the main communication channels and financial resources. If anything, the M5S was able to achieve its success *in spite of* a difficult institutional environment, not thanks to it.

On the contrary, interesting elements emerged from the other two sides. The main organisational aspect of Grillo's party, beyond his personal charisma, is the original mix of new and old means of internal communication. These are Grillo's blog, where the catchphrases of the party are launched and the ideological profile is shaped; the social networks – beginning with meetup.com and extending to Facebook – where new potential activists are recruited and first involved in the internal life of the organisation; the territory, meaning both the assembly of local groups and the 'piazza' of public initiatives during as well as outside the electoral campaign. This organisation has proven to be effective in mobilising a new cohort of citizens, interested in politics, informed, and willing to participate, but kept at distance by delegitimised, unattractive mainstream parties. At the same time, the absence of any supra-local organisational body has prevented the rise of possible challenges to Grillo's leadership.

As far as ideology is concerned, the M5S has been able, to put it simply, to be in the right spot of the political space at the right time. On the one side it managed to monopolise the theme of protest against the establishment at a time when political elites reached their lowest level of popularity, in the midst of an unprecedented economic crisis that they were clearly unable to handle. On the other side, Beppe Grillo was quick to reposition his party on the left-right dimension of competition. Without abandoning the original left-libertarian stances and the links with environmental movements, he added a number of catchphrases appealing to the world of small entrepreneurs, artisans and self-employed workers that were once attracted by Berlusconi's Forza Italia and even more so by the Lega Nord. The result is an ambiguous and contradictory manifesto, talking to different social groups with distant, if not opposite, interests and ideological backgrounds, that was nonetheless suitable to attract voters ranging from the extreme right to the extreme left.

Our interpretation of the success of the M5S raises one more question. How stable is the success of this party? Is it bound to consolidate its position as a leading force in the Italian political system, or might it crumble as fast as it emerged? The two elements that we have proposed as explanations for the success of the M5S, could be useful also for understanding its evolution in the medium-term. Let's start from the ideological profile. Position blurring on the traditional left-right dimension of competition has been a valuable asset, but might turn out to be a weak point if the party is to assume increasing institutional responsibilities. A number of studies, mainly focusing on radical right parties, underline that assuming government responsibilities is likely to lead to major electoral defeats (Heinisch 2003; Buelens and Hino 2009), because participation in government implies taking positions precisely on those issues that emerging parties are more prone to avoid, in order to keep their potential constituencies as wide as possible. After the 2013 elections, the M5S has been repeatedly offered a coalition agreement by the Partito

Democratico, but they have refused. This is the essence of the dilemma between an office and a vote seeking strategy: taking government responsibilities – with the risk of alienating part of the electorate – or remaining (permanently?) in opposition, giving up to the possibility of any policy influence, except an indirect one. In the short run, Beppe Grillo probably did the right thing. The first task for a consolidating political actor is to define its own identity, and this is even more so for an anti-establishment movement, which would certainly be damaged by an alliance with those parties that are constantly pointed to as those mainly responsible for all Italian problems. But also this strategy implies some costs. First, it is likely to create tensions within the movement between a faction of 'hawks', refusing any dialogue with other parties, and a faction of 'doves', open at least to the possibility of temporary alliances in parliament on specific issues. These contrasts have been visible since the very beginning of the parliamentary experience of the M5S, and have occasionally led to internal showdowns and eventually to the expulsion of 19 out of the 163 MPs. The dilemma between those who privilege the loyalty of the movement to its original stances and those who would instead favour immediate policy results is likely to occur again in the future, especially if and when the electoral growth of the party comes to a stop. On a similar note, the M5S could be put under pressure by other parties reacting to the threat of a growing populist opponent by implementing some policy reforms going in the direction of satisfying the pledges of the M5S manifesto. This is, for instance, the case of the legislation for a gradual suppression of public party funding passed by the Italian parliament at the end of 2013, with the opposition of the M5S (Grillo 2013c). Similarly, the M5S has opposed the abolition of provincial elected assemblies, which is included in its own 2009 manifesto, as a 'fake' abolition (Grillo 2014). In general, entering an institutional arena with a significant strength, as the M5S did in 2013, means in one way or another being forced to take hard choices that could be previously avoided, either being challenged by other political forces on one's own core issues, or being forced to diversify one's appeal by taking a position on new and troublesome issues.

The second peril is related to the organisational nature of the M5S as a 'movement party' that is, as such, unstable by definition (Kitschelt 2006). It is even more unstable in the peculiar case of the M5S which, as we have seen, mixes up the contradictory features of a movement party and a charismatic party. Also from this perspective the 2013 general election and the movement's consequent entry in the legislative arena mark a crucial turning point. Until it was acting as a loose confederation of groups organised at local level, the M5S could reconcile the presence of a national leader (the 'megaphone' of the movement, as Grillo called himself) with a relatively autonomous local assembly of activists. However, when the party is expected to take decisions on national policy issues and strategies, this contradiction appears more and more unbearable. As we have argued above, the probability of internal conflicts rises, and thus the need for a strong centralised leadership. At the same time, the stronger the leadership, the more evident the contradiction with the aspiration of the party to keep a totally horizontal structure, where 'each one counts as one'. The hyperbolic (and naïve) narrative that described the internet as the tool to reach the goal of direct democracy and total transparency on all the crucial decisions for the life of the movement has soon proven to be unrealistic. Consultations with registered members have taken place from time to time, when Beppe Grillo has decided so, and according to the procedures envisaged by Grillo himself. What remains of a promise of hyper-democracy is a 'leaderist' party, with few spaces for an internal open debate, mostly restricted to the local level.

In its short lifespan, the M5S has shaken the Italian party system in a way that has no counterparts in the recent history of Europe. Yet its survival and consolidation is not guaranteed. It mainly depends on its ability to adapt to a new institutional environment, something which probably requires changes in the internal organisation, including a redefinition of Grillo's leadership. It also needs to consolidate its electoral appeal to voters on a defined and coherent set of issues, beyond the anti-establishment protest. If the party is able to handle such challenges, it will have a chance to play a leading role on the Italian political stage. If not, it might fade as fast as it appeared.

References

Bartolini, S. 2002. Electoral and Party Competition: Analytical Dimensions and Empirical Problems. In: R. Gunther, J.R. Montero and J. Linz, eds. 2002.*Political Parties. Old Concepts and New Challenges*. Oxford: Oxford University Press, pp. 84–109.

Bartolini, S. and Mair, P. 1990. *Identity, Competition, and Electoral Availability: The Stabilisation of European Electorates 1885–1985*. Cambridge: Cambridge University Press.

Buelens, J. and Hino, A. 2009. The Electoral Fate of New Parties in Government. In: K. Deschouwer, ed. *New Parties in Government. In Power for the First Time*. London: Routledge, pp. 157–74.

De Winter, L. 1998. The Volksunie and the dilemma between policy success and electoral survival in Flanders. In: L. De Winter and H. Tursan, eds. *Regionalist Parties in Western Europe*. London: Routledge, pp. 28–50.

Grillo, B. 2009. Il Programma del Movimento a 5 Stelle *Beppegrillo.it* [blog] 9 October. Available at: http://www.beppegrillo.it/2009/10/il_programma_de.html [Accessed 4 June 2014].

———. 2012a. M5S Sicilia: 1.426.000 euro rifiutati *Beppegrillo.it* [blog] 14 November. Available at: http://www.beppegrillo.it/2012/11/m5s_sicilia_rim.html [Accessed 4 June 2014].

———. 2012b. Programma a 5 Stelle *Beppegrillo.it* [blog] 22 April. Available at: http://www.beppegrillo.it/2012/04/programma_a_5_stelle.html [Accessed 4 June 2014].

———. 2013a. Il M5S rinuncia ai rimborsi elettorali *Beppegrillo.it*, Bersani forse #BersaniFirmaQui [blog] 11 March. Available at: http://www.beppegrillo.it/2013/03/il_m5s_rinuncia_ai_rimborsi_elettorali.html [Accessed 4 June 2014].

———. 2013b. Lettera agli Italiani di Beppe Grillo *Beppegrillo.it* [blog] 6 February. Available at: http://www.beppegrillo.it/2013/02/lettera_agli_italiani.html [Accessed 4 June 2014].

———. 2013c. La mutazione genetica del finanziamento pubblico ai partiti *Beppegrillo.it* [blog] 15 December. Available at: http://www.beppegrillo.it/2013/12/la_mutazione_ge.html [Accessed 4 June 2014].

———. 2014. La finta abolizione delle province: #SfiduciamoRenzie *Beppegrillo.it* [blog] 26 March. Available at: http://www.beppegrillo.it/2014/03/diretta_- _la_finta_abolizione_delle_province_sfiduciamorenzie.html [Accessed 4 June 2014].

Harmel, R. 1985. On the Study of New Parties. *International Political Science Review*, 6(4), pp. 403–18.

Harmel, R. and Robertson, D. 1985. Formation and Success of New Parties. A Cross-National Analysis. *International Political Science Review*, 6(4), pp. 501–23.

Harmel, R. and Svåsand, L. 1993. Party Leadership and Party Institutionalisation: Three Phases of Development. *West European Politics,* 16(2), pp. 67–88.

Heinisch, R. 2003. Success in Opposition – Failure in Government: Explaining the Performance of Right-Wing Populist Parties in Public Office. *West European Politics*, 26(3), pp. 91–130.

Hug, S. 2000. Studying the Electoral Success of New Political Parties. A Methodological Note. *Party Politics*, 6(2), pp. 187–97.

Ignazi, P. 1992. The Silent Counter-Revolution: Hypotheses on the Emergence of Extreme Right-Wing Parties in Europe. *European Journal of Political Research*, 22(1), pp. 3–34.

Kitschelt, H. 1988. Left-Libertarian Parties: Explaining Innovation in Competitive Systems. *World Politics*, 40(2), pp. 194–234.

———. 1995. *The Radical Right in Western Europe*. Ann Arbor, MI: University of Michigan Press.

———. 2006. Movement Parties. In: R.S. Katz and W.J. Crotty, eds. *Handbook of Party Politics*. London: Sage, pp. 278–90.

Legnante, G., Mancini, P., Mazzoleni, G. and Roncarolo, F. 2013. La campagna elettorale sui media. In: Itanes, ed. *Voto amaro. Disincanto e crisi economica nelle elezioni del 2013*. Bologna: Il Mulino, pp. 33–44.

Lipset, S.M. and Rokkan, S. 1967. Cleavage Structures, Party Systems, and Voter Alignments: An Introduction. In: S.M. Lipset and S. Rokkan, eds. *Party Systems and Voter Alignments: Cross-National Perspectives*. New York: The Free Press, pp. 1–63.

Massetti, E. 2006. Electoral Reform in Italy: From PR to Mixed System and (Almost) Back Again. *Representation*, 42(3), pp. 261–9.

Meguid, B.M. 2008. *Party Competition between Unequals: Strategies and Electoral Fortunes in Western Europe*. Cambridge: Cambridge University Press.

Movimento 5 Stelle. 2009. *Programma* [pdf]. Available at: http://www.beppegrillo.it/iniziative/movimentocinquestelle/Programma-Movimento-5-Stelle.pdf [Accessed 4 June 2014].

Müller-Rommel, F., ed. 1989. *New politics in Western Europe: The Rise and Success of Green Parties and Alternative Lists*. Boulder, CO: Westview Press.

Norris, P. 2005. *Radical Right: Voters and Parties in the Electoral Market Place*. Cambridge: Cambridge University Press.

Panebianco, A. 1982. *Modelli di partito: organizzazione e potere nei partiti politici*. Bologna: Il Mulino.

Rovny, J. 2013. Where do radical right parties stand? Position blurring in multidimensional competition. *European Political Science Review,* 5(1), pp. 1–26.

Schakel, A.J. and Jeffery, C. 2013. Are Regional Elections really 'Second-Order' Elections? *Regional Studies*, 47(3), pp. 323–341.

Tavits, M. 2006. Party System Change. Testing a Model of New Party Entry. *Party Politics*, 12(1), pp. 99–119.

Volkens, A., Lacewell, O., Lehmann, P., Regel, S., Schultze, H. and Werner, A. 2011. *The Manifesto Data Collection. Manifesto Project (MRG/CMP/MARPOR)* Berlin: Wissenschaftszentrum Berlin für Sozialforschung. [Online] Available at: https://manifesto-project.wzb.eu/ [Accessed 4 June 2014].

Index